incl tax

Paths to Recovery

Paths to Recovery

Al-Anon's Steps, Traditions and Concepts

▲ AL-ANON FAMILY GROUPS
for Families and Friends of Alcoholics

For information and catalog of literature write World Service Office for Al-Anon and Alateen:

AL-ANON FAMILY GROUP HEADQUARTERS, INC.
1600 CORPORATE LANDING PARKWAY
VIRGINIA BEACH, VA 23454–5617
757–563–1600 / FAX 757–563–1655
E-MAIL: wso@al-anon.org

Al-Anon/Alateen is supported by members' voluntary contributions and from the sale of our Conference Approved Literature.

Library of Congress Catalog Card No. 97–070986
ISBN 0–91-0034–31–1

Publisher's Cataloging in Publication
Paths to Recovery Al-Anon's Steps, Traditions and Concepts /
Al-Anon Family Groups

includes index
ISBN 0–9190034–31–1

1. Alcoholics – Family relationships. 2. Children of Alcoholics. 3. Al-Anon Family Group Headquarters, Inc. I. Al-Anon Family Group Headquarters, Inc.

 Approved by
World Service Conference
Al-Anon Family Groups

2-50M-99-15.00 · B-24 · *Printed in U.S.A.*

Preamble

THE AL-ANON FAMILY GROUPS are a fellowship of relatives and friends of alcoholics who share their experience, strength, and hope, in order to solve their common problems. We believe alcoholism is a family illness and that changed attitudes can aid recovery.

Al-Anon is not allied with any sect, denomination, political entity, organization, or institution; does not engage in any controversy, neither endorses nor opposes any cause. There are no dues for membership. Al-Anon is self-supporting through its own voluntary contributions.

Al-Anon has but one purpose: to help families of alcoholics. We do this by practicing the Twelve Steps, by welcoming and giving comfort to families of alcoholics, and by giving understanding and encouragement to the alcoholic.

— The Suggested Preamble to the Twelve Steps

AL-ANON BOOKS AND THEIR ISBN NUMBERS:

Courage to Be Me - Living with Alcoholism
0-910034-30-3

How Al-Anon Works for Families & Friends of Alcoholics
0-910034-26-5

From Survival to Recovery: Growing Up in an Alcoholic Home
0-910034-97-4

Courage to Change: One Day at a Time in Al-Anon II
0-910034-79-6
0-910034-84-2 Large print

…In All Our Affairs: Making Crisis Work for You
0-910034-73-7

As We Understood…
0-910034-56-7

One Day at a Time In Al-Anon
0-910034-21-4
0-910034-63-x Large print

The Dilemma of the Alcoholic Marriage
0-910034-18-4

Alateen — Hope for Children of Alcoholics
0-910034-20-6

Al-Anon / Alateen Service Manual
P 24 / 27

Contents

Preface

IN 1993, the members of the World Service Conference (WSC) acknowledged the many requests from our Al-Anon fellowship when they passed the following motion:

To produce an in-depth book on Al-Anon's Steps, Traditions and Concepts.

With this direction from Al-Anon's broadest group conscience, our World Service Office (WSO) requested, collected and compiled sharings from Al-Anon members throughout the world. To all who shared their experiences – thank you.

An Al-Anon team, including WSC members, WSO staff, volunteer committee members, a writer, two editors, a designer and indexer, produced, reviewed and revised the manuscript for this text. The result is a collection of individual Al-Anon members' experiences in working and living the Steps, Traditions and Concepts.

To those embarking on this exciting study of our three legacies for the first time, welcome. To those who are enhancing your recovery by seeking new insight, may this book increase your understanding.

We hope all will agree that the spirit and tone of this book embodies the love as well as the experience, strength and hope found in our fellowship. May your individual or group involvement prove a catalyst for continued growth and serenity – One Day At A Time.

AL-ANON'S DECLARATION

When anyone, anywhere, reaches out for help
let the hand of Al-Anon and Alateen
always be there, and – Let It Begin With Me.

Introduction

THIS BOOK, Al-Anon's Steps, Traditions and Concepts are our fellowship's three legacies. It is compiled from the experience, strength and hope of hundreds of Al-Anon members. This comprehensive volume will guide Al-Anon members worldwide as they study our program's three legacies and put them to work in their lives.

Al-Anon's logo is a triangle with a circle inside. The three sides of the triangle symbolize our three legacies: Recovery through acceptance of the Steps, Unity through acceptance of the Traditions and Service through acceptance of the Concepts. All three sides are necessary for the triangle to remain a triangle, just as a three-legged stool needs all three legs in order to stand. The circle within the triangle has been described by some Al-Anon members as a circle of welcome that carries the Al-Anon message of hope to the many families and friends who are living or have lived with the disease of alcoholism. In this simple symbol, we find represented the spiritual principles that unite us in our common bond: recovery from the effects of the family disease of alcoholism.

In the early days of Alcoholics Anonymous (AA), the spouses of alcoholics often found themselves waiting together in the kitchen of a school or church for their alcoholic partners to finish their meeting. As these family members talked to one another about their own difficulties, they realized they had been affected by living with an alcoholic and they, too, needed help. Out of the need to share their own experience, strength and hope, family groups began to develop around the United States. In 1951 the name Al-Anon Family Groups was selected by a poll of the groups. Soon the Twelve Steps and Twelve Traditions were adapted from AA's and adopted; in 1970 the Twelve Concepts were approved, completing Al-Anon's triangle of recovery for families and friends of alcoholics.

Living with the effects of alcoholism can be devastating. However, through the use of the Steps, Traditions and Concepts, countless people around the world have found a new way of life, whether the alcoholic is still drinking or not. Al-Anon is a spiritual program based on the principles found in the three legacies. Anyone who has been affected by another person's drinking is welcome in the fellowship. People from a variety of religions as well as those of no religion can find help in Al-Anon.

We have found that our recovery is based on a recognition of a Power greater than ourselves and active application to our lives of the principles contained in the Steps, Traditions and Concepts. Happily, many of us also discovered that not only do the Steps, Traditions and Concepts help us to recover from the effects of living with another person's alcoholism, but they also guide us to a new way of life filled with serenity and love.

As newcomers to Al-Anon, many of us are overwhelmed with the concept of the family disease. We learn early on about the Twelve Steps. We hear that "working" these Steps is our path to personal recovery. Through study of the Steps, we are told, we will learn new ways to handle our lives; we will discover that we are responsible for our own happiness and that we cannot control other people.

We may hear a little bit about the Traditions when we are new. One or all of these may be read in our group meetings; some groups hold monthly Tradition meetings. As we keep coming back and get a little more involved with service in our group, we will hear more about the principle of unity embodied in the Traditions as well as how they apply to our groups and to our personal lives.

Most Al-Anon members know very little about our

Concepts, which have been referred to as "Al-Anon's best-kept secret." These twelve statements describe the principles at work in the areas of world service – the World Service Conference (WSC), the Board of Trustees, the World Service Office (WSO) – and how these entities relate to each other and to the Al-Anon Family Groups they serve. With study we can come to see how the Concepts are applicable to our local services, to our groups and to our personal lives as well.

The Steps help us learn how to love ourselves, trust our Higher Power and begin to heal our relationships with others. The Traditions show us how to build healthy relationships within our groups, among our friends and in our families. The Concepts help us extend all that we learn to the world at large – our families, jobs, organizations and communities. Through study of these three legacies, we learn not only is our personal recovery through the Steps essential, but also, without the unity as expressed in the Traditions and the service work described in the Concepts, Al-Anon will not survive. By practicing all of these principles, we continue to grow in recovery. In order to keep our recovery, we learn we have to apply it to our lives and pass it on to others.

This book provides guidelines and suggestions for "working" our legacies. Each chapter presents a description of the individual legacy, personal stories from our members and a series of questions for personal and group use in putting the Step, Tradition or Concept to work. As we study the material that follows, we are benefiting from the wisdom of our predecessors in the fellowship who humbly invite us into the circle of love of Al-Anon.

The Twelve Steps

The Twelve Steps

Study of these Steps is essential to progress in the Al-Anon program. The principles they embody are universal, applicable to everyone, whatever his personal creed. In Al-Anon, we strive for an ever-deeper understanding of these Steps, and pray for the wisdom to apply them to our lives.

THE TWELVE STEPS

1. We admitted we were powerless over alcohol – that our lives had become unmanageable.

2. Came to believe that a Power greater than ourselves could restore us to sanity.

3. Made a decision to turn our will and our lives over to the care of God *as we understood Him.*

4. Made a searching and fearless moral inventory of ourselves.

5. Admitted to God, to ourselves, and to another human being the exact nature of our wrongs.

6. Were entirely ready to have God remove all these defects of character.

7. Humbly asked Him to remove our shortcomings.

8. Made a list of all persons we had harmed, and became willing to make amends to them all.

9. Made direct amends to such people wherever possible, except when to do so would injure them or others.

10. Continued to take personal inventory and when we were wrong promptly admitted it.

11. Sought through prayer and meditation to improve our conscious contact with God *as we understood Him,* praying only for knowledge of His will for us and the power to carry that out.

12. Having had a spiritual awakening as the result of these Steps, we tried to carry this message to others, and to practice these principles in all our affairs.

Introduction to the Twelve Steps

AT FIRST GLANCE, understanding the Twelve Steps of Al-Anon can be difficult. Words like powerless, unmanageable, sanity, God, fearless moral inventory, defects of character, amends, prayer and meditation and spiritual awakening may be confusing to a newcomer. It is the experience of millions, however, that proves these Steps work. Notice that they are written in the past tense, echoing the experience of those who have walked this path before us.

Because of the success of the Twelve Steps of Alcoholics Anonymous (AA), the Steps were adopted almost word for word by Al-Anon in 1951. They outline a means of living that have helped our members ". . . to find contentment, and even happiness, whether the alcoholic is still drinking or not" (Al-Anon Suggested Welcome from *Al-Anon/Alateen Service Manual*). The Steps are a path to a new way of life.

We all come to Al-Anon because our lives have been affected by the disease of alcoholism. Many of us enter these doors feeling defeated by this disease. We may have spent our energies trying to get an active alcoholic to stop drinking or otherwise control his or her actions; we may have spent much of our lives struggling with the effects of growing up in an alcoholic home. No matter what our individual situation is, in Al-Anon we discover that we are not alone and that a different way of life is available to us through the Twelve Steps.

The Steps suggest four primary ideas:

"1. ...we are powerless over the problem of alcoholism. When we can honestly accept this truth, it brings us a feeling of release and hope. We can now turn our full attention to bringing our own lives into order. We can go forward to spiritual growth, to the comfort and peace to be gained from the entire program.

2. …we can turn our lives over to a power greater than ourselves. Now that our well-meant aid to the alcoholic has ended in failure and our own lives have become unmanageable, we realize we cannot deal with our problem objectively, perhaps not even sanely.

In Al-Anon we find a Power greater than ourselves which can direct our lives into quiet, useful channels. At first this Power may seem to be the group, but as we grow in knowledge and spiritual understanding, many of us call it God, as we understand Him.

3. …we need to change both our attitudes and our actions. As we become willing to admit our defects, we begin to see how much of our thinking is distorted. We realize how unwise some of our actions have been, how unloving many of our attitudes. We try to recognize and correct these faults.

4. …we keep Al-Anon's gifts by sharing them with others. This sharing makes Al-Anon the vital, forward-reaching fellowship it is. Our great obligation is to those still in need. Leading another person from despair to hope and love brings comfort to both the giver and receiver." (from *Al-Anon/Alateen Service Manual*)

What hope these ideas offer us! We are offered a new way of life that is free for the taking. The requirements for recovery are simple: "If you try to keep an open mind, you will find help. You will come to realize that there is no situation too difficult to be bettered and no unhappiness too great to be lessened" (Al-Anon Suggested Closing from *Al-Anon/Alateen Service Manual*). We will find help; our situation can be bettered and our unhappiness can be lessened.

Remember that we can take one small idea at a time. Working with our Al-Anon literature, our group and a sponsor, we can start with Step One and take whatever time we need to feel comfortable with it before moving to Step Two. There are no fixed timetables for recovery in Al-Anon. All that is required is an open mind and the willingness to do the best we can do for today. We strive for progress not perfection, as we study the Steps on our paths to recovery.

MANY OF US come to Al-Anon filled with despair and hopelessness. Some of us come to find out how to get another person sober; others grew up in alcoholic homes or left alcoholic partners and no longer live with active drinking. We may not see the impact of having lived with alcoholism until we begin to acknowledge that there are familiar difficulties in our present lives and relationships. Many of us would not have voluntarily walked through the doors of Al-Anon if we were not in some sort of crisis or pain that forced us to seek help. Though we may not have labeled it this way, we come to Al-Anon because our lives are unmanageable – we come looking for relief.

The first word of the First Step illustrates an important concept in Al-Anon recovery: We are not alone. In our early meetings, we realize this is true. As the Al-Anon Suggested Welcome says, "We who live, or have lived, with the problem of alcoholism understand as perhaps few others can. We, too, were lonely and frustrated, but in Al-Anon we discover that no situation is really hopeless and that it is possible for us to find contentment, and even happiness, whether the alcoholic is still drinking or not." Just hearing those words may help us to feel that there is hope for us, too.

Once we acknowledge that someone else's drinking has affected our lives, we may want to blame everything on the drinking. We are sure there must be something more we can say or do that will convince the alcoholic to stop drinking, thus resolving our problems. We have no idea that we are as powerless over alcohol as the alcoholic is.

Not understanding that alcoholism is a disease, many of us have tried to take things into our own hands. We may have poured out liquor, made excuses, nagged, pleaded, protected or punished the drinkers in our lives. We may have hidden our feelings, isolated and avoided contact with the alcoholic, thinking our problems would go away. We may have taken

Step One

We admitted we were powerless over alcohol – that our lives had become unmanageable.

over the alcoholic's unfinished projects, answered phone calls or covered his or her mistakes. No matter what we did, our lives did not improve and the alcoholic did not change.

In order to take the First Step and admit our powerlessness over alcoholism, we need first to understand and accept that alcoholism is a disease. Medical authorities agree that alcoholism is a progressive disease that can be arrested, but not cured – it is a lifetime disease. One symptom is an uncontrollable desire to drink; as long as an alcoholic continues to drink, that desire will increase. Some alcoholics try to convince family members that they are social drinkers by drinking only on weekends or by abstaining for a limited time. The compulsion to drink usually returns. The only way to arrest the disease is total abstinence. Many alcoholics successfully recover through a variety of treatments. The Alcoholics Anonymous (AA) program is generally regarded as the most effective. Our experience shows that we cannot force someone to stop drinking. This is an individual choice of the alcoholic.

Alcoholism is a family disease. This means ". . . the alcoholism of one member affects the whole family, and all become sick. Why does that happen? It happens because, unlike diabetes, alcoholism not only exists inside the body of the alcoholic, but is a disease of relationships as well. Many of the symptoms of alcoholism are in the behavior of the alcoholic. The people who are involved with the alcoholic react to his behavior. They try to control it, make up for it or hide it. They often blame themselves for it and are hurt by it. Eventually they become emotionally disturbed themselves." (from *Alateen – Hope for Children of Alcoholics*, page 6).

In Al-Anon meetings we hear the three Cs describing our powerlessness over alcoholism: we didn't cause it, can't cure it, and can't control it. We begin to learn the basic Al-Anon premise of taking our focus off of the alcoholic and keeping the focus on ourselves. Hard as it is to look at our own part in our problems, acceptance of Step One brings relief from impossible responsibilities. We were trying to fix a disease – and someone else's disease at that!

To find peace and serenity in our lives, we have to change – a challenging, and perhaps fearful, thought. We may have to re-learn to take care of ourselves. When we are focused on another person's alcoholism and behavior, many of us develop the habit of putting that person's needs first. We may suffer from low self-esteem and not believe that we deserve to take time for ourselves. Whether we judge ourselves as good or bad doesn't matter; we are always defeated by alcoholism. In Al-Anon, we will find help.

Admitting our powerlessness may be very difficult for us. After all, we are the competent ones who held the family, the job or the world together while the alcoholics in our lives created chaos. How can it be that we, the responsible ones, are powerless? In Al-Anon, we come to understand that our lives may be unmanageable because we are trying to control the people and situations in our lives. It can be hard to conceive that our well-meaning efforts have been part of the problem, but by the time we reach Al-Anon, we are finally ready to try something – anything – new. We have to admit that nothing we do or don't do can control another person's drinking. How can we help an alcoholic? In Al-Anon we learn to accept the things we cannot change (the alcoholic) and change the things we can (ourselves). To recover we have to learn to keep the focus on ourselves.

As we look back on our lives, we are asked to acknowledge our powerlessness over alcohol, the alcoholic and every person and event we sought to control by our own will power. By letting go of the illusion of control over other people, their actions and their addiction to alcohol, we find an enormous burden is lifted and we begin to discover the freedom and the power we do possess – the power to define and live our own lives. Unmanageability lessens. We begin to see the paths to our own recovery.

In Al-Anon we discover principles that work for us and help us relate to others. Al-Anon helps us learn new ways to have healthy relationships in all areas of our lives. Step One reminds us of our proper relationship with others – we are powerless over them. It places us in correct relationship with ourselves – when we try to control others, we lose the ability to manage our own lives. Step One is the true beginning of our path to recovery.

Members Share Experience, Strength and Hope

I ACCEPTED
THE TRUTH

I ADMITTED my life had become unmanageable, but for a long time I could not believe that I was powerless over alcohol. I was certain I could make the alcoholic stop drinking by saying, "If you loved me, you would never drink again." Several statements like that made sense to me at the time. I was a very demanding person. Before Al-Anon, I did not know that my demands were beyond the alcoholic's ability to respond. I didn't know that alcoholism was a disease. He told me that I didn't understand. He said it was not as simple as I thought it was for him to stop drinking.

Some tough questions haunted me and disturbed my peace of mind. What happens if I admit my powerlessness and let go of the situation? Will he drink more if I stop trying to control the drinking? Will he feel I don't love him any more if I stop questioning him about his drinking? Will he think I have lost interest in him and that I may be attracted to someone else? Will he spend more money on alcohol?

What finally enabled me to take Step One was the fact that it made no difference what I did or didn't do. For example, I could cry, plead, get angry, or whatever and he still continued to drink. Gradually he became worse. It took a long time to realize I had no power over this disease. My days in Al-Anon turned into weeks and the weeks turned into months. The more I listened at meetings, the more I knew that I had to "Let Go and Let God." I had to "Live and Let Live." Finally, I let go of the situation and admitted my powerlessness.

I realized if things didn't improve, we would no longer be together. He was extremely ill from the disease of alcoholism, both physically and mentally. I gave up begging and controlling and left the situation alone. I accepted the truth that I did not have the power to stop his drinking. Thank God and Al-Anon that I finally got it right. The alcoholic in my life went to a 28-day program, sought counseling and is now a member of Alcoholics Anonymous. He has been sober for 10 months now. It has been a wonderful 10 months in many ways. Although sobriety is not all roses, thanks to Al-Anon I am able to deal with the changes.

STEP ONE was the hardest thing for me to accept. Powerless over alcohol? A can of beer? A bottle of vodka? They're just objects – lifeless nothings. How could I, a living, breathing human, be powerless over a bottle of alcohol? How could I admit a bottle was the winner, that it could defeat me again and again?

It felt like I was admitting I was powerless over a bar of soap or some other inanimate object. It hurt my ego, it went against all my beliefs. Powerless over alcohol? I hated alcohol. It turned my mother from a nice, rational lady, into a cursing, screaming madwoman. Alcohol caused my husband to lose five jobs in seven years and to have two accidents in the space of two months. I hated the smell of it, the taste of it. I hated looking at it. But I thought I could lick it, that I would be the victor – not alcohol.

It wasn't until I read a passage on page 76 in *One Day at a Time in Al-Anon* that it hit me. Accepting

MY LIFE IS JUST THAT, MY LIFE

this Step didn't mean a weakness of character. It meant honestly admitting there are things that we can't change. Accepting that I am powerless over alcohol puts an end to struggling. It frees me to work on things that can be changed. It means saying to my Higher Power, "I can't do it alone. I need Your help."

Reading that passage was like seeing the light. I could finally be honest with myself. I was powerless over alcohol. I am powerless over alcohol and I always will be powerless over alcohol. My admission took the burden off me. I no longer had to fight and struggle constantly. I could work on other things, such as myself, and free my mind from all-consuming thoughts of the disease.

Before coming to Al-Anon, I could never accept Step One. After being in Al-Anon for over 20 months, I find it is very easy to say this Step and to believe it.

My life had become unmanageable. Thanks to Al-Anon and practicing this Step again and again, my life is just that, my life – to concentrate on and to live the best way that I can.

I COULD SEE THE EFFECTS

BEFORE AL-ANON I wouldn't have accepted any part of Step One. I thought I was fine and that everything would be perfect if I could only get the alcoholic to stop drinking. As I began to study and work the First Step, I found it easier to admit the first part of it than the second part.

I am a visually oriented person. As I looked at Step One and the word alcohol, I visualized a bottle of whiskey. Later, I visualized a person drinking from the bottle. I could see alcohol going into the person and changing him into the alcoholic. I could see I was powerless over the alcoholic when he was drinking, but learning that I was powerless over him at all times took longer. Later my visualization showed me the bottle, the person drinking it, the alcohol flowing from that person to me to family members and business associates, etc. I could see all of us swimming in a sea of alcohol – then coming out, shaking ourselves off and spreading the disease to even more people.

It took time for me to admit that even though I didn't drink the alcohol, the disease could come through me and affect other people. As time passed and I learned more, I came to recognize that anything I contacted could be affected by the alcoholism coming through me. My reactions to other things could be the same as the ways I reacted to the drinking. I began to see how my own reactions had made my life unmanageable. I saw how my role of martyr had taken a sense of responsibility away from other people and lowered their egos. I saw how I had done this not only to the alcoholic, but also to other people in my life.

I finally realized my life had become unmanageable because I was so busy taking care of others that I had no time to take care of me. I laid out clothes for family members so they would be well dressed, but that left no time to see that I was at my best. I arranged for others to have doctor and dental appointments but then I neglected my own. I didn't realize all of these things overnight. They came slowly, but finally I could understand the First Step. I realized that I too have a disease – caused by my contact with all of the alcoholics in my life. Today I know I am powerless over all the nouns and pronouns in my life – other persons, places and things.

By process of elimination, I discovered what I am not powerless over – myself. I am responsible for me. I am not responsible for another person's happiness, nor are they responsible for mine. I know that no one else can control my emotions. No one can make me angry, sad, happy or anything else without me giving them permission to do so. My feelings are my own.

Today I understand that I am powerless over alcohol and that my life is unmanageable. I know with the help of Al-Anon and my Higher Power, whom I choose to call God, my life is becoming more manageable.

WHEN I came into Al-Anon, I was involved in a special relationship with a man whose temper erupted unexpectedly and inappropriately. It especially bothered me to be a passenger in his car. If the person driving the car in front of us didn't take off the instant the traffic light turned green, my friend's temper would explode. If another car cut in front of us, the same thing happened.

Initially, I felt positive my friend was really angry at something I said or did, or at something I had failed to say or do. I was positive that I was at fault. Surely I could fix what was happening. At the very least, I could control the level of his explosion. So, I would get angry and point out his indiscretions on the road, such as not using turn signals when he changed lanes. I chattered about other things to distract his attention from what had occurred. I thought surely there was something I could do to remove my feelings of guilt. Just by being there, I had to have done something that sparked his anger.

Someone in Al-Anon shared the three Cs with me: I didn't cause it; I can't control it; I can't cure it. Slowly, a new perspective, attitude and behavior crept into my awareness. When I thought about it, I could see I hadn't caused the situation. I wasn't driving the other car and I hadn't provoked any anger. I began turning my face toward the passenger window, repeating over and over inside my head "I didn't cause it. I didn't cause it." During this recitation, my stomach flip-flopped all over the place. Declining to take responsibility for my friend's temper was new for me. It gave me a very uncomfortable feeling.

Even though I was completely convinced that I hadn't caused his inappropriate behavior, I still had an overwhelming desire to control or cure what was happening. Once again, I had to sit and feel the discomfort from letting go of his temper tantrums. I watched his behavior over many weeks and I realized that he wasn't concerned with the behavior. He blew off steam and then acted as though nothing unusual had happened. He didn't seem to notice my old behavior of jumping right in to make things better or my new behavior of silence.

With my new awareness, I began to apply the three Cs in many different environments. Sometimes it was more difficult than others to handle the butterflies fluttering in my stomach. But I always survived after applying the three Cs in new situations. That gave me the courage to examine interactions in all areas of my life. I started to make conscious choices about what part I played in various situations. Eventually I learned to say that inappropriate temper tantrums upset me. I learned it was okay to take separate cars. To this day, I still use the three Cs. I am very grateful for many Al-Anon tools.

Working Step One

We admitted we were powerless over alcohol — that our lives had become unmanageable.

EACH OF US is free to create our own solutions using the experience, strength and hope of those who have gone before us. The following questions for self-study or group study may help you with Step One. As you work each Step, remember to appreciate yourself for the effort. Call a friend or sponsor and share your success, too.

* Do I accept that I cannot control another person's drinking? Another person's behavior?

* How do I recognize that the alcoholic is an individual with habits, characteristics and ways of

reacting to daily happenings that are different from mine?

* Do I accept that alcoholism is a disease? How does that change how I deal with a drinker?

* How have I tried to change others in my life? What were the consequences?

* What means have I used to get what I want and need? What might work better to get my needs met?

* How do I feel when the alcoholic refuses to be and do what I want? How do I respond?

* What would happen if I stopped trying to change the alcoholic or anyone else?

* How can I let go of others' problems instead of trying to solve them?

* Am I looking for a quick fix to my problems? Is there one?

* In what situations do I feel excessive responsibility for other people?

* In what situations do I feel shame or embarrassment for someone else's behavior?

* What brought me into Al-Anon? What did I hope to gain at that time? How have my expectations changed?

* Who has expressed concern about my behavior? My health? My children? Give examples.

* How do I know when my life is unmanageable?

* How have I sought approval and affirmation from others?

* Do I say "yes" when I want to say "no"? What happens to my ability to manage my life when I do this?

* Do I take care of others easily, but find it difficult to care for myself?

* How do I feel when life is going smoothly? Do I continually anticipate problems? Do I feel more alive in the midst of a crisis?

* How well do I take care of myself?

* How do I feel when I am alone?

* What is the difference between pity and love?

* Am I attracted to alcoholics and other people who seem to need me to fix them? How have I tried to fix them?

* Do I trust my own feelings? Do I know what they are?

Step Two

*Came to believe
that a Power
greater than ourselves
could restore us
to sanity.*

THE BASIC spiritual principle introduced in Step Two suggests that there is a Power greater than we are that provides hope for sanity, whether we are living with active alcoholism or not. Step Two reaffirms that we may be powerless, but we are not helpless, and we are not alone. For many of us, the introduction of a Power greater than ourselves is difficult to understand. Some initially believe we are speaking of a religious entity. We are not. We are speaking of a loving, caring, nurturing Power that provides us with guidance in dealing with the effects of the disease of alcoholism.

As we consider Step Two, it is often helpful to remember that "Came to believe" is written in the past tense. Like all the Steps, Step Two tells the experience of those who have gone before us and shows that over time we can find the answers to our own dilemmas. Few of us walked into our first meeting firmly convinced that there was a Power greater than ourselves that could bring good into our lives. If there was, why were we so unhappy and confused? Belief grows as we open our minds enough to consider that a spiritual resource could help us with our problems. We listen to the experience of others and want what they have: peace, serenity, happiness, faith and joy. Many members, though filled with plenty of doubts, are willing to seek other possibilities. Willingness to listen and consider an alternative – even a Higher Power – that others have tried opens a door to Step Two.

With Step Two and the support of a loving fellowship, we begin to learn how to recognize and accept our own part in the family disease of alcoholism. In Al-Anon the love and acceptance we find helps us learn to love and accept ourselves with all our imperfections.

Acceptance of Step Two is paramount to working the rest of the Al-Anon Steps. Tripping over Step Two and skipping to other Steps indicates a lack of acceptance of Step One. Many members have difficulty in beginning to work this Step for their personal recovery. Attendance at meetings is only a start; we need the guidance of a sponsor in addition to our group. The wisdom of members who have worked these Steps before us is essential to understanding fully the spiritual answers and guidance we are about to experience. Trusting our group and trusting a sponsor are truly stepping stones to accepting a Power greater than ourselves.

For those who come to Al-Anon with a belief in a God, Step Two may be a very welcome idea; the concept of turning to a familiar God for help with our problems will be reassuring and easy to grasp. Others of us may have developed a fear of our God and have difficulty imagining asking such a punishing God for assistance.

Some of us reject religion of any kind and call ourselves either agnostics or atheists. It is important to hear that, whether we practice a particular religion or not, all of us are welcome in Al-Anon. Yet, when we approach Step Two, we may suspect that a group ideology will be revealed, and we will be forced to conform or leave. Instead the group's members turn us toward defining our own idea of a Higher Power and we come to believe that such a Power could exist and might help us.

In beginning to understand Step Two, we learn that we have choices. If the members of any group in the world were surveyed, each person would respond differently with a personal definition of a Higher Power. If we resist the idea of "God" as our Higher Power, we can begin by using the group as a Power greater than ourselves. In the group we meet people like us who are coping with many of the same problems and finding creative solutions we had not considered or attitudes that make the similar situations in their lives more tolerable. We consider that many heads are better than one and draw on the groups' collective wisdom.

If we struggle with a concept of a Higher Power in any way, we can begin by acting "as if." By reflecting on more serene or peaceful times in our lives, we begin to appreciate today. The slogan "One Day at a Time" takes on new meaning as we commit ourselves to reading a page each day in *One Day at a Time in Al-Anon*, *Alateen – A Day at a Time*, or *Courage to Change: One Day at a Time in Al-Anon II*. With the guidance of our sponsor or group, we begin to pray or meditate, even if we have no idea exactly who is listening to our prayers. We start to act as if we believe not only in a Higher Power, but also that we are loved and supported. Some members share that they once feared the God of their understanding and now speak of a God of love. The Serenity Prayer, often used in meetings, is a universal prayer that helps many members to relate to the God of their understanding:

THE SERENITY PRAYER
God, grant me the serenity
to accept the things I cannot change,
courage to change the things I can,
and wisdom to know the difference.

Whatever our faith or beliefs, whatever our definition of God or Higher Power, we begin to desire increased sanity for ourselves. Motivated, we seek a Power greater than ourselves to aid us in our journey. In Step One we learned that we didn't cause the disease of alcoholism, we couldn't control it or cure it. Step Two offers us an option: sanity. With this new perspective in mind, we truly begin to experience the hope that so many speak of.

Sanity can be defined in many ways. Many share that they no longer purchase alcohol for the alcoholic. Others speak of removing themselves from tumultuous situations. Some share of defusing arguments by merely stating, "You might be right." Taking a bubble bath or going skiing for a day can offer new perspectives on the situation. Gradually and gratefully we develop a faith in a Higher Power. We begin to recognize that the old behavior, if it returns, doesn't have to return for the same duration.

What does faith have to do with a Higher Power? Faith surrounds us in our daily living. When we rise in the morning, we have faith that there will be daylight when we open our window blinds. When we leave home in the morning, we have faith that the car engine will start, that other drivers will stay on their side of the road and that we will arrive safely at our destination. Upon leaving an Al-Anon meeting, we have faith that the meeting will be there week after week. Moreover, when we leave a meeting, we take with us the faith and wisdom of others, the words of love, encouragement, experience and hope that we need for our spiritual growth. We also leave with a new-found trust, trust that we are being restored to sanity.

Here are some ideas members have used to help them increase their faith in a Power greater than themselves.

↭ Saying the Serenity Prayer every morning and every evening or anytime we feel overwhelmed or ill at ease.

↭ Meditating on "God, grant me the serenity," one word at a time.

↭ Being still and asking for help whenever a situation seems too much to take.

↭ Recognizing sane behavior and acknowledging it. Taking notice of small miracles – a bright-eyed child, a bounding puppy, a friend's call just when it's needed.

↭ Acting as if we have faith. Being still, asking for guidance, then going about the day's business assuming it will come.

↭ Laughing; trying to remember some funny occurrence to share at a meeting.

↣ Making a list of the things beyond understanding that have happened in life that might suggest the existence of a Higher Power.

↣ Asking for the "courage to change the things we can" and then completely letting go of the results.

The family disease of alcoholism is as cunning and baffling for us as it is for the alcoholic. In studying Steps One and Two, we are humbled in the realization that we have frailties. Taking these first two Steps provides us with new found hope. The Serenity Prayer takes on new meaning. It can help all Al-Anon members to come to believe that they can be restored to sanity. With this faith we are willing to "Let Go and Let God," and we truly believe in a Power greater than ourselves.

Members Share Experience, Strength and Hope

WHAT MY CREATOR ORIGINALLY INTENDED

SOME TIME ago I read about extensive cleaning and restoration work being done on a very famous chapel. Its frescoes were caked with centuries of dirt, soot and other foreign matter. Artisans painstakingly removed layer upon layer of grime in search of the original masterpiece. Before half the project was completed, a minor controversy ensued. The artist's original hues were far more colorful than anyone expected. They radiated with dazzling brilliance but the world had grown accustomed to the dark, murky forms that had been in the chapel for so long. The cleaned portions appeared quite garish by comparison. These half-bright, half-dark images became a strange paradox. The process turned into a troubling dilemma. Should they complete the restoration, or should they cancel the work and return it to the way everyone was used to seeing it?

As I worked on Step Two during my years in Al-Anon I have faced the same kinds of questions.

Growing up in the family disease of alcoholism, I always saw my life through thick and murky layers of the disease. I had no idea what was underneath. As I began to practice the principles of Al-Anon, changes started taking place. I was so accustomed to the way my life had been that these alterations seemed awkward and ugly at first. Like the half-restored artwork, there were parts of me that didn't fit with the rest. I had two choices. I could stay the way I was, or I could continue being restored to what my Creator originally intended.

Fortunately, like those in charge of restoring the chapel, I decided to trust what my Creator originally intended. In time, the new parts blended in and didn't call attention to themselves in such a displeasing way. The more I was restored, the more consistent I became.

I was hidden under years of pain, shame, guilt and suffering. Step Two made my life brighter and more beautiful than I ever thought possible. The potential had been there all along, waiting for the hand of a loving Power to bring it to the surface. The process is restoring me to a life of beauty, love, serenity and sanity.

ON AN OVERCAST day in the fall, my life felt like it was already in winter with no end in sight. My husband called me at work with another disturbing problem. I felt so upset that I was unable to concentrate on my work. Once again, I became totally obsessed with the alcoholic and our recovery issues.

Earlier that week I had attended my home group meeting. I heard another member share how she removed herself from difficult situations to get a new focus. I thought maybe getting out of the office for a few minutes might help me now.

I put on my coat, rode down in the elevator and decided to get a breath of fresh air. I opened the door to a chilly blast. Alone outside, I looked up at the sky

I IDENTIFIED WITH THE LAST LEAF

and said, "God, I can't handle it. This one is all yours!" At that instant, the last leaf on a nearby tree started gently floating to the ground. I stood there, spellbound.

As the leaf made a soft landing I heard, "It's going to be okay. I can handle it." A tear rolled down my cheek. I realized for the first time that I had "Let Go and Let God." I felt at peace.

Years later I was sitting in a study group that focused on the Twelve Steps. The leader wanted everyone to share a Step Two experience. What I thought about was a cold day in the fall many years before. That's when I came to believe that a Power greater than myself could restore me to sanity. My recovery in Al-Anon produced many unexpected experiences but my Step Two experience was the most poignant.

IT INTRODUCED
ME TO SANITY

OF ALL the Twelve Steps, Step Two is my favorite. When I came into recovery several years ago, I didn't know I was insane. I had grown up in an alcoholic family and the insanity of the disease was all I had ever known. That was just the way it was. It surprises me now that I never thought to question whether there were other ways for life to work. I suppose I had been so repressed from my alcoholic upbringing that, until recovery, asking questions never occurred to me.

It took several years for the meaning of Step Two to begin to sink in. It took longer for me to admit that the way I was living my life was a result of the insanity that the disease of alcoholism had created in my family. I didn't know that living life based on fear, which I experienced growing up, was not the way to do it. I didn't know there was something drastically wrong with the way I grew up.

At first what I heard in meetings frightened me — almost enough so I didn't want to return. My life continued to get worse, however. Looking for answers, I tried a variety of things. I tried counseling, therapy, medication and lots of self-help books. Finally, I became severely depressed and suicidal. It was at this point that I found a kind counselor who recognized that alcoholism might be the underlying problem. She told me Al-Anon was for adult children, too. After gently urging and suggesting, she eventually cajoled me into finding an Al-Anon meeting.

I came back to the program for myself, not to fix anyone else. I had already detected the insanity in my life. In fact, as more of Step Two's message became clear to me, I paraphrased the Step to say it didn't restore me to sanity, but rather it introduced me to it. The insanity in my alcoholic family was all I had known. Abandonment, rejection and negativity seemed normal. A little at a time, however, the caring and gentleness from Al-Anon people began to work for me. I started to attend meetings on a regular basis. That was one of the secrets for me. I needed to keep coming back so I could experience the consistency that I had never found in my home.

Other people's stories shocked me. Physical abuse, violence and sexual abuse had not happened to me. If they had happened to me, I couldn't imagine sharing them with a room full of strangers. I couldn't imagine being that blunt and honest, because hiding had always been my way of life. Though my stories were different from other people's, I realized that we shared the same feelings. A little at a time, I started to share some of what I remembered. I felt very hesitant about it because I didn't know how to trust. Gradually I learned that I could trust people in Al-Anon, but most of all I learned I could trust myself.

I've gotten Step Two's message very slowly. I can see some of my progress each time I have contact with members of my family. None of them are in recovery of any kind, although I keep hoping that one or two will join me. My recovery has been quite lonely at times because I feel alienated from my family. With the knowledge gained from many meetings and the Steps, I can see the insanity in my family where they cannot. Most of my family's insanity takes the form of verbal and emotional abuse. It is very subtle and hard to detect. Not until I trusted my own feelings and reactions could I see how much hurt these forms of abuse could inflict. My denial has been very difficult and painful to break, but finally I had no other choice. The price I paid in pain and losses was too high to continue paying.

I can't say I've become instantly sane since coming to Al-Anon. There are still many times when I am in the grips of this disease. I recognize it faster because it doesn't feel good any more. At these times I turn to my Higher Power and repeat Step Two. I pray to be restored to sanity.

Working Step Two

Came to believe that a Power greater than ourselves could restore us to sanity.

THE FOLLOWING questions may assist us, individually and in our groups, to developing an understanding of the relationship of a Higher Power to our lives.

* What is my concept of a Higher Power at this time?

* What would it take to allow my concept of my Higher Power to change?

* Have past experiences affected my concept of a Higher Power? If so, how?

* What do I hope to gain from accepting the concept of a Power greater than myself?

* Do I sense spiritual guidance in my life? How?

* How do I describe the Higher Power I found in Al-Anon?

* What does "Let Go and Let God" mean to me?

* What does faith mean to me?

* With whom and in what circumstances am I comfortable discussing my spiritual experiences?

* What might I gain from believing I could be supported and loved by a Power greater than myself?

* What does "Came to believe" mean to me?

* What does sanity mean to me?

* How has the alcoholic situation affected my sanity? My life?

* Have I allowed the alcoholic situation to become my Higher Power? How?

* How has my thinking become distorted trying to handle the alcoholic behavior?

* How have I turned to a Power greater than myself in times of great need? Did I call another Al-Anon member? My sponsor? Did I read Al-Anon Conference Approved Literature (CAL)? Did I go to a meeting? If not, why not?

* In working this Step, can I describe a Step Two experience to my sponsor or my group? In a written sharing?

* When have I done the same things over and over, yet expected different results?

Step Three

Made a decision to turn our will and our lives over to the care of God AS WE UNDERSTOOD HIM.

IN STEP ONE we learned that many of our problems may have resulted from our ineffective efforts to manage our own lives; in Step Two we came to believe that a Higher Power could help restore us to sanity. It naturally follows that the next Step would be turning to that Power for help. Some members shorten the first three Steps to, "I can't. God can. I'll let Him." Obviously if our past efforts have been futile, and if we believe that a Power can help us, it makes sense to allow that Power to do so.

The first phrase of Step Three, "Made a decision," shows us that we have choices. We make this decision when we are ready. Everyone works through the Steps at their own pace, in many cases returning to earlier Steps over and over again until ready to move to the next one. No one compels us to turn over our will. We choose to try this because the way of life we created on self-will alone was neither satisfying nor serene.

What decision are we making? We are asked "to turn our will and our lives over to the care of God *as we understood Him.*" Few of us are able to immediately turn over everything in our lives; making the decision to do so is merely a commitment to try. To illustrate this aspect of Step Three, a member posed the following: "Three frogs sat on a lily pad. One made a decision to jump off. How many frogs are left?" The answer is three. The frog merely made the decision to jump – he hasn't jumped yet!

We often have to take one problem or person at a time and work on turning that one thing over to our Higher Power. Most often the alcoholic in our lives is the person we first need to turn over. We learned in Step One that we are powerless over alcohol and the alcoholic and that we cannot control or change him or her. So we can work on turning our desire to change the alcoholic over to God.

Once we turn a few of our problems over to the care of God, many of us feel a great sense of relief.

Depending on our Higher Power can increase our independence from the opinions, needs and demands of others. We need no longer look outside ourselves to other people for validation. Asking for help from a Higher Power is an admission that we cannot do it alone and gives us assurance that we are not alone.

For those of us willing to be helped but still not convinced that God is the one to do it, the last phrase of Step Three, "*as we understood Him*", reinforces our freedom of choice. As in Step Two, we are free to define the God of our understanding, and we do not even have to use the word God. We can seek a Higher Power, a Higher Consciousness or the wisdom and love of the group. What matters is that we set aside our willfulness and determination to be right and believe that our Higher Power, however we may define it, will guide us in the right direction.

Once we have made the decision asked of us in Step Three, we face the question of how to do it. There are as many ways to approach turning our will and our lives over as there are definitions of God. Most find it necessary to ask the God of our understanding to help us. For those from religious backgrounds, the concept of prayer is comfortable; others may find traditional prayer difficult. Thinking of prayer as talking to our Higher Power may help. Again, in Al-Anon we are all free to define our Higher Power as we choose and to decide how we will communicate with that Power. Remember that asking our Higher Power for help does not mean asking for specific results – that is asking God to execute our will! Turning our will and our lives over to God means that we put the outcome in God's hands.

We can practice talking to God. Some members find that starting and ending the day with the Serenity Prayer is helpful. Others ask directly for God to take their will and their life for the day. If we lack confidence, we can ask our Higher Power to provide it. If we have trouble verbalizing our thoughts, we can use a familiar prayer or just say, "Please help me." We can make up our own prayers. One member prays, "God, guide me in my activities today and keep me from idly dwelling on yesterdays and tomorrows." Another simply says each morning, "God, you and I are going to have a good day. And if it's not so good, I know You can handle it." Someone else suggests, "God, help me to live an honest life," while another uses a single word or phrase like, "Be with me today," "Guide me," "Help!" or "Thank you." As in all the Steps, we keep the focus on ourselves and ask for guidance.

A problem can also be handed over to our Higher Power by writing it down and putting it in a special place. Some people make a 'God box' to hold their written requests or prayers; this has an advantage in that it can be revisited several months later. Sometimes we discover with pleasant surprise that problems placed there have literally disappeared, and we have forgotten about them.

As in the first two Steps, Step Three can bring about enormous relief, taking the responsibility for our problems and our loved ones off our shoulders. As we grow in the program, we find ourselves returning again and again to these basic principles when faced with new challenges. Steps One, Two and Three complete our preparation to begin taking action in our recovery with the Steps that follow. We know that we cannot control everything and everyone in our lives; that turning our will and our lives over to the care of God as we understand God is our hope for serenity and peace of mind.

Members Share Experience, Strength and Hope

GETTING TO
KNOW MY
GOD

I REMEMBER trying to make a decision before Al-Anon about which of two blouses to buy. I simply couldn't make a decision – even a minor one. As I look back, I realize many things in my life that required a simple decision seemed to be very complicated.

I came to Al-Anon and began to work the Steps. I was asked to make a decision to turn my will and my life over to God's care. I was more than willing to turn over my life – I knew that I certainly needed help with my life. To turn over my will, now that was different. I was willing to turn over my life if He would do it my way.

Then I heard "turn our will and our lives over to the care of God *as we understood Him.*" The word "care" became my focus. I heard another Al-Anon member say that the word care meant love and concern. That distinction helped me think maybe I could turn my will and my life over to the love and concern of God as I understood Him.

To whom was I turning over my life and my will? This God as I understood Him was important for me. I had grown up going to church with my Baptist father, my Methodist mother, two Catholic sisters and my brothers who attended different churches. One brother and I attended the nearby Presbyterian church. In our family we recognized that while God was the same, the religions were different.

Step Three asked me to make a commitment to God as I understood Him. I realized this made it necessary for me to examine my beliefs. I needed to have my own relationship with God, so I had to do some soul searching. Even though I joined the church when I was in my teens, I learned that this Step was not about church. It wasn't about any specific religion. It was about my own personal relationship with a Higher Power, a Power greater than myself whom I chose to call God.

My concept of God changed. As a child, I had envisioned God sitting on a throne. He looked down on me and saw all the things that I thought I did wrong. I didn't see Him smiling at me. The look I thought

He gave me was pretty much the same condemning look that I received from adults. I was the youngest of six children. I had tried to do things right, but I seemed unable to do things well enough to please all of my family.

Today the God of my understanding is much different. He is a loving God. I no longer think that He judges me through other people. To me, He has a lot of human characteristics. I know that He loves me unconditionally. I know He gives me the privilege of making my own decisions. Sometimes I do the wrong thing and He lets me experience the consequences of my own mistakes. I feel there are times that He looks down on me fondly and shakes His head and smiles and says, "When will she ever learn?"

I know He is always with me. I once heard someone say they carried God on their right shoulder so I decided to do the same. In tough times when I need security, I can reach up and rub my right shoulder to feel His warmth.

My God has a sense of humor. He allows my world to take ridiculous twists. When things go badly He gives me compensations. My God is patient as I make the same mistakes over and over. I can turn something over to Him and then take it back. He watches me wrestle with it until I am willing, once again, to turn it over to Him. To me, God is kind and understanding. He sends people to give me hugs and other caring gestures to show me His love. He answers my prayers. From time to time, He gives me the privilege of helping others. I have learned to listen to Him and to give Him an opportunity to work in my life. I have learned that He helps me accomplish things that I never thought I could.

Today, I am comfortable turning my life and my will over to the God of my understanding. Al-Anon and my Al-Anon friends help me decide when.

My DAUGHTER left me two legacies. One was her black cat, named Ms. Garfield. The cat demands that I stand by her whenever she eats. The other was Al-Anon. This has been a great gift, one that saw me through the grief of losing my daughter. It has also helped me deal with the loss of my son who died years before. Nine months after my daughter took me to my first Al-Anon meeting, her seventh suicide attempt ended in her death. She told me she was an alcoholic and that she was in recovery. She thought Al-Anon would help me. Little did she know what it would come to mean to me. The help and friendship that I received from my Al-Anon friends carried me through very difficult times.

I wanted more. I wanted to be happy again. I really wanted to know how to work the program. A lady in our group told me one day after the meeting that the principles were the important thing. I went home and read through all the books and pamphlets that I had. I still could not figure out what these principles were. The next meeting I decided to ask her if she would be my sponsor. Much to my relief, she said yes.

I met with her at a set time every week. First she had me talk and write about the resentments and anger I had over the deaths of my children. After I could free my mind from these tragedies, we started working on the Steps. We probably spent eight months going through this process. I wrote about my feelings, thoughts and questions. Then I shared them with her. I wanted to know what Steps and principles would help me with any situation that came up. I continued to do a lot of reading and studying from Al-Anon literature. Of course, I continued going to meetings, too.

Eventually, someone asked me to be her sponsor. I told her we could try it but both of us were free to back out at any time. That was about twelve years ago. She is still my friend. In going through the Steps and listening to people's problems, I continued to work the Steps myself. They became a part of my everyday thinking. By sharing and giving to other people what I had learned, I actually helped make the Steps a vital part of my own life.

What became most important to me was turning my will and life over to the care of God, who is my Higher Power. I also had to turn the problems of the people I was sponsoring over to their Higher Power. I did not have the power to solve their problems. I could remember the First Step and practice detachment. That way, I didn't have to worry about what I was to do and how I was to do it. Wherever I was led seemed to be right. Even in my personal life, I had the freedom to do what I wanted. My thoughts, desires and opportunities were put there by my Higher Power, so the Third Step became the most important one for me.

The principles I derived from the first three Steps now guide me to the Step that applies to a specific problem. The principle I got from the First Step is honesty. I really have to search for the honesty of my problem so I can deal with reality. Hope is the principle I received from the Second Step. I know that a Power greater than myself can show me the sane way to proceed. The Third Step gave me the principle of faith. I believe that God can help me handle my situation. These first three Steps are the acceptance Steps. They give me a foundation for working all the rest of the Steps.

ONCE I UNDERSTOOD HIM, THE DECISION WAS EASY

WHEN I worked Step Two, I came to believe there is a Power greater than I am. Step Three asked me to make a decision. It was up to me to decide whether to turn my will and my life over to this Higher Power as I understood Him. Although I believed in a Higher Power, I felt scared and inadequately prepared to make my decision. I realized I did not have a good understanding of Him, which I needed to have in order to turn my life over to Him.

Somewhere along life's path, I bought a bill of goods that God was punishing, rejecting and judgmental. I truly believed that God wanted me to suffer and to be miserable in order to pay for my mistakes. I thought God did not have time for me. I thought I was just supposed to survive and exist. That was what I believed.

In Al-Anon I learned I could have any concept of a Higher Power I wanted. I decided to throw out my past concept of God so I could start over with a clean slate. Cautiously, I began to talk to him. I experimented with prayer and meditation. I spent months getting comfortable with this new relationship. My sponsor let me take my time while she gave me encouragement and suggestions.

When I felt comfortable and safe in this new and special relationship, I began to redefine my concept of my Higher Power. I came to a beautifully simple conclusion – God is my best friend. We talk, laugh and cry together. I can say anything to God. He knows my fears, defects and mistakes. He also knows my dreams, assets and successes. He knows what I need and He provides for me. God gently, with a great sense of humor, points me in the direction of His will for me. When I have questions, I know it is okay to ask. God never makes me feel stupid or wrong. God gives me choices and when I make a mistake – it's okay. We only get closer. My God always has time for me and He makes me feel special.

Working Step Three not only changed my concept of God, it changed my life. I found a friend who will always be there for me. I found a God of my understanding. Once I understood Him, the decision to turn my will and my life over to Him was easy.

Working Step Three

Made a decision to turn our will and our lives over to the care of God as we understood Him.

HERE ARE some ideas and questions to ask ourselves or discuss in our group to begin exploring our relationship to the God of our understanding.

* How do I feel about turning my life over to a Higher Power for guidance?

* How do I know who or what my Higher Power is?

* Am I willing to try to turn my problems over? What could help me to be willing?

* How can I stop thinking, trying and considering, and actually make a decision?

* Have I had a problem making decisions in my life? Give examples.

* If I am unable to make this decision, what holds me back?

* Do I trust my Higher Power to care for me?

* How might Step Three help me keep my hands off situations created by others?

* What consequences have I had by obsessing on problems and other people?

* When I "Let Go and Let God" take care of my life, am I willing to follow the guidance I receive?

* How can I turn a situation over and let go of the results?

* How can I stop myself from taking my will back?

* What can I do when my loved ones make decisions I don't like?

* How can I let my loved ones find their own life paths as I am finding mine?

* What can I do to try to see others as God sees them?

* How can I express God's will in my actions and words toward others, including the alcoholic?

Step Four

Made a searching and fearless moral inventory of ourselves.

STEPS ONE, TWO AND THREE taught us about the disease of alcoholism, that we are powerless over the disease and that a Power greater than ourselves can return us to sanity if we so desire. As in climbing a staircase, we are at the next Step – a Step for spiritual self-discovery. In nine simple words, Step Four challenges us to take a thorough look at ourselves, the positives as well as the negatives.

Al-Anon members worldwide have experienced the power this Step offers. By using the collective experiences of these members, we learn there is no one way to take a Fourth Step inventory. We are repeatedly told that the single key to this Step is to take action by doing it. Many have worked this Step because they were told it would help them in their recovery. Others attempted to begin working this Step without the help of a sponsor or Al-Anon friend and, in fear, abandoned it. By asking for willingness from a Higher Power, working with a sponsor, listening in Fourth Step meetings and reading Al-Anon Conference Approved Literature (CAL), members can continue this incredible journey of self-knowledge. Lovingly we are told to approach Step Four with self-love, kindness, honesty and balance.

The decision to turn our life and will over to the care of our Higher Power is demonstrated when we follow it up with the action of taking our moral inventory. The word searching has an important impact. This word tells us that it is going to take some research into our past, looking for all the personal issues that are a part of our makeup. When we lose our keys, we will search for them until they are found or until we are satisfied that they are gone forever. Similarly the search through our moral character must be equally thorough. This is where we begin to learn that it is important to write out this Step. If we need to make a list before grocery shopping, doesn't it seem logical that, in something as important as the personal study of our lives, we keep documentation as well?

In studying the wording of this Step, we now examine the word fearless. Some members say fear stands for false evidence appearing real. What better way to find out if we fear reality or an illusion than to plunge into the fear itself? With a phone call to our sponsor or program friends, we find that beginning to list our fears is another way to start our inventory. Until we take our inventory, we don't know which character defects blocked us from recovery. "Just do it," we are repeatedly advised. We don't need to do it perfectly, there will be time to do it again. If we don't make a start, nothing about us will ever change. When we courageously and carefully examine where we are, the door to change is opened.

Finally we read the last phrase, "moral inventory of ourselves." The self-analysis required in a fearless, moral inventory is an essential step toward recognizing our responsibilities and finding appropriate, healthful release from our physical, emotional and spiritual experiences. We can begin by writing about the events and people we resent or distrust. Writing becomes important because few of us can remember the many incidents and people that affected us. Writing also helps us to step back and gain a little detachment before we explore our behavior and the characteristics it reveals about us.

A member of Al-Anon asked why she had to write her Fourth Step if she had discussed all her personal issues with a professional. A longtime member shared that she, too, had considered that, but based on the guidance of her sponsor, she decided to begin writing her thoughts. She said that by writing it out she was able to remove herself from some of the specific situations and see herself more clearly. She stated that she had been intellectually analyzing the Al-Anon program using the first three Steps, but was now experiencing a new awareness not only of herself, but also of the many alcoholics in her life.

Another longtime member shared that she heard early in her recovery that some of the issues Al-Anon members share in coping with the disease of alcoholism relate to the four Ms: martyrdom, managing, manipulating and mothering. By writing down each M, she began to use them as the backbone of her inventory. She shared that she ultimately had a long list of situations, persons and events that she wanted to examine closely. She marked each one with a plus or a minus sign to denote how she felt each had impacted her life. She then wrote a brief paragraph or sentence to state what it was she wanted to do differently and how she was going to apply the Al-Anon principles. Her Fourth Step experience provided her with a new-found freedom, and she now believes that she is a good person with values. Most important, she is respected by her family and friends.

Al-Anon's *Blueprint for Progress* is a tool that many Al-Anon members use to begin their inventory and as a measuring tool for growth. A sponsor writes, "I encourage those I sponsor to buy a new *Blueprint for Progress* annually. I then sit down with them and help them compare this year's inventory to the previous year's. Most are amazed and ecstatic with their growth and recovery. Not only is it satisfying to them, but I also glow in the knowledge that some day they will pass this study technique on to someone they will sponsor." He emphasizes that they will grow only by answering the questions with thoughtful narrative. Yes and no answers are not revealing, are not searching and are not fearless.

In 1989, Alateen completed an *Alateen Fourth Step Inventory* workbook, which is used in Al-Anon as well as Alateen meetings. The approach is gentle, yet challenging. In the study, members are encouraged to draw their feelings. An adult using this workbook as part of a thorough inventory may freeze when challenged with the aspect of having to draw how he/ she feels about each of the major inventory topics: attitudes, self-esteem, love, responsibility, feelings, and relationships. After consulting with a teen member, the adult realized that the instructions merely say "draw" your feelings. It doesn't ask you to become an artist and do it perfectly.

An Alateen sponsor shares that, in working with young people, the easiest way to work this Step is to "Keep It Simple." A Fourth Step meeting for this group involves taking one sheet of paper and folding it in half. On one half, the sponsor suggests that members list their assets, all the good things they know about themselves. On the other half, the sponsor suggests that they list their character defects. She suggests that each list should be equal in length. As the teens begin this simple Fourth Step, they are encouraged to talk with their personal or group sponsor when they get stuck. The Alateen sponsor stated that, in this loving environment, this approach toward working Step Four is simple, and for these young people, thorough. She added that it works for adults in Al-Anon, too.

In studying the First Step, we learned that we didn't cause the disease of alcoholism, we can't control it and we can't cure it. Additionally we acquired an awareness of how we contributed to the disease through our actions. Some of our actions were admirable and justified, others were embarrassing and, in our minds, inexcusable. Members have found it easier to dissect specific incidents, situations or relationships by listing these actions in a Fourth Step under columns for cause, control, cure and contribute. For each action they then ask, Did I cause the problem? How have I tried to control it? Is it in my power to cure it? Did this action contribute to the problem? Only one or two of the three Cs may be applicable to each action. A final column is entitled 'Comments.' In this section many members list the names of persons involved in the situation and how their relationships have been affected. Other members write how they would handle the situation differently today by using Al-Anon tools.

With any writing exercise, guidance from a sponsor or Al-Anon member who has worked this Step is helpful. Although there are no specific written rules or instructions in Al-Anon on how to study and work Step Four, the experiences of those who have gone before us are invaluable to our own personal efforts. Studying Al-Anon Conference Approved Literature (CAL) also provides a variety of tools and suggestions for working Step Four.

Living with the disease of alcoholism can destroy self-esteem. Sick family members often point out our faults and shortcomings again and again until we fear taking an inventory. This is not the aim of Step Four. If we are likely to take an inventory only of our faults, it is advisable to return to the first three Steps until enough acceptance and trust in the help of our Higher Power has been achieved to approach Step Four with love, kindness, honesty and balance. It is essential that our inventory include our assets as well as our defects of character.

It is often said at meetings that the words rationalization and justification can become our best friends and our worst enemies. We may discover that we have blamed all our difficulties on the alcoholic and excused ourselves with rationalizations. We probably know most of our own faults intimately and may be unacquainted with our virtues. Self-righteous justification is no longer an acceptable excuse. If we think we don't possess courage, we can ask our Higher Power to provide it and our sponsor or a friend in the program to help us remember it.

What form do we use for Step Four? Any form. Will we do it perfectly the first time? Probably not. It doesn't matter. What does matter is that by completing a first, second or third inventory members learn new facts about themselves. Some compare working a Fourth Step to that of peeling the layers of an onion, one layer at a time, until the core is reached. It matters not how we do it; what matters is that we do it. Working Step Four is an act of self-love, for it helps us take the focus off the alcoholic and encourages us to take time to pay attention to ourselves – the only person we can help.

The suggested Al-Anon closing states in part, "We aren't perfect. . . After a while, you'll discover that though you may not like all of us, you'll love us in a very special way – the same way we already love you." The action of Step Four gives us new-found courage and permission to love ourselves. The door is now open to new horizons of growth and a spiritual awakening we have never before experienced.

Members Share Experience, Strength and Hope

FOR A long time I thought about doing Step Four, but I only thought about it. Then, someone suggested that I try doing one question a day from the *Blueprint for Progress*, Al-Anon's Fourth Step inventory workbook. That idea seemed manageable enough to get me started.

I knew Al-Anon emphasized keeping the focus on ourselves. What attracted me to the Fourth Step was the possibility of discovering parts of myself that I never knew existed. Hearing other members' experiences with the Step gave me the guidance and encouragement that I needed. I heard it was wise to have some time in the program and to have done the first three Steps before beginning to take a formal inventory. While the Step called for a fearless moral inventory, I heard that I might still feel some fear. People compared doing the Fourth Step to opening the door of a closet that has been locked for a long time, or looking into a mirror that I've been avoiding. They

MOVING
TOWARD
THE LIGHT

suggested it was helpful to have a trusted sponsor and other program people to depend on while I went through this process.

Although the *Blueprint for Progress* was one way to do my Fourth Step, it wasn't the only way. Some members said they wrote their autobiography and looked for recurring situations or themes. Others wrote a resentment list. The nicest thing about any of these approaches was that I didn't have to do the Fourth Step alone. I asked for help at meetings and over the phone. Members encouraged me to notice anytime my thoughts told me I should, ought to or must perform some action. They asked me to explore whether my attitudes and assumptions about life were serving my best interests.

By reading the literature and listening to others share at meetings, I could see how the disease had affected the way I was living my life. I got a glimpse of how control, people-pleasing, fear and other shortcomings stood in the way of my serenity. I also saw some of my good qualities that I needed to acknowledge and respect.

Most of all, I learned I needed to be honest, open and willing in order to discover who I really am. Honesty would keep me from excusing my character defects or behavior. I couldn't justify what I did because "they deserved it for what they did to me." From what I heard, it seemed difficult for other people to face negative things about themselves. In all honesty, I had positive aspects in my personality that were even harder for me to accept.

I needed to be open-minded and non-judgmental about examining my life. Step Four wasn't the time for self-hatred or intense self-criticism. The program suggested merely taking stock and conducting an inventory, instead of labeling my characteristics as good or bad. It wasn't appropriate to minimize my behaviors by saying they weren't that bad. Nor was it appropriate to maximize my situation by saying it was the worst ever. An open mind helped me put my life and problems in their true perspective. It helped for me to consider the part that I played in my difficulties. I needed to look at those things that might have kept me stuck.

I needed the willingness to face things – some things that have haunted me from the past and other things about myself that I may discover that I don't like. I needed the willingness to take back my power. I needed the willingness to experience long-frozen emotions, whatever they might be. I needed to be willing to try a new way. I also needed the openness to see myself differently, to drop my roles and to look at alcoholism as a disease that has affected my life.

The Fourth Step inventory was a formidable challenge. It would have been easier to hide and isolate. I could have continued to deny unpleasant and painful truths. Fear was ever present. I wondered, if I did the inventory would the people I was close to stop wanting to be around me? Would I have to get a divorce? Would I have to confront people? Would I like myself when I was done? Being a people-pleaser risking others' disapproval was extremely uncomfortable. My recovery required that I be willing to risk someone else's disapproval in order to gain my own. It meant that, instead of trying to live up to an outside standard, I measured my success by my own yardstick.

To the extent that I was honest, my life improved every time I did an inventory. While it wasn't always an in-depth written one, it helped to examine those areas of my life where the problem just didn't go away. I thought if I did a perfect inventory, I would never have to do another one again. I would know exactly and completely who I was and am. I expected to receive a fully-developed picture of myself when I finished the first one, but it didn't happen. Instead, just like a Polaroid photograph, the color emerged gradually over time. As my ability to deal with life increased, new areas for development attracted my attention. It wasn't that I didn't do my inventory correctly the first time. That's just how my recovery worked. I had been living life in a blinded state. Too much light, all at once, would have been frightening, extremely painful and damaging. Instead, each program experience lit a candle in my darkness. Each spiritual awakening added another measure of light to my life.

I BEGAN TO
SEE MY PART
IN THE
SITUATION

WHEN I was new to Al-Anon, I saw the Fourth Step as a sort of miracle cure. I was flopping around in a puddle of old anger and fear. It seemed that if I'd just write down all of this stuff and follow up with Step Five, I should be all better – right? And, wow, did I want to be all better as soon as possible. So I sat down and started writing. After an hour and six or seven pages, I did feel better. I felt better for about two weeks, when the pit of confusion and self-pity swallowed me again.

I don't think I had a clear understanding of the first three Steps at that time. I expected the program to change me, as I had expected other things to make changes for me – such as a new car, a job, moving to a new location and a hairstyle. Things that temporarily changed how I felt, however, did not change all of my feelings. I thought if I read the Steps and believed them with all my heart and clicked my heels together three times, I would receive that gift of serenity. It took a while to realize that the program didn't work like that for me.

Last year I did another Fourth Step that focused on a particular issue. That time was different. As I answered questions in the format I was using, I began to see my part in the situation. I discovered a starting point for making some changes. Now I could actually use some tools of the program. Instead of expecting the program to change me, I wrote letters and prayed and made phone calls. You know what? My program worked like that!

I RECALL challenging any need for the words, searching and fearless, in my own Fourth Step. I knew why the alcoholic needed to do fearless searching, because drinking had distorted his vision – but I could see everything clearly! As a result, early in my experience with Step Four, I didn't search very far. At the first hint that I might feel fearful about something on the horizon, I stopped searching altogether.

Since that time, I've learned that a lot of things about myself were very deeply hidden. My fear had to do with what I might find. I even thought, What if I've been wrong all my life? What if I've been lying to myself? What if this kind of life is not what I want? What if I am just a fake? What if all my pain was wasted. How dearly I held my misery! How justified I wanted to be in every emotion, every reaction and behavior! But hadn't I also challenged the idea about sanity in Step Two? You bet!

Little by little, I gained an ever deeper understanding of the Twelve Steps. Step Four was an important one for me. I used several different formats to inventory my beliefs. It helped me to realize that I usually acted on the basis of one of my beliefs. When I looked at my actions, or my reactions or my desires, I got clues about what beliefs might still lay hidden beneath my conscious awareness. For example, I began public speaking in junior high. I was always frightened about speaking in public, but I also knew that I got approval from it. What was my underlying belief? I needed to get or earn approval. What was my fear? This next time that I spoke I might not receive any approval. I also saw in the process of all this that I managed to develop a very useful skill.

With or without fear, as I sought out my hidden beliefs and brought them into the light, I found that sometimes I was wrong – but not always. Sometimes I knew truths about myself but I lacked the confidence to stand by them. I discovered I may have wanted something at one time, but that later I changed my mind. Gratefully, my work with Steps Two and Three preceded the work that I did on Step Four. Today I can go on to Steps Five, Six and Seven. I know the early symptoms to watch for in case my actions stray from my conscious beliefs. I also know the remedy to apply when I am suffering again from the disease of alcoholism.

Working Step Four

Made a searching and fearless moral inventory of ourselves.

As we begin to consider the questions below, we need to remember to keep it simple and pray for guidance and courage. The following are not all-inclusive, but rather point to a beginning.

IN PREPARING TO TAKE AN INVENTORY

* Am I willing to look honestly at myself? What stands in my way?

* Have I sought help from my Higher Power, my sponsor or other Al-Anon members?

* What suggestions have I tried to see if they might work?

* Do I understand the spiritual principle of an inventory?

* What do "searching" and "fearless" mean to me?

* What does a "moral inventory" mean?

WE CONTINUE BY EXAMINING OUR ASSETS

An inventory is not just our faults; we must also assess our positive traits and accomplishments. If we are stymied by this task, it can be useful to think about qualities we like in others and whether we may possess that same trait.

* In what ways am I caring? How do I empathize with other people? Am I kind to myself? Am I kind to the elderly? Children? My family? My friends? Those in need of my assistance? Am I agreeable and courteous?

* How am I tolerant?

* Am I open to another's point of view?

* Do I listen in meetings and accept that others have needs different from mine?

* Do I practice patience with a newcomer?

* How am I trustworthy? Do I pay my bills? Am I prompt? Do I fulfill my commitments? Do I act responsible in my job? How much can my family and friends depend on me?

* How am I honest? Do I tell the whole truth? If not, what stops me from telling the truth?

* In what ways do I take care of myself? Do I make needed medical appointments? Do I dress appropriately? Do I eat healthy foods? Exercise? Meditate?

* How am I respectful? Do I take care of material things, whether mine or others'? Do I show respect for the law?

* How am I generous? Do I contribute to my group? To the World Service Office triannual appeal? Have I contributed by volunteering to be a trusted servant?

* In what ways do I look for the good in others?

* How am I kind? Am I considerate of other people? Do I listen patiently to a friend in need? Do I offer help when asked? Do I think to point out the good in others?

* How do I open myself up to others?

* How am I practical? Do I have a budget? How often do I recognize what needs to be done and then do my share?

* How am I dependable? How often do I meet work deadlines? Do I organize well and carry out what I decide to do?

* What are my talents? Do I have any artistic gifts? Do I beautify my surroundings? Do I have mechanical skills?

* Do I make friends easily? Why or why not?

* Do I have trouble with intimate relationships? Why or why not?

* In what ways do I express myself clearly and concisely?

* How do I see the humor in life and express it?

* How am I optimistic?

* How do I practice my faith in a Higher Power? In myself? In others? How do I share my faith? Do I have an attitude of gratitude?

* How am I humble? Do I ask God for guidance and follow it to the best of my ability? When have I allowed others to share their wisdom with me? Do I ever admit mistakes? How patient am I with myself?

We now should have a list of good qualities to fortify us for the rest of the inventory. With each and every good quality we surveyed, we may have considered a quality we find uncomfortable to acknowledge. A thorough inventory, as we stated in the beginning of this chapter includes our positive as well as negative behaviors and thoughts.

Now OUR task is to deal with the difficult issues of our lives, past and present. Nothing will be solved by hiding from the truth. Justifying and rationalizing our actions and blaming others for all the problems in our lives will never produce serenity. Remember, we are only asked to take an inventory, not to do anything about what we learn. If we trust in our Higher Power and the guidance of our sponsor, these issues will be dealt with in a loving way as we continue to work the Al-Anon program of recovery.

* In what ways am I resentful? Do I harbor grudges? Why?

* Whom do I resent from my past? Why? What is my part in it?

* Whom do I resent in my immediate environment? Why? What is my part in it?

* Do I resent authority figures? Why? What is my part in it?

* Do I resent places or things? Why? What is my part in it?

* When do I judge other people harshly and resent their not doing what I think they should?

* Do I hold everyone and everything to an impossible standard of ideal perfection?

* How do I judge myself?

* Am I fearful? What do I fear? Why?

* Am I dishonest? Am I holding secrets? Do I lie rather than "cause a scene"? What dishonesty have I hidden from others?

* Do I feel sorry for myself? Am I filled with self-pity? How do I feel I have been made a victim? What is my part in it?

* Am I a fixer? Do I like to be in charge? Do I get upset when I don't win? What consequences have I had from taking care of others instead of myself?

* In what ways do I trust myself in dealing with others? Do I go to safe places? Do I remove myself from potentially dangerous situations? Even if it's my own home?

* In what ways am I comfortable with my sexuality? Do I enjoy sex? If I am having sexual difficulties, do I know why? Have I sought professional help?

* Do I have a God of love or a God of fear in my life? How can I change my attitude toward my Higher Power?

* Do I take on responsibilities that are not mine? Why or why not?

* Do I do for others what they can do for themselves? Why?

* Do I feel responsible for someone else's learning, marriage or sobriety? How?

In Step Four we have begun the journey to self-trust through self-knowledge. As we continue the journey through the Steps, we gain trust in ourselves, our Higher Power, in other people and in life. The path to recovery using the Twelve Steps – one Step at a time – continues. Before taking the next Step, congratulate yourself, call your sponsor and share at your next home group meeting the excitement and relief you feel from doing your own personal Fourth Step.

In Step Four we made a thorough inventory of ourselves, both assets and defects. Step Five asks us to take another action with what we have learned about ourselves. We are to share "the exact nature of our wrongs" with God, ourselves and another person.

Step Five requires honesty with ourselves and others. It was one thing to get the courage needed to list our deeds and misdeeds, our fears and resentments on a piece of paper; quite another to reveal them to another person. We sometimes hear in Al-Anon meetings that we are only as sick as our secrets. What goes on in alcoholic homes is often kept very private; many of us have been taught not to air our dirty laundry in public. In Step Five we begin to unburden ourselves of our secrets. Step Five does not ask us to show our faults to the whole world, but to our own hearts, to the God of our understanding and to a trusted friend. Step Five gives us permission to talk about things in a healthier manner, rather than make ourselves martyrs to anyone who comes along.

Our first task is to admit the exact nature of our wrongs to our Higher Power. Having spent some time with Steps Two and Three, we have come to understand our God as loving, compassionate and non-judgmental. We also know that God can help us if we are willing to be helped. We can begin work on Step Five by talking to our loving Higher Power about what we discovered in Step Four. We recognize that we are probably not telling God anything new, but this open admission allows us to approach our Higher Power acknowledging our hard work and our willingness to see ourselves as we really are. Many of us feel a sense of relief as we feel the acceptance and love offered despite our wrongs.

The next part of the Step is to admit these same things to ourselves. For some it is easier to tell God about our wrongs than to admit them to ourselves. When we look at ourselves with complete honesty, stripping away excuses and the blaming of others for

Step Five

Admitted to God, to ourselves and to another human being the exact nature of our wrongs.

our behavior, we become aware of how much we deluded and justified ourselves. At this point we may be tempted to condemn ourselves for the difficulties we caused. It is important to remember to love and accept ourselves unconditionally, just as our Higher Power does. We are seeking to grow by facing who we are at the moment; nothing is served by beating ourselves up for the past. Step Five does not ask us to do anything about our past actions; for now all we are asked is to face them squarely and admit them to ourselves as fact.

Admitting to God and to ourselves is not enough; we must break our isolation and share our faults with another human being. This, too, can be difficult, since many of us had criticism and blame heaped upon us if we admitted a mistake. Admitting our faults to another person may seem like asking to be rejected. To admit our darkest secrets to anyone requires us to trust another person and to trust our own value as a human being. Learning to trust is an essential tool of recovery that brings with it relief and serenity.

By the time we reach Step Five, we have usually acquired some degree of trust. We have listened to others share openly and with courage at meetings and have seen them lovingly received. We have likely shared ourselves, called people on the phone and found a sponsor. We have practiced trusting others with some truths about ourselves, and hopefully we are now willing to share our innermost secrets with another human being. We may be filled with anxiety and fear as we approach this task, but we have faith that it is necessary for our recovery.

The person to confide in needs to be chosen with care. Experience has shown it is best not to select our spouse, partner, a family member or the alcoholic. They are too close to us or too involved with the events we will discuss. We do not want to choose anyone who might be wounded by our version of events.

We need someone who is not involved with our individual situation, who can keep a confidence and listen with empathy. We seek someone who will not criticize us, but who will be able to suggest to us any obvious omissions or to give us insight into how the nature of our wrongs has affected us. We may ask them to help us see patterns in our behavior and how a defect is often the flip side of a strength.

We are not looking for someone to tell us how to handle our problems, but rather for a loving witness who can provide perspective on our spiritual journey; one who can appreciate what we are doing and how we are growing. Before we decide on someone, some of us pray and meditate, seeking guidance from our Higher Power, especially if risking and trusting are new to us.

Many members use their sponsors. Others choose a friend, a clergy person, a counselor or even an acquaintance. Whether or not we use our sponsor, their guidance can help us choose the correct person. It is important that we trust the person and that they will hold our experiences in total confidence.

Once we have selected the person, we need to act. We pick up the phone, make our request and set a time and place to share our inventory. We find a place with privacy (it could be a private room in our house, an office, a discreet restaurant, the beach, a park, a hiking trail – whatever works for us) and enough time to talk. It may take more than one meeting.

It is vital to be as honest as we can through all stages of Step Five. Asking our Higher Power for help before we begin to share may be helpful. As we share our inventory aloud, we do not want to deny or excuse our wrongs, but to come to understand and accept them. We honestly face the past and, by sharing our faults, make a commitment to continue to grow and change.

It is important to explore not only the list of events, but also the "exact nature of our wrongs." We seek to know ourselves more fully, therefore we examine our deeds and the reasons for them. Without excusing our behavior, we try to recognize what basic need or fear was operating when we behaved as we did. Taken in context many of our behaviors made sense at the time. For instance, there are experiences where mistrust was appropriate. We may have been dealing with people and events who were out of control or dangerous. The defenses we learned served us well in alcoholic and other unhealthy situations, but now they keep us from living happily and serenely. We can acknowledge these defenses without condemning ourselves for using them. Our confidante is sometimes able to help us understand the exact nature of our wrongs. As we share, we may discover that we need further thought and meditation. In either case, we do the best we can at the time – and move on.

When we complete the Fifth Step, we have accomplished a difficult task and learned more about ourselves and our actions. Some of us feel great relief as we unburden ourselves. We discover that we are not alone in our human frailties and we are not the worst person in the world, as we might have believed. Whether it brings great relief or a small beginning of acceptance, Step Five brings us closer to our Higher Power and helps us learn to trust both God and other people on our spiritual journey.

Members Share Experience, Strength and Hope

A POWERFUL EXPERIENCE
AFTER I had completed a Fourth Step, my sponsor suggested sitting with that Step for a while before we started the Fifth Step. She said we could do the Fifth Step any way that I wanted. She shared with me several of the ways that she had done the Fifth Step with other people. I decided to do mine by reading my Fourth Step to her, one piece at a time. Every week we met for an hour or two. We kept at it until, finally, I

had read all of it to her.

I went through a variety of feelings during those weeks of reading and sharing. Sometimes, I went home tense, overwhelmed or confused; other times relieved or amazed. I had spent many years getting professional help but never before had I experienced this level of personal acceptance and support. I couldn't believe someone would volunteer to spend so much time with me without giving me their judgments, criticisms or comments. It became my first experience with unconditional love. I wanted to pay my sponsor for all the time she had given me. I wanted to take her to lunch or give her a present, but I realized that this was not necessary. The experience with my Fifth Step proved to me what Al-Anon was all about – giving without expectation of results, listening and being present for another who is learning the Al-Anon way of life.

From that powerful experience, I am still learning about the major themes of my recovery – patience, judgment, isolation and detachment. It taught me greater patience and greater acceptance of others as well as greater acceptance of myself. It taught me how to reach out, how to share myself and my feelings. It showed me how to develop a wonderful relationship with my Higher Power, whom I choose to call God. I feel much more connected to other people. I am able to let others live their lives without giving them my advice, even when there is great difficulty and possible danger in a home.

Whenever I feel stuck, angry, or confused, I still work a Fourth Step. It helps me look for my part in the chaos. With experience and time, I find that the Fourth and Fifth Steps help me accept a wide range of human traits that I and all people have. I find comfort and relief in letting go of the need for perfection and becoming more human. I know that God will show me the answers. I no longer need to believe that I am alone in any aspect of my life. Al-Anon poured the spiritual foundation for my recovery when I took Steps Four and Five. They carried me toward my spiritual awakening.

I NO LONGER HAVE TO KEEP SECRETS

STEP FIVE was a very humbling experience for me. Admitting to God, to myself and to another human being the exact nature of my wrongs let me get rid of all my secrets that had kept me from my serenity. Admitting to God meant sharing with my Higher Power something that I did that caused harm to someone else. Admitting to myself meant that I was no longer in denial about my wrongs. Admitting to another human being meant my secrets were out in the open and that I could reason things out better with someone else.

Because my home group had studied the pamphlet on sponsorship, I realized how important a sponsor was when I worked this Step. I had heard others talk about how they selected someone to ask. I looked for someone who was strong. I listened to hear someone who spoke about working the Steps before I found one.

Applying Step Five to my life was not an easy thing to do. When I worked this Step with my sponsor, I felt as though my Higher Power was right there with me, listening to me admit my wrongs. The easiest way for me to apply this Step to my life was to have a sponsor who was willing to listen. Without her my Fifth Step would not have been complete. One of the benefits was my gradual awareness of how much I have grown in my program. By admitting my wrongs and learning from my experiences, I no longer have to keep secrets to sacrifice my serenity.

I MADE AN INDIVIDUAL COMMITMENT

IT WAS not a problem for me to perform the first two parts of Step Five – admitting to God and to myself. Part three, admitting to another human being the exact nature of my wrongs, was a problem.

The admissions to God and to myself were private

and personal acts. The admission to another human being was a public matter. I had spent a lifetime concealing my behavior. Now I found myself in a position where suddenly I had to become an adult. I had to take a quantum leap into adulthood beyond the child-victim role that I had played for so long. These realizations let me know I had more work to do on myself before I could perform the third part of this Step. I needed more information so I could learn techniques for growing up. I needed to run through some rehearsals with myself before I could begin to admit to another human being the exact nature of my wrongs. I had to recognize that time, patience and tolerance were my aids.

One exercise I chose was to make an individual commitment. I chose to read and learn the Twelve Steps and then to put them into practice. This meant I made an initial commitment and I conducted periodic follow-ups. I didn't want to forget what I was doing. I didn't want to slip into a false sense of complacency and forget the purpose and intent of my program.

I recognized I could not make the program work all by myself. It would only work if I did it in concert with other people. I knew doing it solo certainly hadn't worked before! I decided to make a commitment to attend Al-Anon meetings on a regular basis and to go through the exercise of daily readings from *One Day at a Time in Al-Anon* and *Courage to Change: One Day at a Time in Al-Anon II.*

I needed to seek knowledge and help from other Al-Anon members. I needed to share with others, as well as to work with a sponsor. That way, I could keep things in perspective. For five years, I was unable to find a sponsor who suited my needs. That did not make me quit searching. In the meantime, I just kept hanging in there by working my program as best I could.

As a result of working the program, I learned gratitude for what my Higher Power had given me. In order to express my gratitude, I knew I had to give back to the program what it had given me. I began doing service work. I accepted offices at various meetings and I became a group representative so I could serve at the district level. One day, this might lead me into service at the area or world service level.

When I was able to grasp the full meaning of the Al-Anon program, I could accept myself as a mature person. Then I was able to perform the third part of Step Five – admitted to God, to ourselves and to another human being...

SOMEONE LIFTED A BIG BURDEN FROM MY SHOULDERS.

THE FIRST part of Step Five is that we admitted to God. Since God knows all things, I knew that I couldn't hide things about myself from Him. Even though He knows, I needed to admit my wrongs to Him so that I would know.

The next part of Step Five is about admitting to ourselves. I could be quite proficient at justifying my behavior. I whitewashed things, even from myself. When I wrote my inventory and saw it in black and white, I had to let myself in on the truth about myself.

Admitting to myself may not have been easy, but the worst was yet to come. Admitting the exact nature of my wrongs to another human being, the last part of Step Five was really tough. I was taught not to air my dirty laundry in public. My upbringing told me not to let others know about me or they might not like me. Yet, Step Five asked me to do just that.

In Al-Anon meetings I heard the suggestion to take my Fifth Step with one person. I needed to choose someone who understood the Al-Anon program, someone who recognized what I was doing. People suggested I select someone I trusted so I'd know they would not repeat what I told them. I heard this was my Fifth Step and that it was designed to make me feel better. I needed to tell enough about myself to clear away the knots in my stomach. The time and place for my Fifth Step were very important. I needed to make arrangements with the other person so we would both have ample time. I also needed to be sure we would have enough privacy so we would not be interrupted.

When I made my Fifth Step, I found out the things I thought were so horrible about myself were not as gigantic as I thought. Frequently the other person said, "Yes, I did that too," or "I remember when I felt that way."

Doing the Fifth Step was a spiritual experience for me. I learned that I was not as bad as I thought. Mostly, I learned that I am simply human and that I made many normal human errors. On the other hand, being able to talk aloud about things removed my guilty and fearful feelings. Talking about them with another person diminished their size.

In Steps Four and Five, I learned many good things about myself. The character defects that I did find came with enough light to take away my fear. The fear I felt prior to taking Steps Four and Five was like cleaning my house. When I opened the door of a closet, if there was a very scary thing with big eyes in the back in the dark, I could slam the door closed. Deep down I knew whatever was there would still be there. My fear continued to grow. Finally, when I gathered my courage and opened the closet door. I could stick a broom inside and quickly knock the monster out of the closet. When I saw it in the light I realized it was just an old dust mop with two big buttons lying on top. Then, even if I pushed it back in the closet, it no longer frightens me. I could deal with it.

Taking the Fifth Step makes me feel free. I feel like someone lifts a big burden from my shoulders. I also feel extra clean. Sharing my Fifth Step has really helped my self-esteem.

Working Step Five

Admitted to God, to ourselves and to another human being the exact nature of our wrongs.

As WE prepare to admit our faults, we can begin by asking ourselves the following questions or use them for a group discussion.

* If I have completed my Fourth Step inventory, how do I feel about sharing details of my past with another person?

* In what areas of my past am I willing to be completely honest?

* What are some of the advantages I might get from admitting my faults?

* Do I understand the healing relief that honestly admitting my faults can bring?

* What expectations do I have about how I should feel or what I should experience when I admit my faults?

* Am I ready to let these expectations go and allow the God of my understanding to determine the best results for me? How do I know?

* If I do not feel ready to do this Step, do I need to do more work on Steps One through Four?

* Would I be willing to group my inventory into things I could admit, things I might admit, and things I think, "No way! I'll never be able to do that," and then start with the "could" list?

* Am I afraid to admit my faults to my Higher Power? Why?

* Who in the program could I call to discuss my fears about God?

* Could I make a list of my fears and turn them over? What are my fears?

* How can admitting my faults to the God of my understanding help me?

* Can I concede that I am not perfect? How can I quit trying to be?

* How do I try to excuse myself from harms I may have done?

* With whom will I share my Fifth Step? What qualities make me choose this person? Do I trust him or her?

* Do I have any of those qualities myself? Did I list them under my assets?

* What may block me from trusting someone with my truth? Can I share these fears with another person?

* How does my desire to be perfect block me from believing someone could love me unconditionally, even after hearing my Fifth Step?

* How can telling someone else the exact nature of my wrongs enhance my ability to see myself?

* How have I isolated myself? Do I believe that sharing with another person can lead to relief from isolation?

* What is the one thing I don't want to tell another person? Can I start there?

* Can being honest and admitting a mistake have positive consequences? What are they?

* Can I remember when another person admitted a fault or mistake to me and I understood and didn't judge?

* In doing this Fifth Step, what have I learned about the exact nature of my wrongs?

* What have I learned about fear? Honesty? Trust? Acceptance?

* How did I feel after sharing with God? Admitting to myself? Sharing with another person?

* What, if anything, have I left out? If I have completed Step Five, what am I feeling? Is anything different? Better?

SPIRITUAL GROWTH in Al-Anon includes gaining an understanding of our relationship and trust with the God of our understanding. In Step Six we are asked to be entirely ready to have God remove all the defects of character we identified in our Fourth Step and admitted in our Fifth Step. Step Six is a Step of preparation for the next phase of our personal recovery.

The key principle of Step Six is readiness. If we believe we are ready but find we are procrastinating, we need to consider each character defect more closely to see what is stopping us. In most cases we can find several factors that block us from being entirely ready. A longtime member of Al-Anon suggests that, by closely reading, studying and understanding Step Six, some members begin to understand the spiritual basis of this Step. As discussed in Steps One, Two and Three, we learned that we couldn't handle the disease of alcoholism, we acknowledged that the God of our understanding could and that we would let Him. Without true unconditional acceptance of Step Three, the action of Step Six is impossible.

We know we have character defects and have some idea of the pain and difficulties they have caused us; surely it would be a relief to get rid of them. Step Six does not get rid of these defects, it only asks us to become ready. Are we entirely ready? To continue, the answer must be yes. These two words "entirely ready" are not conditional – they are clear and concise in their instruction; we must commit to the action of having God remove our defects of character.

With the guidance of our sponsor or group, we know when we are ready. Some may have taken a break after working the first five Steps, and others of us are fearlessly striving for the serenity sought in continuing our recovery work. Many of us have identified character defects, shared them with God and another human being, and yet we still like them. They are comfortable and familiar – much like our old slippers. We really don't want to discard them, yet logic

Step Six

Were entirely ready to have God remove all these defects of character.

prevails. We get ready. We start shopping for a new pair of slippers. Once new ones are purchased, we make a conscious decision to wear them. The permanent disposal of our old slippers is up to us. With the removal of our character defects, it is up to God. Trust and experience assure us that, by working with our sponsor or group, we will know when we are ready.

Spiritually we are faced with asking our Higher Power – not our friends, Al-Anon members, minister or sponsor – to help us. This is a one-on-one relationship between ourselves and the God of our understanding. Faith of this type is foreign to many of us; it is unconditional. Intellectually some know that their God is a God of love, not a God of fear. Having lived with the disease of alcoholism, our faith has been challenged on many occasions. We are not being asked to trust the alcoholic or another human being. If we trusted God in our Fifth Step, is there any reason to doubt Him now? Further action on our part will take courage and application of the Serenity Prayer.

For some members, working Step Six means prayer; for others it means talking to the God of their understanding by walking on a beach, by a pond or in a spiritual place. Still others share that they write God a letter stating their willingness and fears. The spiritual message of Step Six impacts each member differently. What is important is that we are ready and we know our God.

Our Fourth Step revealed many positive aspects about ourselves, as well as defects, and our sponsor or the person who heard our Fifth Step pointed out some characteristics we had not recognized. Step Six emphasizes that we become ready to release all, not just a few, of our defects of character. There are no exceptions. Our slogan "Let Go and Let God" is applicable to the completion of our work on this Step. Letting go of all our defects does not mean giving up. There is much work to be done in Steps Seven through Twelve. Letting go also does not mean becoming passive or not continuing to learn and grow in the program. Letting go means giving up the struggle of our self-will and turning it over to God.

Now that we have acknowledged our defects, Step Six asks us to be ready to have God remove them. We have learned that we can't do it alone. We need friends, our group, phone mates, sponsors and, most of all, a Power greater than ourselves We reached this point through preparation, action and a promise for solutions. We are now humbly ready to consider Step Seven.

Members Share Experience, Strength and Hope

I FIND myself at Step Six. I've been here before and I'm sure I'll be here again. This time, now that I've been working the Steps for eight years, Step Six is about the six "Ps" for me – perspective, pain, prayer, patience, process, and payoff.

I HAVE SIX Ps

Perspective. My second sponsor described defects of character as "survival skills that no longer serve me." This definition helps me stop being so hard on myself. It helps me understand that for most of my life these defects of character worked for my benefit. Since my Higher Power wants more than mere survival for me now, I can choose to let them go.

Pain. When clinging to my defect or survival skill becomes more painful than my fear of letting it go, I become entirely ready to have God remove that defect of character.

Prayer. Step Six says God removes all these defects of character, not me. My part is to pray for openness and willingness. God chooses which defects He will remove. I just do the footwork.

Patience. Since God is in charge, God gets to choose when and how fast He will remove my defects of character. A couple years ago, when I humbly asked

Him to remove my arrogance, God proceeded to first show me how terribly arrogant I was and how it affected so many of my relationships in a negative way. I was able to accept that perhaps I humbly asked a little too soon.

Process. Becoming entirely ready involves a process for me – a grief process – where I walk through my denial, anger, bargaining and depression. As I complete the grief process, I become ready to have God remove a defect or former survival skill. It is helpful for me to pretend the defect is a friend by writing it a thank-you and good-bye letter.

Payoff. When I struggle with a defect, my current sponsor asks, "What's the payoff?" In other words, since I'm having a hard time letting it go, "What's still good about it?" Lately, I've been struggling with forgiveness. If I remain unforgiving, the payoff is that I can savor thoughts of revenge. I can feel sorry for myself for the hurt that was inflicted on me. I can justify my actions and remain distant. I don't have to work toward a closer relationship with that person if I remain unforgiving.

LETTING GO OF WILL-POWER. STEP ONE helps us realize that we need to change. Steps Two and Three give us trust and faith in a Higher Power so we can begin our recovery. In Step Four we examined ourselves to determine our beliefs about right and wrong. In Step Five we admitted to God, to ourselves and another human being how we deviated from our personal principles.

Now is the time to prepare to let go of these defects of character, some of which have been with us for many years. We are carrying a lot of excess baggage such as resentments, fear, jealousy, self-pity, dishonesty and blaming. We realize this excess baggage has been a terrible burden to us and that now would be a good time to let it go. But sometimes we still cling to it.

At first when I tried to work this Step, I thought I

needed to remake myself. I thought I would have to really work to achieve an immediate and complete metamorphosis. I thought I could cast away my skin like a snake and gain a new one. That way, I would be a new and different me. I thought I really needed to work hard, because I had to do all this changing to make myself perfect.

Then it was pointed out to me that I am not God. All this Step asks is that I become ready or willing to have God remove all of my defects of character. The word all in this Step became a hurdle for me to cross. I realized that I had already turned my will and my life over to His care. Surely I could turn my character defects over to Him as well. I found that I could turn them over and over, because old habits die hard. Sometimes I take them back and allow myself to suffer a little more before I turn them over again.

I pictured God removing all of my defects very suddenly and making me a completely different person. It didn't happened that way for me. Instead it has been a very slow process.

I learned that when something is removed it is always filled with something else. If I dig a hole, air replaces the dirt. I learned to replace my defects with assets. Now I have peace and serenity where my defects used to be.

Many years ago I bought my first electric sweeper. I brought it home and put it in the living room where it didn't do a thing. I tried to push it around the room. While it was hard to push, I could move it but it didn't remove the dirt. When I plugged it into the wall, however, it began to hum. The power was there. To get it to do the work, all I had to do was put my hand on the handle. From then on, it was easy.

Step Six has been very similar. To get rid of my defects of character, I have allowed my Higher Power to guide me. I could not do it by sheer willpower. I could not say, "You do it," without being willing to follow where He guided me. My willingness has meant recognizing my defects and working the program with all of the tools I can find. In this way, I am opening the door and inviting Him into my life.

Working Step Six

Were entirely ready to have God remove all these defects of character.

THE FOLLOWING questions may generate thought and discussion on Step Six.

* Have I completed working the first five Steps to the best of my ability? Am I willing to go back and look at them if I feel overwhelmed in working this Step?

* What have I learned from my sponsor or another Al-Anon friend on how they worked Step Six?

* As a result of working Step Five, am I grateful that there is a Step Six to work?

* Do I clearly understand the concept of readiness?

* How do I know if I am ready?

* If I am not entirely ready, how might I turn these fears over to the God of my understanding?

* What fears block me from being entirely ready?

* Can I ask God for the willingness to be ready?

* In what ways do I trust the God of my understanding in working this Step?

* Am I willing to let go of all my defects of character? Why or why not?

* Which ones would I prefer to hold on to? What advantages do I see to holding on to them?

* Which defects of character also contained assets?

* What does "have God remove all of my defects of character" mean to me?

* How do I trust and feel confident that my Higher Power is there for me?

* Do I understand why this Step speaks only of my own relationship with God? What does this mean to me?

* How am I grateful that I now know the God of my understanding?

* Can I make a commitment to share in an Al-Anon meeting how I worked this Step?

* How have I encouraged those I sponsor to work this Step?

* Will I consider chairing a meeting or workshop on the power of this Step?

* What evidence do I see in my life today of my Higher Power's willingness to help me improve my behavior? How can I do my part?

* Do I make demands on God, praying for a specific result rather than trusting God to know which defect is most important to remove?

* How can I look at all these characteristics from a fresh point of view today?

* Other than "Let Go and Let God" what other Al-Anon slogans or tools can help me with this Step?

Step Seven

Humbly asked Him to remove our shortcomings.

THERE IS a natural progression through our Steps; we are never asked to do anything before we are fully prepared and ready. In the same way, Step Seven is the natural follow-up to Steps Four, Five and Six. Now that we have taken our inventory, discussed the "exact nature of our wrongs" and become "entirely ready" for God to remove our defects, it follows that the next Step would be to ask Him to do so. We were not asked to turn our will and our lives over to God in Step Three until we had admitted that we were powerless and had become certain that God could help us in Steps One and Two.

On the surface Step Seven appears fairly simple. We have identified and examined our shortcomings in previous Steps. We are ready to have them removed. Now we must humbly ask that God remove them. What does this mean? We may have experienced humiliation in the past – this is very different from humility.

Humility, the state of being humble, is often misunderstood; it is not a state of weakness, but of strength. It does not mean inferiority, resignation or submission; these imply that we are still resisting our need for help. When we are humble, we are totally willing to accept God's help, knowing that without it we cannot progress further. In humility we possess self-esteem, accept ourselves as we are, assets and defects alike, and extend the same acceptance to others. We are learning to recognize humility in others; we are attracted to them and we learn from them.

Humility also helps us to see our true relationship to our Higher Power. Throughout the Steps, we are steered to turn to the God of our understanding for guidance and support in our efforts to change. By the time we reach Step Seven, we know we don't have to beg or demand things from God. We simply ask. We learn to trust God's way and pace as we go about our business. Humility is also the recognition of all the components of ourselves discovered in Steps Four and

Five and total acceptance of the daily action in Step Three.

How do we humbly ask God to remove our shortcomings? As we learned in Step Three, there is no set way to communicate with our Higher Power. Some of us will read our list of imperfections over and over, asking our Higher Power to remove them. Some of us find it helpful to pray and meditate on our relationship with God. Some of us get on our knees and ask God to remove our shortcomings. However we choose to ask, turning everything over can offer a wonderful release that enables us to continue our recovery confidently.

It is important to remember that all of our defects will probably not disappear immediately. We will always fall short of perfection; that's part of being human. Even after repeatedly praying for their removal, we will find that old behaviors and thinking may stay with us. Recovery is a process, and there is no quick fix for what ails us. Fortunately, Al-Anon reminds us to be gentle with ourselves and to turn to our Higher Power for help, again and again. This is true humility. It can be a hard lesson, but we will learn to have compassion for ourselves and others. To change, we need to accept ourselves as we are, stubborn shortcomings and all. Our Higher Power knows better than we do the extent and timing of each change that is right for us.

At the same time, we must take some action. Sitting back and behaving in all the same old ways while asking God to remove the defects is not effective. We cannot continue to do the same things over and over and expect different results. Recovery is a journey not a destination.

In turning to the God of our understanding for removal of our shortcomings, we find we are given countless opportunities to see our requests answered. New situations appear in our lives, giving us opportunities either to repeat our same old responses or to practice something new. By knowing our own short-comings and looking for alternative ways to act, we find new, positive options for old, negative behaviors. We become aware when old behaviors appear and can imagine a big stop sign in our minds. We can use the slogans to help us; "Easy Does It" or "Think" may be appropriate. Though it can be awkward at first to stop amid a criticism or sarcastic remark, our group will appreciate the changes. Even if they don't, we can give ourselves a pat on the back to acknowledge ourselves and learn to see the humor in catching ourselves in the same old patterns.

As we change we may be dismayed to discover new shortcomings. Once again as we peel away the layers of an onion, we discover new layers which shows our spiritual growth. Recovery continually reveals new aspects of our personalities to us until we come to fully know ourselves. When we use the tools found in the Steps, we become resilient, able to laugh at our humanness and to love ourselves for it.

Step Seven is a spiritual Step. It reminds us that our Higher Power understands better than we do how our shortcomings can be removed. We may also find there are assets hidden in our faults. For example, judgment is a negative trait when used to wound and criticize, but judgment is positive when it allows us to recognize quality and distinguish good work from mediocre. Our Higher Power can help us remove the criticism while retaining good judgment.

Fear can be a major stumbling block at any stage of recovery. Whenever we feel stuck, it is often useful to ask ourselves what we fear. Then we can ask God for the courage to change the things we can. We find with relief that God will help us. Our trust that God knows when and how to help us change grows. Our job is to cooperate with God and then move on to Step Eight.

Our willingness to take action for our own recovery, combined with our willingness to let God remove traits that no longer serve us, gives us spiritual muscles to continue our spiritual growth. We are learning how to surrender. As we give up each shortcoming, we experience change in ourselves and we know we are not alone. We know we can rely on a Power greater than ourselves to be with us in facing life's challenges.

Members Share Experience, Strength and Hope

I WORK Step Seven by asking God for the courage to change the things I can. I've discovered that God doesn't take away any of my shortcomings on His own. I must ask. What's more, I have to be ready to cooperate when I ask, which means I must acknowledge the defect and be prepared to practice different behavior. I don't just ask for all of my shortcomings to be removed and "poof" they are gone. God doesn't take them until I am ready to let go completely.

Before I'm ready to do something different, what I have been doing has to glare at me with the message that it's not working. If I don't change, nothing changes. That means if I'm miserable, I have to change so I won't be miserable. If all I do is wait for something to happen, I get to stay miserable.

Sometimes I need to know how a defect has benefited me. That way I can tell what it will cost me to give it up. Then I have to find another way to receive the same benefit. If I can't think of an alternative, I have to admit that I just don't want to get rid of it, yet. For example, I've always liked to be funny and amusing. Being sarcastic brought me a lot of laughs, usually at the expense of someone else. With sarcasm, I was clever and popular on the surface – but I also lost the trust of my friends.

Today I want to live a God-centered life, not a self-centered one. But giving up sarcasm was hard for me. As I asked for help, I realized I did not have to give up

TEAMWORK

my sense of humor in order to bring the sarcasm to a stop. I simply needed to redirect my humor into more harmless channels. Even if someone is hurting me, I try to confront the situation honestly, instead of being sarcastic.

As I cooperate with God to lessen my character defect, He does for me what I can not do for myself. He helps me create kindness in humor. If I need to stand up for myself, He gives me courage so I don't need to use sarcasm to push people away. He doesn't just make me a better person, because I have to do my part. I have learned that my serenity is based on humility. When I willfully take charge, I have no humility and soon I have no serenity. When I give up participating altogether, nothing changes. Humility for me means balancing God's responsibility with my responsibility, so we can be a team.

ALL MY
TRICKS
FAILED

FEAR AND CONTROL were hard for me to let go because I wasn't sure I wanted them to go. Those sometimes comfortable and sometimes painful shortcomings felt so familiar. If God was going to remove them, for heaven's sake, what was He going to come up with as replacements? I might not like the replacements! On the other hand, I really did want this program and what it might give me if I worked it.

I became quite ill with viral meningitis. I felt as if everything important was in jeopardy – speaking a whole sentence, working, keeping my job and my home. Everything was on the line. I was a nurse, so believe me, I tried everything I could think of to heal myself – except surrendering to my Higher Power. All my tricks failed, however. In humble desperation, I literally put myself in the hands of my Higher Power. I felt as if I was in a foxhole and it was closing in on me. I realized then I could not take a breath, speak, walk or do the simplest of tasks without the desire of my Higher Power. Who was I, so arrogant to think I was in control of anything? At that point, it became easy to ask my God to remove whatever He thought was best for me – I'd take whatever was His desire.

My Higher Power decided to return me to a wholly functioning human being. He has given me a life beyond any dream I would have come up with. Today I am married and have a lovely family, both inside and outside the program. I thank God for reminders to let go, absolutely, and trust in Him. He knows what is best for me. He made me a walking, talking miracle!

WHAT A strange word to use in the Al-Anon Steps – humbly. After considering that the Steps were originally written for AAs and adopted by Al-Anon pioneers, I could certainly see the wisdom of a humble attitude for alcoholics, but not for Al-Anons. After all, I was trying to rid myself of my humble attitude. One of the character defects I found in the Fourth Step was my subservient behavior in my marriage. At meetings I heard, "If you think you have humility, you don't really have it." So this humble stuff, which while growing up I thought belonged to saints and quiet church ladies, was just not even on my list of things to consider.

MY CHERISHED BELIEFS NO LONGER GAVE ME PEACE

At meetings there is often a chance word that leads to serenity; no one ever said the chance word would be heard while riding to the meeting. But one night, after picking up a car full of members, I hit a huge pothole in the street making everyone in the back seat literally hit the ceiling. When I told them I was sorry, one of them asked, "Why would you apologize for that?" Good question! Apologizing meant more than just saying the words. With my exaggerated sense of responsibility, it had become almost a way of life. This was something to think about.

I didn't connect this insight to the Seventh Step until several years later. Just before making the painful decision to leave my marriage, I went to many extra meetings. This took place in July, the seventh month, and at those extra meetings the Seventh Step was discussed every time. I wanted to hear about anger, courage, decisions and action ideas, but "humbly ask" kept being repeated. Listening with less of a filter than in my early Al-Anon days, I heard that humility might mean having an attitude of honesty and simplicity along with a mind set of being teachable. While I became more open to looking at humility as a positive, I knew working toward it would mean digging deeper into my attitudes about myself and my investments in my character defects.

If my original thoughts on humility were wrong, and real humility had nothing to do with the subservient attitude reflected in all those "I'm sorrys," then years of cultivating the belief that a wife and mother always puts others first and acquiesces had to be replaced. What beliefs would define me? My cherished beliefs about how I should respond to life's situations no longer gave me any peace. On the other hand, just thinking about the kinds of internal changes I would need to make so that my behavior honestly reflected my thinking was too frightening. I kept trying to make old habits fit these new ideas about humility.

I needed to make consistent root changes in my thinking, to be really honest. To make it harder, I knew this couldn't all take place in my head. I would have to act on this new honesty which would upset many people. I wasn't certain I could do it. The attitudes and values I was giving up were so close to me – I felt they were me. I was still thinking that God helps those who help themselves.

But the God of my understanding, mentioned in the Third Step, cared. By now His care was part of our relationship. To humbly ask Him to remove my shortcomings was my only out. Trusting that honesty, simplicity and openness are moves in the direction of humility helped. Relaxing my grip on everything I cared about came in flashes. Making it routine is something I am still striving for.

Did working on this Step change my decision to separate after 15 years of marriage? No, but it did change the way I approached God for help in living out all that accompanied that decision. When I humbly ask and don't get what I ask for, I can be more at peace – most of the time.

Working Step Seven

Humbly asked Him to remove our shortcomings.

IN WORKING Step Seven, some of us pray for the willingness to release our shortcomings and then trust that God will take them from us. Questions for thought and discussion:

* What does humility mean to me? List people I know who possess this trait.

* How am I humble? What can help me be more so?

* What old behaviors get in the way of my being humble?

* What defects am I ready to have removed?

* Do I believe that my Higher Power can rid me of my defects? How do I know this?

* Am I ready to ask God to remove my defects?

* How do I humbly ask God to take my shortcomings?

* Which shortcoming is causing me the most trouble right now? What benefits do I get from it? What problems does it cause?

* How can I treat myself with compassion in my recovery and ask for the willingness to keep trying?

* Do I have a sponsor? If I don't have one, how can I ask someone to help me?

* What character defects will I have to overcome to allow myself to turn to a sponsor for help?

* What can I do to cooperate with my Higher Power in removing my shortcomings?

* What positive changes can I make in myself?

* What positive trait do I want to develop or substitute for a trait I want to eliminate?

* What can I do this week to practice a positive trait?

* Have I had any fears removed from my life? Which ones?

* What negative behaviors or traits are lessening or have been removed?

* What slogan could remind me to find a substitute for a negative behavior I wish to release?

* Am I able to see challenges as opportunities to practice new character traits?

* Am I able to laugh fondly at my mistakes and not be devastated when I am not perfect? Can I love and celebrate my humanness while working for balance?

* As I turn my defects over to God, are new shortcomings coming to light? If so, can I continue to ask God for help?

* As I work Step Seven, do I see a change in my relationship with my Higher Power?

In Step Eight we are given a new task to perform and specific direction for approaching the recovery work needed. Our specific assignment is to make a list of persons we have harmed. The second part of Step Eight challenges us to become willing to make amends. Many a member has jumped to Step Nine without considering the power this Step offers. Obtaining a clear path through willingness gives us a fresh starting point for our continuing growth and recovery.

Many Al-Anon members, having completed their Fourth Steps, already have a list of persons they have harmed. Looking at our Fourth Step inventory provides us with a base to build on. We probably have written about the people in our lives whom we have harmed. As we recall, it wasn't easy to figure out whom we have harmed or exactly what we have done that caused another's pain. By working our Fourth and Fifth Steps, we have overcome numerous obstacles and become more self-aware.

How do I make a list? One member shares that she made the following column heads: the person harmed, their relationship to me, my harmful act, the reason for my amends and my willingness. It is here that she transferred the names from her Fourth Step inventory and began adding new ones.

Some of us start our list with anyone about whom we still feel any discomfort. With the help of our sponsor, another program friend or by writing, we examine the list carefully. Some names are obvious; we know we have done something we feel badly or guilty about. Others require us to search carefully for the reasons we feel discomfort. Still others seem to be people who have harmed us, but we have not actually harmed. If we still resent them, our own peace of mind is best served by forgiving them. Some of us find that our lists are endless. This may be a clue that being overly responsible is an issue and we are harming only ourselves. As members we are often

Step Eight

Made a list of all persons we had harmed and became willing to make amends to them all.

encouraged to put ourselves on the list first. Knowing that others before us have experienced this self-awareness provides us with a sense of gratitude for the fellowship and for our fellow members who still love us in a special way even though we may not love ourselves at this moment.

After we carefully examine and review our list for thoroughness, we are ready to tackle the second part of Step Eight – become willing. Step Eight directs us to take action and continue to try until we are willing. If we keep the focus on ourselves and our part, whether it is 5 percent or 95 percent of the problem, we are better able to become willing. How do we acquire this willingness? Many seek prayer and meditation. Others call upon the experience of other Al-Anon members or their sponsor.

In working each Step, members become more aware of a Power greater than themselves, the option to "Let Go and Let God" and the opportunity to begin a new partnership with that Power in ridding themselves of the past. Can we begin a future without dumping the garbage of our past? Most would emphatically state, "No!" Wanting to carry a lighter load, we begin building a belief that this action Step will be spiritually guided. One member shares she learned long ago that it was okay to make plans – but not to plan the outcome. It is the same with Step Eight – we are only asked to become willing to make amends.

Some categorize their list in order of willingness. First on the list are those of whom we can say, "Yes, I want to make amends." The second category is those to whom we might be willing to make amends; the third category is those to whom we still feel like saying, "No way!" Our willingness to make amends starts with the "yes" category and, by building our spiritual strength, continues with the remaining people on our list. When we begin to feel stuck, we pray for the willingness. Sometimes we have to pray for the willingness to be willing.

Some of the people on our list have also harmed us. Do they really belong here? We may have put them on the "never" list and find we are experiencing difficulty in becoming willing to make amends to them. It is possible that, with the help of our sponsor, we can "Let Go and Let God" and continue to pray for willingness to make amends.

In living with the disease of alcoholism, a non-drinking parent's reactions to the drinking parent may have caused harm to the children in the family. As a non-drinking parent, we may feel our behavior was justified, although our words and actions were harmful. These actions may be difficult to see, but taking responsibility for them is necessary. They are worth our willingness to consider as we continue to work our program – "One Day at a Time."

Some of those we harmed may also have harmed us. Expecting amends from another person only blocks us in our own recovery and keeps us from becoming willing. "One source of frustration we seldom recognize is in expecting too much of others or expecting too specifically what we feel they ought to be, say, give or do" (*One Day at a Time in Al-Anon*, p. 217). Our job is to look at our role. We can't take another's inventory or do their Eighth Step. By keeping the focus on ourselves we again ask, are we willing?

It is very important to use all the tools we have available to us. We share our list and talk about our willingness with our sponsor; we attend Al-Anon meetings to remind ourselves that we are beginning to respond in healthy ways to a powerful and insidious family disease. We are at last doing something about our part in the whole picture. Attending meetings and talking to newcomers helps us see how far we have come. Praying keeps us in conscious contact with the God of our understanding and helps us to accept and forgive ourselves.

Until we accept those who have harmed us for who

they are, becoming willing to make our amends is an extremely difficult task. Step Eight reminds us that only we can unlock the door of our past and walk away. Our list is complete, we are now willing. We ask for courage and remember that we do not really need to like or want to do something in order to be willing to do it. Willingness is all that is asked of us. With willingness and a desire for increased recovery in our lives, we turn to our Higher Power to help us move on to Step Nine.

Members Share Experience, Strength and Hope

I FOUND
MYSELF PANIC-
STRICKEN OVER
STEP EIGHT

WHEN I came into Al-Anon, it seemed to me that fault in any matter was black or white, all or nothing. Initially, as I learned more about the disease of alcoholism, I easily placed the blame for everything squarely on the alcoholic. Gradually I learned to take responsibility for my part in situations.

After years of work on a Fourth Step inventory, I finally took Step Five. I meditated and prayed on Steps Six and Seven until I found myself facing Step Eight. I remembered how I periodically worked and procrastinated with my Fourth Step, because I was fearful of Step Five. Now I found myself panic-stricken over Step Eight because I was afraid to face the people I had harmed.

Although I heard, "One step at a time – they're in order for a reason," my fear overwhelmed me. I could not write the list. My sponsor suggested that I think of a staircase with each step exactly the same height. Each step required the same effort and willingness to climb. She reminded me that I could stand on Step Eight as long as I wanted. She said making a list of all persons I had harmed and being willing to make amends to them did not mean I had to make the amends, yet.

The things that my sponsor said helped me to

make my list. I included family members, co-workers, friends, many of the important people in my life. I went to a Step Eight meeting and heard a woman share about putting herself at the top of her list. That idea hit home. How many times had I beaten myself for things that were not my fault? So I put myself on my Eighth Step list.

Once I'd made the list, I started to work on the second part of Step Eight. I discovered that I didn't need to decide how to make my amends. All I had to do was be willing. I felt more willing to make amends with some people than with others. But the Step said became willing, so that gave me the time and permission for my willingness to develop. Prayer, meditation and writing helped me a lot. Step Eight gave me the freedom to acknowledge my wrongs and to move forward. I forgave myself. Step Eight released me from the baggage of guilt I had carried around for so many years.

THE EXPRESSION "look before you leap" applied to me when I came to Step Eight. The word from Step Eight that I focused on was willing. It was important for me to avoid the temptation to jump ahead and actually make my amends. Step Eight was not Step Nine, so I needed to slow down. In becoming willing, I needed to look at what my amends might be. I needed to think about what I was doing, instead of leaping into action. Another important word for me to consider in Step Eight was the word all. This word taught me to avoid clinging to some of my old hurts, angers and resentments.

The first part of the Step said, "Made a list of all persons we had harmed." It was suggested that I divide a sheet of paper into three columns with the following headings:

1. Whom I have harmed;
2. How I harmed;
3. "Appropriate" amends.

I was surprised when I heard that I should put my own name at the top of the list. I didn't realize that I had harmed myself more than anyone else. It took a little time to learn the details of how I had harmed myself.

I didn't know that I needed to put the alcoholic on my list, because I thought he had harmed me. What I found out was that he had not harmed me – but that I had harmed myself. An example was the time he was going to take the car to get something to drink. I held onto the car door handle to keep him from going. He drove away and my hand was injured. I cried and said that he had hurt my hand. Step Eight taught me that he did not hurt my hand. I caused my hand to be injured because I put my hand where it didn't belong. The alcoholic wasn't aware that my hand was getting hurt. My angry accusations, however, were harmful to him. This incident was one more example of me playing the "blame game."

Eventually, I realized that I also needed to put God on my list, because I had withheld my trust and faith in Him and I had turned away from Him. Now I know that God belongs on the very top of my list, because He was always with me. He helped me even when I thought that I was the only one who was taking care of me.

When I started to make my Step Eight list, I thought I had harmed many, many people. As it turned out, my Step Four inventory really helped to guide me in this. As I studied the column, "How I harmed," I noticed I had put people on the list whom I had not harmed. For example, if I had bad thoughts about someone, those thoughts were harmful to me because they affected my attitude. On the other hand, there were people I didn't put on my list because I had only done something to them because of something they had done to me. I discovered that this justification didn't work because this was my list. I was not responsible for their behavior, nor did blaming them vindicate my wrongs. I also learned that I was harboring guilt for things I had done to hurt another person, even though the other person wasn't hurt. All I needed to do was to change my attitude. I even listed people who blamed me for hurting their feelings before I learned that I'm not responsible for how another person feels.

Some of the harm I caused came from things that I did, and some came from things that I failed to do. Because so much of my focus had been on the alcoholic, I frequently neglected myself and others, so I needed to put these acts of commission and omission on my list.

The third column, "Appropriate" amends, would not be completed until I had thoroughly studied Step Nine. But, I could begin to think about how I might make amends to the people on my list. I was the kind of person who was inclined to go too far with things. For instance, I thought that to make amends meant that I needed to be punished. If I wasn't careful, I could add to the list of harms that I had done to myself.

One of the most important things that I learned in Step Eight is that I only needed to be willing to make amends. I also learned that Step Eight is for me. If others reap some benefits from my Eighth Step, that is a bonus. If I make the list and become willing to make appropriate amends, one thing is for certain – I will reap the benefits.

Working Step Eight

Made a list of all persons we had harmed and became willing to make amends to them all.

AL-ANON MEMBERS have offered various approaches to this Step. The following questions may provide further guidance.

* Have I resisted making a list? If so, why?

* Did I use my Fourth Step as a tool in preparing my list? How?

* Did I consult with my sponsor or others in Al-Anon on how they made their list? What suggestions did they make? How can I learn from them?

* Am I willing to make amends? If no, why not? If yes, am I willing to write about my experience?

* How have I used rationalization or justification to block me from becoming willing?

* Do I understand that willingness is different than making the actual amends? Describe the differences.

* Have I considered praying for the willingness to become willing? How patient am I in allowing myself to grow into the willingness for making difficult amends?

* How willing am I to be completely honest?

* Which people on my list am I willing to contact first? Why?

* Have I included myself on my list? Why or why not?

* How does the God of my understanding play a role in this Step?

* Can I share with my group my thoughts, feelings and challenges with this Step?

* How can I encourage those I sponsor to begin working this Step based on my own personal experiences?

* As I work Step Eight, how do I envision it helping me in my relationship with the alcoholics in my life? My co-workers or friends? My extended family?

* In reviewing my list, is there a pattern reflecting new defects in my character? Can I see how those defects harmed those on my list? Is this a pattern I identified in working Steps Five and Six?

* Do I recognize when my minding someone else's business may have harmed them or others? Am I willing to recognize the need for my amends?

Step Nine

Made direct amends to such people wherever possible, except when to do so would injure them or others.

STEP NINE is an action Step in which we become humble enough to verbalize our regrets, if appropriate, to the people we have harmed. Identifying the persons we have harmed in Step Eight took courage. Because of our thoroughness, we build character by calling upon our Higher Power for the courage to change the things we can. We cannot undo our past, and we cannot expect those we approach to respond positively, but we can admit our part and do whatever is possible to mitigate the consequences of our past errors.

When all of the persons we have harmed are listed, the task of making amends may seem overwhelming. To make it manageable, we approach one person at a time and one event at a time. To begin, it is best to refer to our Step Eight list and begin with the "yes" list. Working through the easier amends helps us build courage for considering the harder ones at a later time.

Another way to divide up the work is to categorize our list by noting those whom we see regularly, those whom we might have to wait to see until an opportune time arises, and those to whom direct amends are impossible because of death or having lost touch. The member who has used the column approach to making a list from Step Eight may find it helpful to add a final column for the action they decide upon. Keeping it simple is important. Having an action plan is equally important. Over the years, members have shared how, much to their surprise, once they sincerely started seeking to make amends, some "lost" people miraculously reappeared in their lives, and the members were able to use the opportunity to make amends.

In making amends, we need to understand that we are not necessarily making an apology. There are differences between amends and apologies. In making an apology, we usually say, "I'm sorry," expecting a response of acceptance, pardon or forgiveness. In making amends, we may state our errors, our role in the incident and that we will correct our behavior for the future. We may or may not ask for forgiveness, and we may or may not experience a positive response. In many cases our changed behavior indicated stronger amends than words could ever be. If we have any expectations of the response to amends, we are setting ourselves up for disappointment.

Some amends need immediate attention, and in most cases we can do this by changing our behavior. Financial amends often fall into this category. While we may not be able to pay our debts immediately, we can make a plan for repayment. A change in behavior also keeps us from creating new wrongs. Making amends by changing our behavior may be considered by some to be taking the easy way out. In most cases changing our behavior is the only way that we can affirm our desire to improve our relations with others. If we say we are sorry for being late to work and keep coming in late, we have not amended our behavior. We need to arrive on time. Amends require a change in our attitude and behavior. When the other person resists our amends, we have to continue doing our part and detach with love.

Step Nine calls for direct amends except when to do so might cause further injury. We want to be careful that we aren't trying to achieve our personal serenity at the expense of someone else. Reviewing our intended amends with a sponsor or another Al-Anon friend helps us consider our motivation and the consequences of our intended actions. An example could be marital infidelity. While everyone involved may be knowledgeable of the situation, we have to consider whether or not our amends will open old wounds. We can start by replacing the neglect of our partner with loving, focused attention rather than imposing details that create further pain. In consideration of all the parties involved, indirect amends through changed behavior may serve us best.

The key is that we do not avoid making amends in order to spare ourselves discomfort – that will only increase our guilt and prevent our healing. In some cases, we need to stop doing something, such as gossiping, complaining or controlling. In all cases, when we are not sure which type of amends is called for, we remember that making direct amends is our responsibility except when someone else would be harmed. We pray for guidance as we approach each task. It helps to call our sponsor to check out our intentions and to talk about what we have in mind. A sponsor can help us to look at our motives and to plan our approach.

How have others approached this task? With prayer, common sense, support from other members and the realization that we need not do it perfectly to do it sincerely. It is best to meet the person in a quiet, neutral location. With family members, it may mean going for a drive or a walk, away from the day-to-day activities at home. When direct contact is not feasible, we may use the phone or write a letter.

How can we approach someone we still dislike? We start with prayer, perhaps asking to see them as God sees them. It may help to slowly sort out facts from feelings, imagined or real. Keep in mind that we need to amend the actions or inaction that caused harm, not our feelings. If we need to relieve ourselves of secret feelings, we discuss this with our sponsor or another friend who will not be further harmed. Our future interactions with a disagreeable person call for us to be accepting, courteous and respectful. Amazingly, our own feelings will soften as we let go of our own feelings of resentment.

It is often more difficult to make amends to those closest to us. A commitment to changed behavior over time and patience in ourselves and others usually yields positive results in the long run. If we want renewed trust, we have to earn it. Some of our actions cannot be undone. If in our bitterness and frustration we neglected our loved ones, we cannot change our past behavior, but we can pay attention today by being more loving.

Indirect amends to those who died or are unavailable can be made by doing good deeds for their family members, making contributions of time or money to a favorite charity or by treating others as we wish we had treated the departed. Some of us find it useful to write a letter to the person and read it to God or to them in a special place that reminds us of them. A member shares that one way she made amends for her behavior in raising her children was by making herself available as an Alateen sponsor. She stated that she was able to listen and share with the teens with great understanding as a result of the self-knowledge gained in recovery.

Then there are the relationships that pose the greatest challenge – those with loved ones who have harmed us or those people who think anything we do harms them. Honesty, balance and realism are essential tools to keep at hand as we approach these amends. If we are leaning toward self-justification, we may find it useful to remember the Golden Rule, which asks us to treat others as we want to be treated. When we have not followed this rule, amends are needed. The amends also need to fit the situation. If we cut someone off in traffic, it is probably better to start driving with more caution and courtesy than to chase down the other driver and apologize.

In Step Nine we learn that, by using good common sense, appropriate timing, our sponsor, courage and spiritual faith, we can complete the task assigned. By using all of the tools we have learned in the previous Steps, we know that by cleaning our slate we are now free to continue our journey to Step Ten.

A PERFECT
RELATIONSHIP

SEVERAL PEOPLE from AA made a Twelfth Step call on the man who was soon to be my ex-husband. A friend of mine said there was also a program that could help me. Being the people-pleaser that I was, I could not tell her that I did not need any help. My attitude was, "He's the one with the problem." Nevertheless, I paid a friend of mine $50 to drive 25 miles to my house so we could attend an Al-Anon meeting that was four blocks away. I did not want to go alone to something that I did not know anything about.

Step Nine was the topic of the very first meeting I attended. I was not at all impressed with Al-Anon or Step Nine. In fact, I was disgusted with the meeting. My comment to my friend was, "If those women think they are going to make me feel guilty for what he made me do, they're nuts." I did not get any literature or phone numbers, nor did I give my phone number to anyone. I did not want any of what I had seen.

I am so grateful I kept going back to the meetings. I did not go for what I could get, but rather to keep my friend off my back. I thought it was very noble of me to attend one meeting each week. Of course, I got very little out of the meetings because I put very little into the meetings.

That marriage did not survive – but I did!

For a long time, I knew I had to work Step Nine with my father. I had moved 3,000 miles to get away from him. It took me a long time to make my amends. For the next 10 years, most of the amends I made to both of my parents was to be the kind of daughter they deserved. Along the way, I made many surface amends when I visited them each year.

My God, with his sense of humor, arranged for my new husband's job transfer to bring us within 90 miles of my parents. For one year, I had the chance to get to know my parents and to let them know me. They even got to see what I had become as the result of this wonderful program. There was still one big amend, however, that I needed to make to my father. I attempted it on several occasions. Every time, something happened to prevent me from following through.

On my way home one day, after another unsuccessful attempt, I told God I was willing to do it in His time, not mine. Then I promptly forgot about it. A short time later, I visited my parents before my husband and I left on a two week vacation. Suddenly Dad and I were sitting alone in the back yard, and out came my amends. We both cried. He asked me for my forgiveness, although that was not in my script. Of course, I assured him that he had my forgiveness and that our slate was clean. Mother came outside where we were sitting and we continued our visit. When I went home, I cried all the way, thanking my God for this special time that I'd had with them.

My husband and I went on our vacation, but it was interrupted by a phone call from my mother. Daddy suffered a ruptured aorta and was not expected to survive. We arrived at the hospital one hour before he died. I never had another word with my father after I made my amends. My God had given me the opportunity to have a perfect relationship with my father – total forgiveness on both sides.

For most of the time I was in Al-Anon, until the time of my final amends to my father, I had been afraid of Step Nine. My Higher Power showed me in a very clear way that Step Nine wouldn't bring me more fear – only freedom. The amends I am making to other members of my family include being the best wife, mother, sister and daughter that I can be. My family members know they can depend on me now. They can trust me and love me without the fear that I will use or abuse them. The Twelve Steps have brought me a long way. I remember I am the one who said, "If those women think they are going to make me feel guilty for what he made me do, they're nuts." Who would think someone like that could ever experience total forgiveness?

Thank you for giving this to me.

MATURITY MANY OF the words I heard at my first Al-Anon meeting didn't make much sense to me. I was very self-righteous and angry. I already made up my mind that the world had dealt me a rotten hand. I heard "release," but I couldn't even think of releasing my grasp on the situation. I might lose my mind. Serenity? I didn't have a clue what serenity meant.

I didn't hear very much that made me want to come right back to Al-Anon. I was nineteen years old, expecting my second baby, worried sick over the unpaid bills. I needed someone to love me the way I thought I needed to be loved. I could see no reason for a "program."

I know now that it was natural for me to have married a drinker. There were so many unresolved relationships with drinkers in my life. I felt I needed one of my own to control. I married, had a baby and the merry-go-round continued. My husband and I were classic adult children of alcoholics. I was an inconsistent mother and an unhappy wife. We fought over everything. If I didn't get my way, I became violent with my husband.

I went back to Al-Anon to save my marriage. I began to see that I carried so much baggage from my family that our marriage had only a tiny chance to survive. The baggage was the way I related to my parents and my siblings. I needed to deal with all that baggage, but I felt so much guilt about it that I just avoided seeing them.

After several months of crying silently and listening in Al-Anon meetings, I began to share. I began to search for standards and ideals. I embraced the Twelve Steps and Traditions. I renewed my faith in God. I began to make amends to the family whose only fault had been not being what I wanted them to be. I began to accept. I prayed to see the reality of the situation, instead of what I fantasized. I carefully wrote an inventory and included my bad deeds. I was still very guilt ridden so I didn't find many assets.

Once the lights began to come on in my head, however, I just kept flipping switches. I had been the first in my family who could easily have gone to college, but I dropped out of high school. As a result, I became one of my parent's biggest disappointments. So I got a sitter for our sons, went back to night school and graduated. I did this for me as much as for my parents.

Al-Anon became a joy for me. I liked being secretary, Group Representative, coffee maker, cookie baker, whatever. I belonged. I did the Steps, wrote, picked up newcomers, answered the phone and went to lots of meetings. I began to get involved in other things, too – including the PTA, the kids' school, our neighborhood and church. I never said no. I was also the main transportation for my parents, because they didn't drive. It was at this time that my dad got cancer.

I made amends to my folks according to the part of Step Nine that said "except when to do so would injure them or others." I knew time was running out with my dad. I had never said the words "I love you, Dad." I didn't remember hearing these words around our house when I grew up, but I was saying them a lot to my own children. It was easy with them, but I froze when I thought about saying that to my dad.

I took him to the hospital, to chemotherapy and to doctor's appointments. I helped out any way I could. I let go of many other responsibilities so I could be with my mom and dad. It seemed like he was free of pain when he could be with his grandbabies. My children didn't mind playing at Grandma's, so I took them there as often as I could. We just didn't speak those words to each other. He died shortly after my twenty-fifth birthday.

It may be that I didn't love my Dad. That could be why I didn't say it. I haven't found where it is written that one has to love one's parents. Al-Anon helped me see the reality of my situation. I can give myself permission to let go of the guilt. I answer to God, and I've learned that guilt has a purpose. I try to not misuse it.

My mom and I developed a loving adult relationship. She seemed relieved when my dad died, and I can understand that. We were able to say the words, I love you. She passed away many years later. I shared my program with her, but she felt she was set in her ways and didn't see much reason to change. I see so much of my mother in me and I rejoice about that rather than resent it. It used to be that I never wanted to be seen with her, let alone be like her. The Al-Anon program has given me so much maturity but I have so far to go. I still have six brothers and sister and my alcoholic husband.

Most of the words that frightened me when I first came to Al-Anon are part of my daily conversation today. I know exactly what serenity is, and I love it! I gladly release the problems in my life to God. I know what footwork is, and I do it. I thank God that our program exists and that we have so many meetings. I pray that the help I found will always be available to others who need it.

FREEDOM TO GROW

I LEARNED that direct amends can take many forms. In some cases, when the other person knew I had wronged them, I needed to go face to face to try to mend the relationship. My amends, however, could also be an act of kindness or consideration. A change in my attitude oftentimes was the best possible amends. Leaving the door open to allow a relationship to redevelop slowly was a helpful approach, too.

I also learned that my amends needed to carry with

it a commitment for better behavior in the future. Whether someone accepted or rejected my amends was none of my business. I needed to make my amends as honestly as possible, but there were instances when the other person needed more time. To accept my offer, some people needed to see that I had really changed my attitude and behavior. Of course, there were those individuals who could not or would not accept my amends, but I was not responsible for their decision. Occasionally, I found people I thought I had harmed who were completely unaware of what I did. While I was anguishing over the terrible damage I had done, they remained unaffected. Once again, I was not as powerful as I thought.

In Step Eight, when I made a list of the persons I harmed and how I had harmed them, I became aware of what I did or what I failed to do. Although I needed to become willing to make amends to them all, Step Nine told me to make amends wherever possible. It was not up to me to move mountains in order to make my amends. Rather, it was my job to be open and willing to take advantage of opportunities that God provided.

It was important for me to remember that I worked all of the Steps for me – including Step Nine. If someone else benefited from my amends, that was wonderful. The real purpose of this Step was to cleanse me. It was to help me get rid of my guilt so I could grow. If people could accept my amends, of course I felt good about it, but I still needed to realize that acceptance came in God's time, not in mine.

Along the way, I needed to make amends for damage I had done to myself. Changing my attitudes and taking better care of myself helped a lot. Forgiving my weaknesses and accepting my strengths really freed me to grow.

Working Step Nine

Made direct amends to such people wherever possible, except when to do so would injure them or others.

HERE ARE some questions to ask ourselves or discuss in our groups to assist us in proceeding with making our amends.

* Which people on my list do I need to make direct amends to first? What's stopping me?

* How can I plan what I am going to say in my direct amends to be clear and concise and to avoid blaming any other person?

* What doubts do I have about my amends injuring someone? Can I discuss these doubts with my sponsor? Pray to be guided? Write about them?

* What are my motives for making amends? Am I willing to accept the outcome, whatever it may be?

* What is the difference between an apology and making amends? Which amends will be best done by changes in my behavior?

* How can I be sure I am not just ducking an embarrassing situation?

* What amends am I putting off? Why?

* Do I have any amends to make that could result in serious consequences for my family, like loss of employment or a prison term? How can I use my sponsor or a trusted friend to help me sort these out?

* Who on my amends list will never be available for direct amends? Can I make amends in another way? Can I do something for another person?

* What harm have I done to my children or immediate family? Can I make some amends by respecting them now as adults?

* Am I willing to pray to become willing to make amends in the future?

* How can I forgive myself for all the difficulties I've caused myself? What can I do this week to begin my amends to myself?

* Could I write an amends letter to myself?

* When I have finished this action Step, what can I do to celebrate? Have I remembered to appreciate and reward my good deeds? The good deeds of others?

Step
Ten

Continued to take personal inventory and when we were wrong promptly admitted it.

STEP TEN is the beginning of what some members refer to as the maintenance Steps. Others call them the continuous-growth Steps. Step Ten helps us to keep the principles and tools of the previous Steps working in our daily lives. To maintain our serenity and continue to grow, we continue to inventory ourselves and make amends to others.

If we have been thorough and honest in our work on Steps One through Nine, we have begun a process to clear away much of the damage of our past. We have turned our defects of character over to our Higher Power; now we apply continual effort to changing our old behaviors for the better. We have begun to take care of ourselves and our needs; instead of reacting to life and the alcoholic, we act on our own behalf. With Step Ten we try to keep our slates clean in order not to slip back into self-destructive patterns. Slips are especially likely to occur during times of stress, when it is natural to retreat into old, defensive behaviors. Recovery does not cure us of every human imperfection or eliminate all pain in our lives. But it gives us the tools to deal with our problems and to continually work to improve ourselves.

There are numerous ways to continue to take personal inventory. Members share that they find three types of inventory useful: a spot check, a daily check-in and a periodic long-term check. A spot check can be used anytime throughout the day when we feel that something is not right. We can then take responsibility immediately for our part, if only by stopping in the moment to acknowledge the problem and ask ourselves what we can do differently.

We may not catch every mistake as it occurs, but a daily check can help us become more adept at recognizing and changing our behavior. We can take a few minutes each evening to review the day for both positive and negative experiences. Some of us choose to make it a part of our end-of-day rituals, just like brushing our teeth. This needn't be a lengthy written inventory; it can be done mentally or perhaps by taking just a couple of quick notes on what went well and what we could improve. We can plan to amend any errors the next day. If we ask for the courage and willingness to do our part, we may find that we can drift off to sleep and start the next day with a clear conscience. Those who are morning people may prefer to take stock as part of a morning ritual, perhaps while driving to work, or during a call to our sponsor at some regular time.

Periodically we may want to take a more detailed inventory. Regular yearly or twice-yearly inventories shared with our sponsor can help us work on more deeply imbedded characteristics and consider new ones that appear as we evolve spiritually. An inventory can remind us to reward ourselves for the progress we have made but have not noticed on a daily basis. Sometimes we take fairly detailed inventories, using our *Blueprint for Progress: Al-Anon's Fourth Step Inventory* or the *Alateen Fourth Step Inventory* booklets. We may review our original inventory. At times we concentrate on just one particular area of our lives. Each time we renew our commitment to continue our self-examination, we grow spiritually. If making a change is frightening, we find that by simply and honestly making an effort each day, the fear lessens.

Just as it was in Step Four, it is very important to include in any inventory the things we did well in addition to the mistakes we may have made. We can ask ourselves where we see improvement in our behavior or what positive characteristics we exhibited. There may be many days where we handle ourselves well and exhibit none of our old behaviors!

The second half of Step Ten says, "...when we were wrong promptly admitted it." Continuing the process of admitting our mistakes and making amends to ourselves and others when called for keeps us humble and helps us to accept others as they are. Disciplining ourselves to do this again and again reminds us of the ancient wisdom in the words, "To err is human; to forgive divine." Both our humanness and our spirituality expand when we accept and forgive the mistakes of ourselves and others. We discover that it is a relief not to feel we always have to be right. We can let other people gain the benefits and suffer the consequences of their own decisions. We become more and more comfortable with who we are.

As we work Step Ten on a regular basis, we will continue to turn to our Higher Power for help. When we inventory our day, we admit our shortcomings to God, become ready and then humbly ask God to remove them. We list the people we have harmed and make the appropriate amends. In taking our Step Ten inventories, we are actually using all of the previous Steps, remembering to treat ourselves with compassion and love. Because we have experienced the pain caused by our shortcomings, we do not want to return to them. We keep working our program as if the quality of our lives depends on it – and it does!

Completing Steps Four through Nine does not insure that our lives will now be totally serene and free of problems. There will be times when we may feel like we are back in our first day in Al-Anon with every single character defect unaltered. Working Step Ten helps us keep our bad times fewer and farther between. Continuing to take personal inventory keeps our slates clean and, maintains our spiritual, emotional and physical health to better deal with the rough times that occur in everyday life.

Members Share Experience, Strength and Hope

BEST
FORGOTTEN

WHEN I first started coming to Al-Anon, I spoke rather harshly to a co-worker, feeling quite justified in what I had said. I soon realized that I really hurt her feelings. I found myself justifying my action – if she hadn't done so and so, then I wouldn't have…then, thank goodness, Step Ten came to mind.

Suddenly I realized when I find myself making excuses and trying to justify what I have done, it is time to practice the Tenth Step and simply say, "I'm sorry."

Knowing this and practicing it have saved me from spending many hours building up resentments and reliving incidents that were best forgotten.

I have no idea what that long-ago incident was all about. I do know that my co-worker and I are still friends.

IN STEP TEN, one of the words that stood out in my mind was "continued." It reminded me that I began my personal inventory in Step Four. Likewise the words, "and when we were wrong, promptly admitted it," reminded me of work I had already done in Steps Five, Eight and Nine. All of these Steps represented a thorough, personal housecleaning for me. But I knew my house wouldn't stay clean if I didn't do a few daily chores.

WE NEED DAILY MAINTENANCE

In order to work Step Ten, the experience I acquired in the nine Steps that led up to it showed me what I needed. Specifically, I needed to recognize my powerlessness over other people. I needed to believe that God could help me. I needed to make the decision to allow my Higher Power to take care of me. I needed to inventory my behavior so I could recognize my good points as well as my bad.

As I learned in Step Four, it was important to find my positive characteristics so I could build on them. When I found areas where I was lacking, I needed to examine the specifics. I needed to admit to myself where I was wrong and push aside all of my excuses and justifications. I didn't have to accept the guilt for what other people had done, but I needed to stop using others as scapegoats. With this new understanding of myself, I needed to admit my wrongs to God and to another human being.

Step Ten helped me recognize that certain character defects still prevailed in my life. It didn't excuse my errors, however, so I needed to continue checking myself to see whom I had harmed and to make the appropriate amends. I appreciated hearing the practical suggestion to do Step Ten every evening. When I started following that suggestion, I began to feel better – and I liked the feeling. Then I learned that I didn't have to do this just one time a day, so I started doing a daily inventory after work, by doing this I cleaned away my work day so I wasn't carrying home my feelings from work. It taught me to leave outside the home those things that don't belong at home.

I found something else that helped. In the Twelve Concepts I learned to determine my primary purpose in any given situation and then to try to hold my focus. As a result, I started doing a noon time inventory. I cleared away any interactions that I'd had during the morning. If I had harmed another person and was feeling guilty about it, clearing it away helped to improve the quality of my afternoon.

Eventually, I set up other little stop gaps for myself – on my way to work, mid-morning and mid-afternoon. As time went by, I found myself automatically inventorying my actions, thoughts and words. By dealing with things and letting them go, I made myself feel better. I stopped going around feeling like I needed to kick myself for something. I put my tools to work.

Recently, I read a card for an Al-Anon friend. It presented an acronym for "Think."

T – *Is it Thoughtful?*
H – *Is it Honest?*
I – *Is it Intelligent?*
N – *Is it Necessary?*
K – *Is it Kind?*

If so, then it is probably okay for me to say it.

Working Step Ten

Continued to take personal inventory and when we were wrong promptly admitted it.

SOME MEMBERS find it useful to make a chart that includes a list of typical personal weaknesses and strengths that can be checked off before going to bed. A mental review of the day chronologically or taking note of any event that produced uncomfortable feelings also works. The following questions may help develop the habit of continual inventory.

* What is the purpose of Step Ten?

* How do I feel about continuing to take a personal inventory?

* What means of taking daily inventory is comfortable for me?

* What will help me continue to apply program tools when life gets rough?

* How can I be patient with myself if I feel I'm not growing fast enough?

* When might I need to take a spot-check?

* What can I do with my spot-check inventory?

* In a daily inventory, I can ask myself:

* What were the major events of the day?

* What feelings did I experience?

* How did I deal with them?

* Did I get myself involved in any situation today I had no business being in?

* What can help me to accept myself as I make mistakes again and again?

* Did fear or faith rule my actions today?

* How can I admit my wrong despite my pride and fear that it will be used against me?

* Am I at fault for trying for peace at any price? What are my motives?

* How do I know when to make amends and when not to?

* What positive traits did I exhibit today?

* What negative traits did I exhibit today?

* How did I try to fix anyone today?

* How can I "Let Go and Let God"?

* Did I abandon my own needs today? How?

* Have I been too accommodating, saying "yes" when I wanted to say "no"?

* Was I afraid of an authority figure? Of anyone? Why or why not?

* What small things can I do to practice standing up for myself?

* How did I take on anyone else's responsibility today?

* What am I afraid will happen if I don't take on extra responsibility?

* If I was wrong, did I promptly admit it?

* What can I do to take good care of myself today?

* Is there something that I need to take a longer look at? What is it?

* Have I done something difficult or particularly well today? How can I appreciate myself for it?

* How could sharing my daily Tenth Step inventory with another person, such as my sponsor, help me?

* What characteristics show up most often in my inventory?

* Why do I resist having them removed?

* After practicing the Tenth Step, how have my feelings about it changed?

Step
Eleven

Sought through prayer and meditation to improve our conscious contact with God AS WE UNDERSTOOD HIM, *praying only for knowledge of His will for us and the power to carry that out.*

THE RELATIONSHIP we have with the God of our understanding, compared to when we first walked through the doors of Al-Anon, is now more powerful as the result of our experience in working Steps One through Ten. In Step Two we "came to believe that a Power greater than ourselves could restore us to sanity." Some of us call that Power God. In Step Three we experienced the power of making a conscious "decision to turn our will and our lives over to the care of God *as we understood Him.*" In Step Five we became more intimate with our God by admitting "the exact nature of our wrongs;" in Step Six we became ready to have Him remove our "defects of character," and finally in Step Seven we "asked Him to remove our shortcomings." Each Step offers new spiritual guidance. In Step Eleven we can maintain our growth with new energy through prayer, meditation and knowledge of His will.

Although referred to as the second maintenance Step, Step Eleven does introduce new action – the action of seeking through prayer and mediation to improve our conscious contact with God. What is prayer? What is meditation? How are they different? An important note to make is that this Step guides us with the words prayer and meditation, not prayer or meditation.

To some, prayer is seen as a religious act of placing one's hands together, getting on one's knees and talking to God. Others ask their sponsor, an Al-Anon member or a spiritual person to guide them. In Al-Anon some begin with simple prayers, such as the Serenity Prayer or "not my will, but thine be done." Some pray every morning or evening, some pray throughout the day. Reading the prayers found in Al-Anon literature opens the door for others. Many read daily from *One Day at a Time in Al-Anon, Courage to Change: One Day at a Time in Al-Anon II* or *Alateen: A Day at a Time*, using the day's message as a form of prayer. Writing letters to God works, too. We learn to pray from example and from other's personal experience. To some of us, it may feel artificial. Sometimes prayer works and we are delighted, while at other times nothing seems to happen. Accepting God's will and God's time can mean saying a prayer and letting go.

Meditation has been used in many cultures as a spiritual practice for thousands of years. Finding a quiet time in our busy lives can be difficult. Many find it helpful to schedule a specific time at a set location to meditate. In the beginning we may not need a great deal of time. In fact, success may come by trying for a few minutes at a time until we become more comfortable with the action. Almost all of us can find the few minutes needed, if we want. As we have success disciplining our minds, these brief periods of meditation will increase.

"What is meditation? Al-Anon leaves that a question open for each of us to answer in our own way. Drawing upon the experiences of other Al-Anon members can help us to find our own path. Here are only a few of the ways members of the fellowship have shared:

"To me, meditation is a higher spiritual awareness. I practice remembering that every action can serve a spiritual purpose.

"I go to a quiet place, close my eyes, and repeat the words of the Serenity Prayer to myself in a gentle voice.

"I need to get beyond my thoughts, so I concentrate on my breathing, counting from one to ten over and over as I breathe in and out.

"I simply step back and watch my thoughts as if I were watching a play. I try to keep my attention on the present day only, leaving the past and the future alone.

"I focus on a flower. When my thoughts stray, I accept that my mind is just doing its job – thinking – and then gently return to my subject.

"In my mind, I picture my Higher Power's hands. One by one, I place my problems and worries, my joy and my gratitude, into those hands, and finally, I climb in too."

(from *Courage to Change: One Day at a Time in Al-Anon II*, p. 338)

In meditation some people find taking long, slow breaths helps relax the body and still the mind. While some people experience flashes of new ideas and solutions to problems during meditation, it is not our intent to try to solve a specific problem. We try not to spend the time worrying or thinking about a problem; what we seek in meditation is to find peace and enough silence to hear the still, small voice within. We should all feel free to meditate in any way that works for us.

Together prayer and meditation are actions we consciously take to open our hearts and minds not only to the powerful recovery found in Al-Anon, but also to the experience, strength and hope of others. Our wish and need for the knowledge of God's presence is experienced and cherished by many a member. It has been said in many Al-Anon meeting rooms by wise members that prayer is talking to God, meditation is listening.

Improving or making a conscious contact with God is not always simple and at times the path may seem rocky or uneven. Even after years of meditating and praying, most of us, at one time or another, find ourselves in a place of frustration or discontent. By using Step Ten, we can usually identify challenges that are blocking us from successful prayer or meditation. We may find that we are back to exercising our own will. Being gentle with ourselves and remembering that we are human beings on a spiritual path with twists and turns is helpful. As we say in our suggested Al-Anon closing, "We aren't perfect." We learn not to be too hard on ourselves and discover, much to our relief, that our loving Higher Power waits patiently for a renewed contact.

The second part of Step Eleven, "…praying only for knowledge of His will for us and the power to carry that out," focuses our prayers in a specific direction – God's, not ours. Asking only for God's will means surrendering our own. Working previous Steps has helped us to become willing. Before recovery some of us accepted unacceptable behavior in others, believing we were doing God's will. Despite sincere efforts, we are not always able to separate God's will from our own, but we can strive for improvement. When we experience a new joy, we now celebrate with newfound gratitude. When we make a mistake, we learn from it and continue to grow – "One Day at a Time."

In experiencing God's will, some members find a deep sense of awareness and peace. At other times we learn to risk personal discomfort for changed behavior. We ask our Higher Power to increase our desire to do what is good for us and to diminish the desire to do what isn't. We can accept that each time we feel even slightly more sane or loving, it is a response to our prayers and meditation. Strong feelings sometimes provide strong messages. If we get a strong message and wonder if it is our will or our Higher Power speaking, we find it is usually wise to check it out with a sponsor or another Al-Anon member before taking action.

Seeking, prayer, meditation, improvement, conscious contact, understanding, knowledge, His will and power are all the gifts of Step Eleven. With newfound energy we are learning to follow God's will. Our faith and competence grow daily as we pray and meditate. There are thousands of paths to a Higher

Power and we can choose any one of them. Gratefully we choose at least one and step out on our continued journey to recovery.

Members Share Experience, Strength and Hope

A MIRACLE STEP ELEVEN is a very special Step. I liked it from the moment I first heard it. Before I came into Al-Anon, I had been interested in oriental religions. I found the idea of meditation appealing. But it seemed all of my attempts at meditation failed. I could not keep my mind quiet for more than 30 seconds. Since I did not get it right the first time, I believed I was hopeless so I gave up.

When I came to Al-Anon, I got a sponsor right away. I asked her if I could begin meditating even though I was just starting the Steps. She told me to go ahead, that prayer and meditation were tools I could always use. Again I tried to meditate, sure that now I was going to get "it," whatever "it" was. I felt very frustrated when I realized I still couldn't keep my mind quiet. Thoughts passed through my brain at about 3,000 miles per hour, so I gave up.

I continued to use the Steps. I progressed to Step Nine, changed sponsors and worked through the Steps again until I finally reached Step Eleven. Even though I worked all those Steps in about five or six months, I changed a lot. I was willing to be willing. I tried to meditate and pray as best I could. I didn't give up if it didn't work perfectly the first time.

Although my outlook on life changed considerably, I still had a very hard time getting up in the morning. Most days, I laid in bed until it was a decent hour to call my sponsor. After talking with her, I felt I could go on with my day. When I began practicing Step Eleven, I decided to do it first thing in the morning.

I woke up resentful about being alive, not wanting

to do anything. I started saying short prayers that my sponsor suggested. I read spiritual materials and tried to listen to my Higher Power. Often I read aloud because I found that would help to quiet my thoughts. I was so surprised when an hour or so of such endeavors completely changed my attitude! I felt happy and ready to tackle the day. Even deciding what to do first came easier! It was amazing. I began to follow this sequence every day. Invariably I experienced a change of attitude. Some days it was quick, and others took longer. I just kept going until, for some unknown reason, my heart filled with joy and hope. It always seemed like a miracle.

Even when I felt like giving up, I continued my routine every morning because I remembered the miracle of my changed attitude. I was to receive an even bigger gift for practicing Step Eleven. One day, I woke up happy and full of energy! I could not remember the last time when that had happened. For over a year now, I have almost always awakened ready to tackle the daily challenges of living life. I can't tell you how wonderful it feels to wake up and look forward to the day – to wake up and feel as though I am part of the universe.

THE ELEVENTH STEP was not an easy one for me to talk about. My relationship with my Higher Power felt more private than sex. I remember my husband saying once, shortly after he was in recovery, that he would like us to pray together. Just the thought of it terrified me. I didn't answer him. I pretended I didn't hear what he had said.

My mother was the religious one in my family when I was growing up. Her relationship with God was also very private but I could tell it was based on fear. The only time my dad mentioned God was when he was cursing us. I know these experiences didn't get me off to a good start with a Higher Power. Living with an alcoholic for years didn't help, either. God didn't answer any of the prayers in which I asked Him to fix my husband. I began to think that God didn't care about me.

With the help of Al-Anon and the Second, Third and Eleventh Steps, I know differently today. I know God loves me and cares for me. All He wants is for me to be happy. It took a long time for me to learn this because the God I knew was judgmental and punishing. I saw people in the program who had the good relationship with their Higher Power that I wanted, but I didn't know how to get it. As for prayer and meditation, I learned that prayer wasn't necessarily the same as what I memorized when I was growing up. Prayer could be simply talking to God, which wasn't so hard, because I was already doing that. All meditation meant was to listen to God – just being quiet and clearing my mind of worrisome thoughts so I could hear what God was saying to me. The Eleventh Step also said my relationship with God didn't have to be perfect. I just needed to try to improve it.

The part about God's will for me seemed much harder to do, until I heard it described very simply. "How do we know what is God's will? That's easy – just get up every day, keep moving and when you hit a wall, turn left!" It sounded too simple, but how many times had I come to those walls and just stayed there, doing nothing? How many times did I continue throwing myself at the wall, totally exhausting myself and getting nowhere? How much easier it was to make a simple turn and keep moving forward.

WE ARE SPECIAL

I BROKE Step Eleven into four parts. Prayer is talking with God about what His will is for me. Meditation is quietly listening and focusing on the Power of God that is inside of me. Conscious contact is making myself deeply aware of God's presence. Knowledge and power is when I stop giving directions and start listening for God's will. In this way, I develop a deeper relationship with God. I can feel His strength, wisdom, peace and love. I receive the courage to carry out His will with love, humility, dignity, kindness and sometimes even humor.

My prayer is that everyone will find a Higher Power's love, strength, wisdom and understanding. I pray that everyone finds unconditional love on the way to loving themselves. May all know that we are special and that we are children of God.

Working Step Eleven

Sought through prayer and meditation to improve our conscious contact with God as we understood Him, praying only for knowledge of His will for us and the power to carry that out.

* How do I define the difference between prayer and meditation? Can I talk to my sponsor, another Al-Anon friend or someone I am sponsoring about the difference?

* Am I willing to try prayer and meditation today?

* What can I do to add prayer and meditation to my life today?

* Do I have a special time and place to pray and meditate? What can I do to create one?

* How have I sought to improve my conscious contact? Have I sought out help from my group? My sponsor? Anyone else in Al-Anon?

* What personal spiritual experiences can I draw on to help me improve my conscious contact with a Higher Power?

* What does it mean to me to pray only for God's will and not my own? How can I distinguish between God's will and my self-will?

* How have I been mistaken about God's will? How has my self-will caused me difficulties?

* How am I willing to be guided today?

* Is something blocking me in this Step today? What is it? What Steps can I review to help me feel connected again?

* What do I need to have the power to carry out God's will for me? Have I asked God for that power?

It can be said that the entire Al-Anon program is summed up in Step Twelve. We acknowledge the results of our efforts – a spiritual awakening – commit ourselves to sharing the gifts we have received and recognize that living a spiritual life is an ongoing process. We have found a new way of life in Al-Anon, and to keep what we have found, we have to continue appreciating the gift and giving it away. The three parts of Step Twelve raise the following questions: What is a spiritual awakening? How can we try to carry this message? What are these principles that we practice in all our affairs?

One of the wonderful experiences of working the Twelve Steps is a spiritual awakening. How do we know when we have it? Some of us have had vivid, dramatic experiences that clearly were spiritual awakenings. We felt changed in some obvious, permanent sense and knew that we would never be the same again. However, most of us found our spiritual awakening to be a much slower, more subtle experience, more like a flower opening petal by petal than like a flash of lightning.

When awakening is slow, internal and quiet, it can often be overlooked. We sometimes question if, indeed, anything at all has happened, especially when familiar problems continue to appear in our lives. What does a spiritual awakening look like to us? Obviously it varies with each individual, but many of us have similar experiences. Instead of obsession or constant crisis, we find more inner peace. We may have less interest in judging others and ourselves, or act spontaneously instead of with fearful control. Moments of appreciation for little things happen more frequently. Some of us experience feelings of connection with and delight in nature, or find ourselves relaxing and going with the flow. We find ourselves giving and receiving unconditional love. Suddenly we may become aware that some of these good feelings have come into our lives but not know

Step Twelve

Having had a spiritual awakening as the result of these Steps, we tried to carry this message to others, and to practice these principles in all our affairs.

exactly when it happened.

Being aware that we have spiritually changed, we are now ready to try to carry the message to others. Before Al-Anon many of us were lonely and isolated. Attending meetings and sharing the program helped us break our isolation. We have learned to reach out and ask for help from our Higher Power, a sponsor and our groups. Now it is our turn to give back.

When we freely share ourselves with others we discover that it fills us with satisfaction. We support our meetings with our attendance because we want them to be available when anyone needs them. When we take phone calls, we often hear something we need to hear. When we accept a group, district or area service position, we find participating with other active Al-Anon members expands our own understanding and capabilities. Sponsoring a new member challenges us to continue working our own program; working with newcomers who are in pain reminds us of how far we have come and, possibly, of how far we may have to travel. Even the task of keeping coffee and cookies available as part of a group welcome is important Twelfth Step work.

Sometimes we discover that our character defects are magnified as we apply ourselves to these endeavors. In the past many of us spent too much time taking care of others; enabling the alcoholic; or trying to control his or her drinking. A big part of our growth has been learning to keep the focus on ourselves and not put others' needs ahead of our own. We may have had to learn to say, "No." Twelfth Step work may tempt us to give advice or overmanage another person's situation, often with unhappy results. Maybe we have irritated our family and friends by trying to make them see the light. We need to learn to give up expectations about outcomes and catch ourselves when we are trying to fix anyone. We look to find a balance between taking care of ourselves and helping others; we can be available to those we want to help without taking on all their burdens. We share our experience, strength and hope, offer love and acceptance and then let go. We can give ourselves credit for the compassion and care we feel for others; each time we make well-meaning mistakes, we learn from them and continue to grow.

Carrying the message can take many forms, from giving encouragement to a newcomer to participating in service at any level from group to the world service level. Many members share that they always seem to get back far more than they give in Al-Anon – sometimes just when they need it most. Our best message is to be a good example of Al-Anon. This is the best thing we can do for ourselves as well as others.

Living the principles describes the final part of Step Twelve which says, "...to practice these principles in all our affairs." The principles we need to practice have been learned in our study of the Twelve Steps. We know that we are not in charge of everything – a Higher Power is – and we can continuously seek guidance from and turn our lives over to the care of that Power. We are continually taking our own inventories and making amends as needed. Through prayer, meditation and working the Steps, we have had a spiritual awakening, and our trust in God and other people is expanded. We are able to give and receive unconditional love. Step Twelve invites us to stay on our path to recovery. We must continue our maintenance work so we won't slip back into old patterns. To continue, we need to share all that we have been given with other families and friends of alcoholics. To keep it, we have to give it away.

In our Al-Anon meetings, we share our experience, strength and hope with others on this path to recovery. In meetings and with our Al-Anon friends, we practice the Al-Anon principles together. Practicing these principles "in all our affairs" is the real test of recovery and the challenge that keeps us coming back. Life continually provides us with new challenges and opportunities to put our Step work into action.

Dealing with our loved ones – our closest, most important and often most troublesome relationships – can be a strong test of our recovery. These are often the people who were responsible for our seeking out Al-Anon in the first place. We may be connected to them financially, emotionally and legally. We need to apply our Al-Anon program continually in all areas of these relationships. This is usually the place of greatest challenge and thus holds the potential for the greatest healing. To learn to act lovingly in intimate relationships is an important goal for many of us. To do so requires continual practice of all the Steps as well as the tools found in the Traditions and Concepts.

Practicing the principles of the Steps in all our affairs – at work, in our community and religious institutions, with family and friends – is important to our recovery and serenity. We find that applying these principles works as well with people who have never heard of our Twelve Step program as with our loved ones. They are universal spiritual principles that help us negotiate life with love and serenity.

All of us are faced with challenges in life – bereavement, disappointment, poverty, to name a few. Recovery doesn't protect us from life. It enables us to live more fully and deal with life's problems as they arise. Al-Anon gives us human support, a Higher Power to guide and support us and Twelve Steps to live by.

Carrying out the actions of the Twelfth Step renews our spirit on a daily basis. Reaching out to others helps us gain perspective on our own lives. We are encouraged by the examples of others. Everyday irritations shrink and life's big problems seem more manageable. Practicing these principles in all our affairs clearly demonstrates to us that the Twelve Steps are a way of life like no other.

SLOWLY, BUT surely, I became aware of God working in my life. I became aware of a new and closer relationship with my Higher Power, whom I chose to call God. Just as in Step Two, I came, then I came to and then I came to believe.

My spiritual awakening progressed in the same way – very gradually. I admitted my powerlessness, realized that He could help me, and learned to turn my will and life over to my loving Higher Power. Having the faith to make the Fourth and Fifth Steps, I learned to trust Him in my Sixth, Seventh, Eighth and Ninth Steps. Using Steps Ten and Eleven brought me to a new awareness of His love and care for me. As I worked the Steps, I came to recognize the common principles of honesty, compassion, love, trust, humility, willingness, forgiveness and freedom.

I saw many people designate certain principles to match specific Steps, but that didn't work for me. I found many principles that applied to each Step. I also learned to work the Steps in order, because each Step depended on the ones that preceded it. When I reached Step Twelve, it helped that I knew something about the message that I was supposed to carry to others. Even so, I was glad to know that I only had to try to carry the message. I was not responsible for the way other people understood it or accepted it.

The last part of Step Twelve reminded me to practice these principles in all my affairs. It told me to take what I learned in Al-Anon and use it in my dealings with all people. It was not enough for me to be compassionate and forgiving and loving in my Al-Anon meetings. I may be the only example of Al-Anon that some people will ever see. Each time I interact with people, I am carrying a message. Step Twelve reminded me of the question in our *Blueprint for Progress* regarding attitudes, "Are mine worth catching?"

It is my belief that I am supposed to carry the message of love, especially God's love, to all people. Because I worked each of the Twelve Steps for my own benefit, I came to see that I had to love myself before I could love others. I had to help myself before I could help anyone else.

AT THE end of every meeting, my group reads, "...though you may not like all of us, you'll love us in a very special way – the same way we already love you." During my first year in Al-Anon, there was one member I not only did not like, I positively could not stand her.

She had this terrible character defect of talking too much during the meetings. Every time she raised her hand to speak, I groaned inside. I knew she would talk for 20 or 25 minutes, often about the very things she'd shared at the last meeting.

During her long-winded sharings, I tried all sorts of ways to signal my displeasure. I stared into space with a very bored expression. I sighed. I glanced at my watch frequently and thumbed through my *One Day at a Time in Al-Anon* book. I knew she also bothered others, because several people offered pointed suggestions about limiting our sharing. None of it did any good. I got to the point that if I walked into a meeting and saw her there, I almost walked out.

One day, something happened that can only happen in Al-Anon. I was sitting in the meeting, muttering in my mind about how selfish and inconsiderate she was. She hadn't even shared, yet. I was just anticipating. Suddenly a thought banged its way into my head: "Do you think that by resenting her, you are going to change her?" I just about fell out of my chair. Oh, my Lord! I was doing to her exactly what I had done to my alcoholic for all those years! I was trying to change her, and I was making myself crazy in the process.

I let go of my controlling thoughts, and something

happened that I can only describe as a miracle. Suddenly, I was flooded with total love for that woman. I no longer saw her as a selfish, inconsiderate problem, but as a sweet, gentle woman with whom I had a lot in common.

Today, the same woman is one of my favorite people in the program! When I walk into the room and see her, I can feel my whole face light up. If that isn't amazing enough, I also find her sharings incredibly interesting. She seems to have one beautiful insight after another.

Now, I'm not saying that it's okay for people to talk and talk and talk, especially if the meeting is short and others want to share. I really don't know what the solution is, other than a group conscience to limit sharings. Members sharing too long is still a major problem to some people at my meetings. I tell them that we need to be patient with everyone. From personal experience, I found that getting all hyped up over other people's behavior is a trap. My mind sets the trap to divert attention from my own unacceptable behavior. If I let go of control, I can get the focus back on myself, which opens the door for a lot of miracles.

I INVOLVED myself in Al-Anon service work for many reasons. I wanted to escape from home. I wanted to stake my claim in a program specifically designed to heal me. What I found was unconditional love, acceptance, serenity, wisdom and courage. I found an opportunity to invest my talents in my own growth. When I wanted to feel as if I belonged, I found that each small task I accomplished helped me feel a sense of ownership.

I wanted to enjoy the camaraderie of friends who shared spiritual goals. I found friendships based on the Twelve Traditions, a combination of ideals and safe boundaries that I needed so much in my personal life. I wanted to keep my mind from reeling. What I found was if I concentrated on a service project I became too busy to obsess about other people's problems. The same was true when I wanted to solve the problems in my home. As I took the focus off my problems, my life smoothed out and the problems found their own God-given solutions.

When I stopped reacting to negative criticism, I studied what my reactions had been. I learned useful information about myself that helped me build my self-esteem. When I tried to assess my value as a person, I found that service magnified both my assets and my defects. All of this self knowledge made it possible for me to become the integrated person I wanted to be. When I tried to learn how to make decisions based on facts, I found out how to trust the facts to my intuition without losing my power to impulses and fear. When I wanted to learn how to form and retain an opinion, I found many opportunities. I found I could have strong opinions, express them and allow others to have equally strong opinions as well.

I did not intend to give so much of my time and energy to carrying the message. It just happened that way when I couldn't say no to program people who offered me a better way to live. Their enthusiasm and invitation led me toward this exciting, rewarding, Al-Anon way of life.

Most of all, I wanted to receive and keep recovery. What I found was the joy of giving it away, the same way others so generously gave the gift of service to me – with love, respect and compassion. I found all these treasures and more when I thought I was seeking much less. I call that my spiritual awakening.

Working Step Twelve

Having had a spiritual awakening as the result of these Steps, we tried to carry this message to others, and to practice these principles in all our affairs.

THERE ARE many spiritual awakenings and many ways to carry the message. Al-Anon members offer these ideas and questions to help us explore the meaning of the Twelfth Step.

* Have I experienced a spiritual awakening(s)? Describe.

* In what ways do I downplay my spiritual growth? What can help me to acknowledge it?

* What have I received from Al-Anon that I would most like to share?

* What are the different ways I can carry this message to others?

* Did I see a friendly face early in my recovery? What can I do to be a friendly face to someone else?

* What is the difference between carrying the message and giving advice?

* When trying to carry the message, what have I experienced?

* How can I recognize a cry for help without meddling in other people's affairs?

* How can I best carry the message to my family members, especially those who resist the ideas?

* How can I practice these principles in my financial affairs? Is my job merely a means of earning money or an opportunity to practice my recovery?

* What does the Twelfth Step say to me about Al-Anon service work?

* What part has service to Al-Anon played in my recovery?

* What would change if I viewed service as my goal in every area of my life?

* What are "these principles"?

* How can I apply them in my daily life?

* In what areas of my life do I need to start practicing these principles? What can I do this week to make a beginning?

* How am I living the message of the program?

* How am I a good example of Al-Anon recovery?

The Twelve Traditions

The Twelve Traditions

THE TRADITIONS that follow bind us together in unity. They guide the groups in their relations with other groups, with AA and the outside world. They recommend group attitudes toward leadership, membership, money, property, public relations, and anonymity.

The Traditions evolved from the experience of AA groups in trying to solve their problems of living and working together. Al-Anon adopted these group guidelines and over the years has found them sound and wise. Although they are only suggestions, Al-Anon's unity and perhaps even its survival are dependent on adherence to these principles.

1. Our common welfare should come first; personal progress for the greatest number depends upon unity.

2. For our group purpose there is but one authority – a loving God as He may express Himself in our group conscience. Our leaders are but trusted servants; they do not govern.

3. The relatives of alcoholics, when gathered together for mutual aid, may call themselves an Al-Anon Family Group, provided that, as a group, they have no other affiliation. The only requirement for membership is that there be a problem of alcoholism in a relative or friend.

4. Each group should be autonomous, except in matters affecting another group or Al-Anon or AA as a whole.

5. Each Al-Anon Family Group has but one purpose: to help families of alcoholics. We do this by practicing the Twelve Steps of AA *ourselves*, by encouraging and understanding our alcoholic relatives, and by welcoming and giving comfort to families of alcoholics.

6. Our Al-Anon Family Groups ought never endorse, finance or lend our name to any outside enterprise, lest problems of money, property and prestige divert us from our primary spiritual aim. Although a separate entity, we should always cooperate with Alcoholics Anonymous.

7. Every group ought to be fully self-supporting, declining outside contributions.

8. Al-Anon Twelfth-Step work should remain forever nonprofessional, but our service centers may employ special workers.

9. Our groups, as such, ought never be organized; but we may create service boards or committees directly responsible to those they serve.

10. The Al-Anon Family Groups have no opinion on outside issues; hence our name ought never be drawn into public controversy.

11. Our public relations policy is based on attraction rather than promotion; we need always maintain personal anonymity at the level of press, radio, TV and films. We need guard with special care the anonymity of all AA members.

12. Anonymity is the spiritual foundation of all our Traditions, ever reminding us to place principles above personalities.

Introduction to The Twelve Traditions

Lois W., our co-founder, wrote, "Al-Anon...holds together by means of a loving understanding among its members. Al-Anon is united – without organization, without management, without a chain of command or a set of rules – by its members' willingness to be obedient to the unenforceable." Al-Anon's Twelve Traditions are guides for the conduct and unity necessary to maintain healthy groups. They are as much a part of our spiritual foundation as the Steps. Since Al-Anon has no rules or regulations, the Traditions form the framework of common consent within which we may best carry out our activities. The lessons learned by studying the Traditions form a framework for our personal lives as well as for our groups.

For Al-Anon members, the study of the Traditions creates new insights and goals. The journey through the Traditions includes recovery topics such as membership, group purpose, money, property, public relations, leadership and anonymity. These principles and others suggest the basic spiritual guidelines that are invaluable to our growth; they guide our paths to recovery in Al-Anon.

We voluntarily follow the Traditions to the best of our understanding because experience has shown that, when we stray too far from them in any direction, our groups become less effective or even fall apart. The health of our groups is essential to our recovery, and loving application of the Traditions can resolve almost any group problem. We need only contribute our personal experience, strength and hope honestly; listen to each other respectfully; refer to the Traditions and trust a Higher Power with our groups as we have learned to trust a Higher Power in our personal lives.

Using the Traditions in our groups reveals another

great Al-Anon gift. The principles that guide us through conflict in the naturally different points of view within our diverse fellowship are useful as personal standards in any group – families, jobs, clubs, churches – just about anywhere. In Al-Anon we learn how to live in a variety of relationships without losing ourselves or forcing our ideas on others. By including study of the Traditions on our paths to recovery, we learn how to have healthier relationships than most of us have ever known.

In Al-Anon we have learned that as individuals we are very important and that, if we don't take care of ourselves, "Who will?" Tradition One speaks to our need for "common welfare." It speaks to us as individuals, as members of a group and to our group. It suggests that, by caring for the well-being of all participants, we will be able to discern what will best serve the individual growth of most members and foster our own well-being. Within a loving, spiritual community, each of us has the best chance for personal progress and Tradition One sets the foundation for creating and maintaining that community.

Remembering our common welfare helps us learn how to use our meetings effectively. What is common welfare? For Al-Anon members it means familiarity with our primary purpose – to help families and friends of alcoholics. It means recovery, sharing at meetings, personal growth, group growth, participating in the worldwide fellowship and understanding a common problem – alcoholism. Although spoken and written in many languages, by reading the suggested opening, reciting the Serenity Prayer, Steps, Traditions and Concepts, using Conference Approved Literature (CAL) and reading our suggested closing, we are assured that the message of Al-Anon is spoken worldwide.

This does not mean that all groups are exactly alike. Groups follow different formats: some hold literature study meetings, have monthly or quarterly chairpersons, begin meetings by reading all Steps and Traditions or by reading the Steps and one Tradition. Some groups are non-smoking, some meet in hospitals, some focus on children or parents of alcoholics and some are primarily for men, women, gays or lesbians or newcomers, but all groups have a framework of Al-Anon principles. All groups seek to relieve the pain of living or having lived with an alcoholic.

As new members of a group, many of us withhold our thoughts and experiences, either out of consider-

Tradition One

Our common welfare should come first; personal progress for the greatest number depends upon unity.

ation for others or from fear that we might be embarrassed, thus depriving our group of our wisdom. Through the unity and leadership of the group members, we learn that by speaking we share the responsibility for keeping our meetings healthy. Longtime members often withhold sharing in larger meetings, believing it is essential for the newer members to talk first. They forget that, by sharing, they may be providing wisdom and encouragement to a newcomer or another longtime member with a new problem in his or her life. It is essential that we nod in understanding to the pain of the newcomer, to the parent living with a child who slips in and out of recovery or to the longtime member discovering that yet another relative is suffering from the insidious disease of alcoholism. Sharing our common experiences and the Al-Anon solutions at meetings is what makes a meeting alive and unified in purpose.

Practicing the Traditions helps us maintain unity and a sense of familiarity. As individuals each of us is free to find a group where we feel most at home. At the same time, because of our unity of purpose, we are assured that we will find some familiar ground in any Al-Anon group we attend.

Sometimes, however, members consciously or unconsciously disregard the Traditions. In such instances each of us has a responsibility to remind them of the Traditions in a caring, loving way. When making such a suggestion, it helps if we remember that guidelines are for group harmony. Our Traditions are suggestions that we each adhere to voluntarily, using the best understanding we have of them at the time. We have learned that as our recovery expands, our ability to benefit from the Traditions also expands.

Over the years, many groups have faced common problems. As new members, we find it far easier to talk about the alcoholics in our lives than to focus on ourselves. Later we learn that taking excessive time dumping a great many details on the group is not beneficial for the group or for us. It is often at this point in our recovery that we learn about the role of a sponsor and the many purposes of sponsorship. A sponsor is a person with whom a member can share and discuss personal problems or questions in detail, who will willingly share their Al-Anon experience, strength and hope one-on-one. A sponsor serves us better than the group for lengthy discussions. Sometimes desperate newcomers may need to unburden. Allowing them some meeting time to share and making an offer of personal contact after the meeting are ways to offer loving understanding in this situation.

A good source of unifying material is our own Conference Approved Literature (CAL). "Conference approved" means that what is contained in our published literature was written by Al-Anon members and has passed through a rigorous World Service Conference (WSC) approval process. It is an accurate reflection of the ideas and experience of our fellowship as a whole. It is appropriate for use at all Al-Anon meetings and events. What we read outside meetings is our own business and becomes a part of our personal experience. In meetings we share from our personal experiences and from CAL. With all the research, popular writing and media attention to alcoholism, we in Al-Anon cannot review and discuss everything that is published. We keep it simple when we use the literature that we know reflects our Al-Anon approach to alcoholism. Using CAL also has the advantage of allowing us to access the experience, strength and hope of members in our large, diverse, worldwide fellowship. Through CAL, we share the suggestions we know have helped us.

Some people may wonder how an entirely volunteer fellowship can survive without enforcing rules. Ours is a spiritual program. Again and again we must place our trust in a God of our understanding to lead us to decisions for our common good and we must practice the principles we know have worked for others in our fellowship. We are not perfect; we often have strong conflicts, but we work our way through them with the Traditions and our trust in a Higher Power. So far we have found that if each of us seeks our best personal understanding of the principle of unity, accepts our diverse backgrounds and keeps faith with ground rules established by the group conscience, the program works. It may be amazing that it works, but that is further evidence for trust in our Higher Power.

Many Al-Anon groups close their meetings by reciting the Al-Anon Declaration, Let it Begin with Me "When anyone, anywhere reaches out for help, let the hand of Al-Anon and Alateen always be there and let it begin with me." This is a common message and it speaks to the welfare of those who have not yet found meetings as well as to the unity of members of our world-wide fellowship.

Members Share Experience, Strength and Hope

I SAW A
GLIMMER
OF HOPE

How DID Al-Anon come alive for me? It wasn't through the Steps as it might have been for most members. For me it was on a special night in a meeting on Tradition One. That night I was receptive. I heard how Al-Anon worked in other people's lives, and I understood some of my part in this disease. I felt the pain. I realized how deeply alcoholism had affected our family. As I sat in the Tradition study meeting, I really listened to each person share. It became clear to me that these Traditions could apply to my home. After all, I saw Tradition One working in our group. I even saw it applied very successfully in our business meetings. I saw a glimmer of hope, a new direction, a real tool I could use in my recovery.

Tradition One spoke of unity – something that I longed for in my home. This Tradition made me look at my part in our dis-unity. Somewhere in the family disease of alcoholism, I had taken control. I took it upon myself to make most of the decisions. After all, I was not the alcoholic, so I was okay. The decisions I made and my motives for making them were to keep the family together and the alcoholic in line. I know today that most of my decisions were made in times of anger, resentment, deep despair and insanity. I had no balance, no serenity and no Higher Power. I had retired God many years before this and I had been fueled by self-will ever since.

Today I know that for unity to exist in my family or in my group, all of us must have a voice. No one voice is more or less important than anyone else's. I have a responsibility to listen, to share and to accept. Tradition One lifted the burden of control off my shoulders. I no longer had the right to make decisions for everyone. The people in my home deserved to make their own decisions and to be given the same respect that I desired for myself, whether they were in recovery or not. This new freedom for me and the other members of my family was a miracle from Al-Anon. When I see Tradition One applied at the group level, it reminds me again how important unity is in my life. The reminder always brings me back into balance.

WHEN I first came into the Al-Anon program, I didn't understand the Steps, let alone the Traditions. After a while I began to look at the Traditions, but I interpreted them according to my own behavior at that time. I always put my needs after those of the alcoholic and my friends. If they told me what they wanted, I did it. I kept thinking someday my turn would come, but it never did. As a result I interpreted the Traditions to mean that everyone in the group had to be happy or we would lose our unity. If someone wanted to ban smoking, I thought we had to ban smoking. If an AA member wanted to discuss the Big Book in a meeting, I thought we should all be courteous and listen. If a member shared the same story week after week without taking any action to improve the situation, I felt my job was to be there for him or her, even if he or she kept taking valuable meeting time to rehash the same old problem.

One week we studied the First Tradition. The leader said that in Al-Anon each person's opinion counts and that no one person should force the group to do anything. I was floored. How could we possibly have unity and still let everyone speak? A fight always started when I expressed my opinion at home. I always gave in to keep the peace. In Al-Anon I learned a different way. Tradition One meant the group could set aside time to discuss the issues and then we could vote. That way no one forced the rest of us to do anything. During our group conscience meetings, I actually saw people disagree without getting angry. After we voted and made a decision, we held hands and said the Serenity Prayer. Even the people in the minority were pleasant because they had had their say. In the end everyone accepted the group's decision.

Learning about the Traditions also helped me in my private life. I began to understand that even at home I didn't need to take it personally when we had different opinions. I could state my opinion and let go of the results. As I began to detach and not force solutions, even the alcoholic began to change. Sometimes we agreed to disagree. Other times we talked about our problem and came to a mutually acceptable decision. Al-Anon taught me that I don't always have to win or lose. Sometimes I can just participate.

I began to understand that common welfare meant I needed to object to things that would divide and confuse us in our meeting. If someone dominated the discussion or tried to bring outside issues into the meeting, I needed to stand up and say something. Eventually I had the courage to speak up when members discussed their religious convictions or political beliefs. I gently reminded them that we come to Al-Anon to share our experience, strength and hope about living with alcoholism. I found they responded positively when I gave them my reason instead of shouting, "We don't do that here!" Sometimes I spoke to someone after the meeting to explain a Tradition and then listened to them. Again, people responded with acceptance.

Tradition One has taught me that unity does not mean uniformity. It has also shown me that what is good for the group is probably good for me as well. If it isn't good for me, I can always find another meeting or I can take a closer look at my own feelings. I am certain that Tradition One is there to keep my Al-Anon meeting an important part of Al-Anon as a whole. We don't need to be an isolated entity. We don't need to ignore the Traditions and enforce our own self-will, either. That was what I was like before I came to Al-Anon. Tradition One has given me tools to change some of the things I can. That's why I keep coming back for more.

TRADITION ONE gives me balance. On the one hand, it is not good for me to control or dominate my group. On the other, I do not need to become a shrinking violet and submerge my needs under everyone else's. The simple truth is that I am a group member, equal in importance to everyone else.

OUR COMMON WELFARE MUST COME FIRST

I do not take up too much time sharing, because the Tradition tells me that everyone has the right to share. When I share I try to stick to the topic, because that is how the greatest number will benefit. It is better for me to apply a topic to my life than to dwell on my problems. I try to share my experience, strength and hope for the good of the group. Even if I am in pain, I can share what I am learning from that pain, because it is part of my experience.

I take responsibility in the group and do various jobs. I find speakers, set up the room, chair meetings. I do not take too much responsibility because it is our group, not my group. Our common welfare means that everyone needs to pitch in and do their share.

All of this leads to unity. Unity means that we work together for our common goal. In our recovery from the effects of someone else's drinking, the goal is personal progress for the greatest number. We work together best when we carry out the Traditions, because the Traditions unite us rather than divide us.

I try to remember Tradition One outside of Al-Anon. At work, if I remember our common welfare and unity, I am more likely to work well and enjoy it. I am less likely to spend the day depressed and wishing things were other than the way they are. At home I try to remember that I am not the boss. Everyone's opinions and ways of doing things are just as valid as mine.

I recently took a trip with two US friends, a mother and her daughter, who were visiting England. I drove them around a particularly beautiful part of England. The daughter was getting crabby, and I started feeling miserable. I thought the mother and daughter were paying far too much attention to each other and very little to me. How dare the young woman moan about being tired when I was doing all of the work! I was driving down treacherous country lanes, not knowing for certain where I was going. Where was the appreciation?

I decided to stop myself. My friends had traveled thousands of miles to be with me and to see England. They might never come back. What was the good in being divided like this? The two of them were angry with each other and I was feeling sorry for myself. I thought, "Our common welfare must come first," and my attitude changed. They were my friends and we were having a vacation. It was up to me to be a part of our little group. I was the driver but I was not responsible for their moods. I suggested that we see a few more villages and then stop for tea. They still may have been angry with each other, but we took time to refresh ourselves. My focus pleasantly changed from myself to our trip.

I had time to wonder at the simple wisdom of the Traditions and to try, through attraction, to give them to someone else.

Working Tradition One

Our common welfare should come first; personal progress for the greatest number depends upon unity.

* How can I apply this Tradition to my everyday life?

* How do I use this Tradition in my meeting?

* How does this Tradition give me the right to offer my opinion? How can I do this without dominating or having to 'win'?

* What does "common welfare" mean to me? My group? In other areas of service work within Al-Anon?

* What does "unity" mean to me? My group? In other areas of service work within Al-Anon?

* Do I consider myself to be open minded? Always?

* Am I willing to respect others' views? How?

* Am I willing to accept and appreciate what others are able to give?

* Am I expressing myself for unity or for manipulation and control?

* How do I keep Al-Anon unity in mind when expressing my opinion?

* How am I flexible?

* Am I bringing anything positive to this group? My family? My personal relationships?

* Do endless sharings at meetings hinder the unity of the group? If so, how can this be handled?

* What other ways do groups suffer when members dominate meetings?

* How can I be a part of the solution of my group's problems not a part of the problem?

* Am I giving with love? How?

* Do I listen with love to those I dislike or don't agree with?

* Am I an informed Al-Anon member, supporting my group, district, area and World Service Office in all of their affairs? How can I become informed?

* Do I welcome newcomers in the same manner as my long-time Al-Anon friends? Am I willing to change?

* When I share, am I honest in sharing the good as well as the bad? Do I listen to the wisdom of long-time members? My sponsor?

* Do I understand that there are no rules, but that there are suggested guidelines created for the common welfare of Al-Anon groups worldwide? How will this change my participation in Al-Anon? In my family? With others?

Tradition Two addresses both leadership and the unity, respect and integrity of our groups. Obviously for a group to continue to be available to us week after week, some tasks must be undertaken and some decisions about structure need to be reached. Tradition Two shows us how to practice the first three Steps as a group. We admit our own limitations, come to trust a Higher Power to guide us and then turn the group conscience over to that Power.

Each of us is an integral part of the group conscience and we learn to share our thoughts on matters that affect our group. Through trial and error, we learn that it is best not to force a particular decision or to continually restate our views. That is controlling. When there is no group conscience taken, we find that factions, cliques, a single dominant individual or the absence of anyone taking responsibility can create chaos. By being part of an informed group conscience, gathering the information we need, letting our loving God guide us, and remaining trusted servants, we are all a part of the group and support its decisions.

When a group or a family is in trouble, placing authority in a Power greater than ourselves is critical to clear judgment. When tempers flare, listening for guidance is hard but important. How can we know when it is a message from a loving God, our own will or the voice of another member? We start by trusting a Higher Power and continue by learning to trust each other. In the process we learn that we can participate in honest disagreement with integrity and flexibility even when things do not go exactly our way. For some of us it is the first experience of positive conflict resolution we have ever had.

In Al-Anon we learn that many of our reactions to the alcoholic's behavior were out of fear. It is easy to transfer the same responses into our meeting rooms if we do not understand Tradition Two. If we trust ourselves to do our best, each asking for guidance along

Tradition Two

For our group purpose there is but one authority – a loving God as He may express Himself in our group conscience. Our leaders are but trusted servants; they do not govern.

the way, we won't be drawn too far off course. We learn to pray for guidance before we launch into our opinion on a controversy. Learning to listen respectfully to each other – especially those who oppose us or who we do not particularly like – helps us grow in tolerance. Listening also helps us discover the wisdom hidden in unlikely sources. The member who disagrees or doesn't understand must be heard and given fair consideration. Sometimes the minority opinion can bring forth new information. From discussion, the group may find compromises upon which they all can agree; sometimes a vote must be taken to reach a decision.

If our own position is not that of the group as a whole, we learn to support the decision reached. Over time we learn to recognize and accept that in the long run the wisdom of the group, informed by thorough discussion and guided by a Higher Power, ultimately will be the best for the group and its individual members. It takes time to trust in the group conscience process. When we all seek God's will, there can be no winning or losing, but only a journey to greater understanding.

Everyone – from the person who makes the coffee to group representatives, district representatives, area delegates, trustees and World Service Office (WSO) staff members – is a trusted servant. Each relies on guidance from a Higher Power and direction from the group conscience. It is amazingly effective, both personally and collectively. To be trusted is both humbling and elevating. For our group to trust us with service is an honor and a serious responsibility. Our self-esteem grows as we fulfill our offices to the best of our abilities.

Rotating leadership and remembering that our only authority is a loving God can help us with our defects of character. Members accustomed to dominating may be unhappy when reminded that we rotate leaders and that we are to serve, not govern.

Longtime members learn about letting go and letting others serve. Rotating leadership also draws those of us with little self-esteem or leadership experience into positions of trust and authority. Although we might prefer to let someone else do it, we won't always like the results. In practicing the Second Tradition, we can't just stand by and gripe if we haven't contributed to the group conscience or offered to take an office.

Many beginners in Al-Anon marvel at how a group can function with such a loose structure. We find this structure is intensely practical because of its broad base. When we all do our share, no one gets burned out. When we share decisions, we each play a part in the solutions reached. When we are careful to consider each person's needs, our groups serve us and we want to come back.

Service to our groups goes beyond holding a group office, setting up the chairs or finding speakers. It can mean helping make decisions and speaking up when we believe our Traditions are being violated. It is leadership, but not governing. What, then, is the difference between Al-Anon leadership and governing? Generally governments have rules and laws with some means of enforcing them. Al-Anon offers suggestions, experience and our Traditions without absolute rules and regulations. We are asked to practice obedience to the unenforceable. We let newcomers know the meeting structure and important group conscience decisions so they will not be embarrassed by ignorance; we share our experience when we believe our group might be going astray. Ultimately we lead by example, trusting that our Higher Power will guide us in the right direction.

WHEN I first began to recognize that my Al-Anon group had its own structure, I wondered how the organization could make decisions and still maintain any consistency from group to group. I watched as one group elected their officers by ballot, another group by a show of hands and a third group by asking for volunteers. At first I didn't pay a lot of attention to these differences.

Most of the time, when a problem arose about how to do something that we didn't normally do, longtime members quoted the *Al-Anon/Alateen Service Manual.* Usually the group went along with whatever the manual said. One time a newcomer, who was obviously in distress from the smoke in the room, brought up the subject of whether to allow smoking to continue at our meeting. The meeting secretary asked the question, "Will all who are in favor of a non-smoking meeting please raise your hand?" She didn't suggest looking at the manual. She didn't even suggest any discussion.

The group representative calmly asked the secretary to withdraw the question so that an informed group conscience could be formed. We all asked, "What is that?" She explained that changing the character of the meeting was not something to be taken lightly. She also suggested that we could decide not to smoke for this night to help out the newcomer. Before any permanent decision could be made, she said we needed to take into account the feelings of regular members who weren't present. Since the purpose of the meeting was for recovery, we couldn't spend sufficient time to allow all the members to express themselves prior to a vote in a single meeting. The group decided instead to speak about the topic for a few minutes before the meeting for several weeks. After everyone received an opportunity to speak, then the group voted.

Over the years, I used this story to illustrate how to make an informed group conscience. I discovered from experience that there are at least six possible answers to a question when it is first placed before a group. I knew about "yes" and "no." I also recognized a couple of other possible answers – "I don't know" and "I don't care." It was later that I also found other possible answers – "I don't want to discuss it" and "I don't want you to discuss it." I was able to identify several feelings around these six answers – agreement, disagreement, ignorance, confusion, resentment and anger.

I found that for any serious matter presented to my group, district or area, first I needed to acknowledge how I felt about it. Then I needed to postpone my personal decision until I heard all the people who wished to share. For most decisions in Al-Anon, I think it is more important to allow each of us to share our opinion than it is to allow the lack of time to dominate an issue. Today I believe the process of discussion, review of our literature and a vote is a good way for our group to make decisions that just about everyone can accept.

I OFTEN feel like an outsider in school. The more popular kids have a lot to say about things that affect my life. They say what kind of clothes are fashionable and what music groups are cool.

In Alateen I see that we are all on the same level. We trust our Higher Power to help us with our group. No individual person makes a decision for everyone else. All of us have the opportunity to share and express our views when we take a group conscience. Each of us has a voice. Alateen is the only place where I know I am equal with all the other members of my group.

WE ARE ALL ON THE SAME LEVEL

TRADITION TWO performs a pivotal function for me. It is similar to the way Step Two helped me understand and work all the other Steps by teaching me humility. Tradition Two helps me learn how to apply this humility when I practice the Traditions in my relationships with other people. I have learned through leadership to accept a responsibility, be accountable for it and be responsible enough to carry it out with the help of my Higher Power, without being prodded by another person. Tradition Two also teaches me to share my responsibilities with other members of the group. It reminds me that I am a trusted servant of my fellow Al-Anon members and of my Higher Power.

I learned that in this Tradition we are not speaking of a servant as a menial thing, but as a person who is highly esteemed and trusted to do this vital work.

In a group, various members have various jobs and responsibilities for and to the group. However, the group has certain responsibilities, too. For example, members of the group are needed in order to have a group conscience. The treasurer needs the respect of being allowed to give a treasurer's report on a regular basis.

Rotating service in a group is very important for two reasons: 1) giving everyone an opportunity to serve, 2) keeping the person serving from feeling self-important.

Sometimes a person takes on a job in Al-Anon and everyone is willing to let that person keep serving year after year. This situation is not good for either the person serving in one position too long or for those depriving themselves of the growth gained by service. When a term is over we need to rotate to some other form of service. In our manuals there are suggestions for the term length for different responsibilities.

In my home I am a trusted servant of my Higher Power to carry out His message of love. Our children are not our possessions, but are on loan to us from

God for our love and guidance. I cannot own another person. If I try to keep another person a prisoner, then I, myself, become the prisoner.

When I think of my Higher Power, I recognize that in His love He gives me a free will and allows me to make my own decisions, even though they are frequently wrong, and He allows me the privilege of suffering or enjoying the consequences of my behavior.

This Tradition teaches me the importance of group discussions. We learn to keep in contact with our Higher Power and to listen to others. We learn that we need to treat each other with respect and not talk or do anything distracting when someone else is talking. In the home we can also listen to others; it doesn't mean that we have to heed them. Just as the group representative (GR) listens to all the ideas of the group and collects all pertinent information available before deciding how to vote at the assembly, so I have to learn to listen to others in my home and collect any available information before I decide what I will do. What others say may or may not influence what I do, but they will feel better for having had the opportunity to express their feelings.

This doesn't mean that we always cave in to what others think or believe, neither do we resist something that is good just because someone else thought of it. It means that I have to decide what is best for me. I have to learn that "be good to yourself" also means "good for yourself." I must consider all of the facts and examine the possible consequences. I have to learn to take time and think things through. However, I need to be careful of people offering advice. Is this person an authority on the subject? If the question is legal, I need a lawyer not a bricklayer. If I want to lay bricks, then I need a bricklayer. Advising is not Al-Anon. If I give you advice and things go wrong, then you may blame me. If you don't follow my advice, I might be sick enough to get mad because you didn't listen.

Practicing Tradition Two takes time and patience.

Like our recovery, it will move slowly. This Tradition helps me to keep my priorities in order — God, self, family and others. It also reminds me that each person in my life has a God, and I am not it.

Working Tradition Two

For our group purpose there is but one authority — a loving God as He may express Himself in our group conscience. Our leaders are but trusted servants; they do not govern.

* Am I willing to take time to discuss all points of view before reaching a decision? Does my need to be right get in the way? How?

* How do I participate in my group's business?

* Do I listen to others in group discussion with an open mind?

* What am I willing to do for service work?

* Does my group practice rotation of leadership positions?

* What can I do to contribute to service in my group and elsewhere?

* Has my group ever taken a group conscience?

* Does everyone in our group participate in the group conscience process?

* What can I do if one member starts to dominate a group?

* What is the difference between Al-Anon leadership and governing?

* How am I willing to I support the group conscience even if I don't agree with it?

* Am I contributing to the health of my group? How?

* Do I bring my concerns to group level with love? How?

* How am I a leader and a trusted servant? How can I be a leader without "being in charge?"

* Am I being honest with myself and others?

* Am I trying to control? Convince others that I am right?

* Do I give up my responsibilities and then blame others if things go wrong?

* Am I listening for God's words in others? What do I hear?

Tradition Three

The relatives of alcoholics, when gathered together for mutual aid, may call themselves an Al-Anon Family Group, provided that, as a group, they have no other affiliation. The only requirement for membership is that there be a problem of alcoholism in a relative or friend.

To LEARN how to join Al-Anon or form a group, turn to Tradition Three, which tells us that any individual can join Al-Anon simply by deciding he or she is troubled by another person's drinking. A group can be formed whenever two or more persons get together to use the Al-Anon principles to help themselves. The only stipulation is that the group itself not affiliate with any other program, religion or cause. This stipulation is intentionally simple and inclusive. It insures that when anyone, anywhere, reaches out for help in dealing with the effects of another's alcoholism, Al-Anon will be there.

Most organizations have specific requirements for membership and some way to see that only those who qualify are admitted. Applications are created and obligations are spelled out. Al-Anon is different. If you think you are troubled by a drinker, you are welcome. Al-Anon's non-affiliation with any other cause or organization keeps our purpose clear and helps us avoid controversies that could hurt our unity. Although there are many good, related endeavors, our experience indicates that we lose the vitality and effectiveness of our Al-Anon program when we stretch ourselves too thin by trying to be all things to all people.

Practicing this Tradition brings us personal growth and expanded recovery. For all who come through the doors and claim by their presence that they have a problem, we extend the hand of fellowship. We offer them unconditional love and acceptance. It is simple. If they say they need help, they are welcome at our meetings.

Once we have some personal recovery, it is tempting to shout it to the world and go out and help others. We have found that we can best serve ourselves and others by keeping it simple and focusing as a group on our Al-Anon approach to the family disease of alcoholism. In recovery, other problems often surface that may be better addressed in therapy or in another organization. When we keep our focus clear and our group consistently Al-Anon, we as individuals can then confidently seek whatever helps us in addition to Al-Anon.

Does this mean we refuse to participate if a local hospital has a treatment program for alcoholics and their families? No. It means we do not affiliate with their program. When requested we may set up beginner meetings in institutions and support those meetings by having experienced members volunteer to attend and share. An institutions group meeting, however, is still created as an Al-Anon meeting and any Al-Anon member may attend, subject to the institution's regulations. Carrying the message is important to our own recovery. If people are interested, they can be given literature, a meeting list or help to start a meeting.

Because of our extensive network of groups, Al-Anon sometimes is viewed as an attractive place to advertise products and services or to offer therapies or philosophies that relate to alcoholism. Discussion or announcement of such things could be interpreted as affiliation with them, diverting us from our primary spiritual approach to recovery.

We are always free as individuals to seek help and spiritual comfort wherever we desire. Al-Anon is a spiritual way of life, which blends positively with many different belief systems. Members belong to churches, synagogues, temples and religious groups of their choice. Some participate in therapy, treatment plans, other Twelve Step programs or community events that they find helpful. They do this in their capacity as free individuals, not as The Friday Night Al-Anon Family Group. Similarly, a group selects a name that does not imply affiliation with another entity, such as the church or institution in which the group meets.

The only requirement for membership is a problem of alcoholism in a friend or loved one. It is up to each of us to decide whether we belong. In our Al-Anon groups we discover – sometimes for the first time – how much we have in common with people who seem very different from ourselves. Soon we want to be sure that any newcomers, no matter how different they appear, will feel welcome and will be able to decide for themselves whether or not they belong.

Within the fellowship we have many different special-focus groups. As individuals we have widely varying opinions, politics, values and notions of spirituality. Unity is preserved when we remember that anyone in Al-Anon may attend any Al-Anon meeting. Focusing on a particular area of recovery does not change the fact that our similarities outweigh our differences. We have all been affected by another person's drinking. When facing the disease of alcoholism, we learn to stand together, to love unconditionally and to practice the principles daily as best we can.

In Al-Anon we talk about how the disease of alcoholism in a loved one has affected our own thinking and behavior. By sharing our Al-Anon recovery, we offer others the courage and wisdom we have found, from the perspective of having lived with an alcoholic. By concentrating on the Al-Anon message, we are challenged to search within ourselves to determine how we can best apply Al-Anon principles to our own personal recovery. "Sharing" then becomes beneficial for both the newcomer and for the messenger.

In addition, while it is important for newcomers to realize that alcoholism is a disease, it is far more important that they find safety in our meetings. Many members come to Al-Anon as a last resort and have little or no trust left in anyone, especially the alcoholics in their lives. More often than not, an Al-Anon or Alateen meeting is the safest place that a member can go while living with an alcoholic. Many Al-Anon members belong to other Twelve Step programs as well; in Al-Anon meetings we leave our other affiliations outside the door and focus on the Al-Anon message of recovery.

We do not use our group for other purposes or link our group to other causes, treatment programs or outside endeavors, however worthy they may be, because we want to be sure Al-Anon is always available to us and others in need of the help we have found so useful. Al-Anon has grown from a handful of dedicated individuals to a respected worldwide source of help for families and friends of alcoholics. Our experience is a valuable gift to many suffering people who want to learn how to help themselves in a fellowship of loving, caring equals. Tradition Three insures that Al-Anon remains Al-Anon.

Members Share Experience, Strength and Hope

WE WOULD only hurt ourselves if we were to ramble from one issue to another at our meetings. What brought us to Al-Anon in the first place was one thing: alcoholism. By keeping our focus on this problem, a solution will come for each of us as we follow the guidance of our Higher Power and the Twelve Steps. There is no instant cure, as some people or programs may promise. Because we did not get the way we are overnight, it will take time for us to return to healthy thinking.

I do not have to tell people whether they belong at an Al-Anon meeting. As we read the Traditions, they will become aware. They will soon learn that we qualify for Al-Anon when someone else's drinking bothers us. Each of us must decide for ourselves whether we meet the requirements for the program as stated in Tradition Three.

I am thankful when I attend a meeting where others' experience with alcoholism is similar to mine. I get help when I listen to people who have been where

EACH OF US
MUST
DECIDE
FOR
OURSELVES

I am. They share their experience, strength and hope in ways that no one else can. Because our time in the meetings is so short, it is to everyone's advantage to put all other issues aside. Sticking to the principles of the program allows me to Let Go and Let God. By facing the problems of alcoholism, the power that this disease has over me diminishes. When I find release from its grip, it becomes easier for me to get on with my own life.

Al-Anon is a spiritual program. By keeping a spiritual focus at meetings, I can use the principles of the program to help me with problems that are caused by someone else's drinking. In Al-Anon I find a spiritual way out of my own private torment.

I want Al-Anon to be there for all the people who will be affected by alcoholism in the future. It is so important that we do not allow our program to become a hodgepodge of ideas that have not been proven to work. If we try to be a fix-all for everyone we will get sidetracked from our main aim. Let's keep it simple. Al-Anon will work for us if we stick to the "unenforceable" guidance that we find in the Traditions.

Sometimes we get so caught up in the disease that we obsess about how we can keep someone else from drinking. Accepting that alcoholism is a disease keeps us on track with our primary purpose, learning to live a full life despite the effects of someone else's drinking. As an individual I can support any cause I choose, but if I value my recovery, I will stick to Al-Anon principles in Al-Anon meetings and with those I sponsor. Our program really works, when we work it.

I KNEW I BELONGED

I FELT a warm feeling during my first Alateen meeting. I knew I belonged there. I was with people who knew what I was going through because they understood my feelings. I was so glad it didn't matter what clothes I was wearing, what school I went to, what grades I earned. I didn't even have to pay to belong, like in a club. Everyone accepted me and I felt very much a part of the group.

All that was important was that my mom was an alcoholic. I could participate in Alateen because of that. I learned that we all get together at our Alateen meetings to help each other live with people whose drinking bothers us. Our sponsors and the members of our group always remind us to share about how we are dealing with alcoholism. That way we can always welcome new members to our group. It is our primary purpose to help other teenagers of alcoholics.

WHEN I came to Al-Anon and found the help I needed, I thought that everyone in the world needed Al-Anon. Then I learned several things. One was that when I try to make others fit into Al-Anon, I am being judgmental of them and their needs. Another thing I learned was that our uniqueness lies in our similarities. We relate to each other because we know where the other person is coming from. I learned that Al-Anon is not for those who need it, but for those who want it.

I believe almost every alcoholic has an "and" with the disease. Alcohol and gambling, alcohol and overeating, alcohol and drugs or some other problems like wife abuse, child abuse and other things. These side issues are different, but we relate through the disease of alcoholism and we keep the focus of our program on the effects of alcoholism in our lives.

Tradition Three has taught me the importance of establishing a purpose and sticking to that purpose instead of splintering into many different directions. As individuals we can do whatever we feel helps us, but when we come to Al-Anon, we leave those other activities outside.

Who can belong to Al-Anon? Anyone who feels that his or her life has been affected by alcoholism. It makes no difference how much or how often the

I CAN'T ALWAYS HAVE MY OWN WAY

drinker drank, or what other side issues might be involved. If someone's life has been affected by the drinking of a friend or relative, then that person is eligible for Al-Anon.

The Al-Anon program has worked in many people's lives, and there are many imitators of the Al-Anon program. We do not need to incorporate these things into Al-Anon – it has already proven itself and doesn't need to be fixed. Accepting Al-Anon as it is helps me to accept myself where I am and to recognize that I have strengths and weaknesses.

Learning to find the singleness of purpose in my Al-Anon fellowship has helped to teach me to find the singleness of purpose in other facets of my life. I have learned that I can't be all things to all people all the time, that I must learn to have balance. It has taught me that I can actually damage myself and others by trying to do things in which I have no expertise.

I use our Service Manual as well as Al-Anon's Twelve Steps and Twelve Traditions to remind me of why we do what we do. As I restudied these materials, I was reminded of the importance of being a part of a group or a family and learning that I don't need to try to fix the whole family or group. Studying Tradition Three has helped me to learn be a functioning member of a group. I can't always have my own way; I need to have consideration for others. Those in my family can have their own interests, and I don't have to be a part of everything in their lives. This Tradition reminds me of the slogan "Live and Let Live."

Working Tradition Three

The relatives of alcoholics, when gathered together for mutual aid, may call themselves an Al-Anon Family Group, provided that, as a group, they have no other affiliation. The only requirement for membership is that there be a problem of alcoholism in a relative or friend.

* Do I give each newcomer a warm and loving welcome?

* Do I welcome all who attend our meeting even if they are different from me in age? Sex? Scxual orientation? Socioeconomic background? How can my group be more welcoming of those who are different from us?

* Are there members to whom I have not reached out?

* Do I treat each member and potential member with unconditional love?

* How does my group encourage all members to share? Do I encourage all members to share?

* How can my group welcome members of other programs and maintain our Al-Anon focus? What can I do to make them welcome?

* Have I alienated anyone that might have needed Al-Anon because I thought another meeting might be better for them?

* How can I help my group remain open to new ideas while assuring that we not affiliate with any other cause or group?

* Do I leave my other affiliations and interests outside the doors of Al-Anon?

* Am I being understanding and encouraging?

* How can I treat others with acceptance, tolerance and love?

* Am I accepting myself and others as we are? How?

* How can I apply Tradition Three to other areas of my life?

THE AUTONOMY described in Tradition Four allows each group to decide what works best for its members within Al-Anon guidelines and principles. Without such autonomy at the group level, every meeting would be exactly the same. Autonomy makes responses to our members' needs possible and gives us room to make mistakes and to learn from correcting them. The worldwide fellowship of Al-Anon is richly nourished by the experiences of the various groups, as they are shared with the larger whole through district and area meetings and the World Service Conference (WSC). However, the Tradition cautions us to be sure that decisions made by our group do not affect another group adversely or present an unfavorable or inaccurate picture of Al-Anon or AA as a whole.

When Al-Anon first started, members brought writings, articles and good ideas from outside of Al-Anon to the groups. These tools were often useful and some were widely circulated. As Al-Anon grew, its literature expanded. Our trusted servants wanted to be sure that what we used conformed to our principles. The WSC decided in the early 1960s to create a procedure for review and publication of our own literature and to refrain from endorsing or using other material. Policies for writing and approving Al-Anon literature were created, and the term Conference Approved Literature (CAL) was adopted (CAL is identified by the Al-Anon logo, with the letters AFG in the circle and the words World Service Conference within the triangle). Members are now encouraged to use only Al-Anon literature at meetings. Through CAL the whole fellowship can be united by reading materials developed and approved by Al-Anon's WSC. Such action effected Al-Anon as a whole in a positive way, encouraging unity.

Unity through literature has also helped us communicate with each other in terms that represent the fellowship as a whole. On occasion members may use brief excerpts or ideas from outside literature that

Tradition Four

Each group should be autonomous, except in matters affecting another group or Al-Anon or AA as a whole.

they have found helpful as part of their personal sharings, but the exclusive use of CAL at meetings limits confusion and fosters unity in the fellowship.

Al-Anon adapted the Twelve Steps and Twelve Traditions from Alcoholics Anonymous. These two legacies (with the third legacy, our Twelve Concepts) create our paths to recovery and provide the framework for Al-Anon worldwide. The World Service Conference has given them special status; they cannot be easily changed. A single word change in any of these three legacies would require a great deal of consideration, discussion and voting of the WSC and the vote of three-fourths of all Al-Anon groups worldwide. Although our "unenforceable" legacies offer some flexibility in interpretation, it is important to keep Al-Anon's foundation firm. When members or groups take it upon themselves to deviate from these guidelines or not to use them at all, confusion follows that can affect our fellowship as a whole. When anyone, anywhere attends an Al-Anon meeting, it is important that the meeting be based on these well-established principles.

Al-Anon groups are free to decide how to structure their meetings, what topics will be discussed, whom to invite to speak, how to allocate funds and what kind of focus the meeting will have. Reading selections may differ from group to group, and each group has its own flavor and tone. Tradition Four assures us that wherever and whenever we seek out an Al-Anon meeting, the principles of recovery will be the same.

We come to Al-Anon seeking a greater understanding of the disease of alcoholism and how it has affected us. We attend meetings because of this one single common denominator. We are asked to be obedient to the unenforceable. Our Traditions are guidelines, not rules; no one is forced to follow them. No one individual or group can exclude another because of the individual's or group's autonomy.

Sometimes groups don't live by the principles embodied in the Traditions, often because members are unaware of the history and experience behind them. A member familiar with the Traditions then has the responsibility to speak up and inform the group of its options – group autonomy is one of them. If a discussion follows, the knowledgeable members can share experience and understanding and encourage all group members to participate. The group probably will become more aware of Al-Anon's principles through discussion and any questions may be resolved. Even if a problem persists, the group likely will benefit from study and deeper understanding of the Traditions. Our Traditions come from members' and groups' experiences and provide guidance for most group difficulties.

As in life, freedom in Al-Anon carries with it responsibility. We wish to preserve the working principles of the fellowship that have served us well and have helped us recover. Each member of every group is responsible for helping accomplish that end. As a group and as individuals, we need both unity and independence to flourish. How are we to keep a balance of these apparent opposites? When we catch ourselves insisting too loudly or too determinedly for one or the other, we step back and consider if we are trying to control the group. On the other hand, if we ignore the discomfort we feel when our group seems to wander too far from the Traditions, we ask ourselves if we are seeking peace at any price as we may have done in our alcoholic homes.

Certainly we make mistakes, and occasionally groups fold because of too much rigidity or disregard for our suggested guidelines; but overall, we learn to trust ourselves and our groups to voluntarily follow Tradition Four. Constantly turning to the guidance of a Power greater than ourselves, we find safety even in the process of trial and error. We learn how to achieve harmony with others from our own mistakes. From such lessons a group often is stronger than before.

Does this mean that in Al-Anon anything goes as long as the group agrees to it? Certainly not. There is an important principle that needs to be observed to avoid severe difficulties – autonomy is necessary "except in matters affecting another group or Al-Anon or AA as a whole." Each of us is charged with the responsibility to think about the possible effects of our decisions on Al-Anon itself. As individuals and as individual groups, we are the face of Al-Anon. People who come to us for help often see only our group, rather than the worldwide fellowship of Al-Anon, for months or even years. If we do not present a favorable picture of Al-Anon, not only might we discourage a newcomer, but also many others who still suffer might never find the help we have to give. Acting thoughtfully, responsibly and kindly means that Al-Anon, as well as ourselves, can continue to flourish.

Tradition Four keeps Al-Anon flexible, yet strong. Learning to act autonomously while keeping an eye out for harmony with others is a vital skill. As we practice using it in our Al-Anon groups, taking it up through each level of the fellowship, we discover what a useful principle it is in all areas of our lives. We learn the importance of being our individual selves, but don't need to impose our perceptions on everyone else in order for those perceptions to be valid. Tradition Four is democracy in action. With it, we can step out into the world well-balanced between freedom and responsibility.

Members Share Experience, Strength and Hope

TRADITION
FOUR
HELPED IN
MY GROUP

My FIRST recollection of Tradition Four at work in my home group was at our monthly business meeting. A member expressed her uneasiness about saying the prayer that we used at the close of the meeting. She went on to say that through Al-Anon she was seeking her Higher Power and her own definition of spirituality. She also noted that our meeting was only a few miles from a major university and that we had a diverse population of new members from a variety of religious backgrounds.

Another member shared that she was an agnostic. Prayer in the group was the only reason she had seriously considered not coming back! The group was emphatic that we didn't want to lose any members and that a resolution was essential. The group representative suggested that we read the Traditions to decide which ones applied to this issue. She also suggested that we review our Service Manual and hold a special meeting the next week to discuss our options.

The group representative opened the discussion meeting by reading Tradition Four. She explained that each group was autonomous, and that different groups close their meeting with different prayers and statements. What she emphasized was the second half of Tradition Four, "...except in matters affecting another group or Al-Anon or AA as a whole." She stressed that our decision needed to be for the good of the group as well as for the good of Al-Anon. After lengthy discussion, we took a silent ballot. More than three-fourths of the members voted to close the meeting with the Serenity Prayer.

It wasn't until a few years later, as I stood in my living room discussing a new crisis with my husband, that I realized how applicable Tradition Four is in family situations. Specifically I realized that what my husband or neighbor does is none of my business, except in matters that affect me or my family as a whole.

Our neighbor toppled a tree that landed in our yard, breaking down our fence and splitting our peach tree in half. I was upset. My alcoholic husband, though sober, blew up and became too furious to deal effectively with the problem. Our neighbor was very apologetic, but we still had a conflict over timing and whose responsibilities were whose. Our neighbor wanted to wait for his insurance company to handle the whole matter, but we needed a fence fast so we could confine our dogs. If we didn't act quickly, the situation would affect our whole neighborhood.

Tradition Four helped me sort out the difficult issues. On the issue of autonomy, we contacted our insurance company and got our own bids. We separated the matters affecting our neighbor and his insurance company from those that affected the neighborhood as a whole. We even confined our dogs at a very reasonable speed. Tradition Four helped me keep my head and my focus on solving these problems. As a result, we were taking care of ourselves autonomously in a matter of days. The effect on the neighborhood was minimal, considering what could have happened if our dogs had roamed free. My relationships with my spouse and our neighbor returned to how they were before the tree fell.

IF THE GROUP DECIDED

I REMEMBER a time when some members of my group wanted to change the format of our meeting. They wanted to read a specific piece of Alateen literature. Some other members got upset because the meeting might change. If it changed it wouldn't be like the other meetings in our area.

Our Alateen sponsor explained that the word autonomous in Tradition Four means that we could change our format if the group decided to. She said not all Alateen meetings have to be the same. She suggested we take a group conscience so everyone could participate in the decision and express their views. As long as we were using Al-Anon Conference Approved Literature, following the Traditions and making a change according to Alateen principles, our sponsor said it was okay to change the format of our meeting to suit our group's needs and wants. The decision was up to us.

WHILE TRADITIONS are usually considered part of the business side of the program, I have heard it said that when applied on a personal level, they help in recovery. These same ideas can be used to resolve individual, family or work difficulties.

A passage in *When I Got Busy, I Got Better* relates to group autonomy. It says we could "run our group as we saw fit, except when our actions or decisions affected the unity of the fellowship or of AA." On a personal level, we can run our lives as we see fit, except when our actions or decisions impact unfairly upon someone else. While this Tradition gives us freedom, it implies that there are limits. We can learn what our limits are by using basic courtesy, principles above personalities and guidance from a Higher Power. Listening at meetings, being in service and reading Al-Anon literature are ways to learn about realistic limits. We also learn what is reasonable compared to the extreme behavior we experience in living with a mental, physical and spiritual disease.

Autonomy refers to the right of self-government; it comes from two Greek words: autos, meaning self, and nomos, meaning law. In the disease we often learn ways of reacting that require no self-government at all. When a certain situation occurs, we think, say or do what we always have. The button is pushed and the old tapes play. We act like automatons – machines that act mechanically, automatically. There is no thought, just routine reaction to whatever is going on.

Al-Anon says we should focus on ourselves and act in our own best interests. Autonomy is the attitude that my actions are my own choices. It puts me in the center of my life and in charge of what is happening at the moment. Choosing autonomy means giving up safety; there may be consequences to my actions. What if he gets mad, she doesn't like me, or I'm too scared to change. It also means I don't have to wait until someone else changes before I change. Waiting for someone else to change is like volunteering to be a victim. One of the benefits of relying on other people for directions on how to live my life is that I can blame them when it doesn't work out. I never have to be responsible for the situation I'm in.

Seeing myself as a separate individual is often difficult. I often have strong beliefs about how life should be but people I live or work with want me to live or work their way. I say "yes" when I mean "no". I withhold information and try to get people to go along with me and not be angry. I become a people-pleaser. I take care of people with the hope that some day they will take care of me. Most of the time that bargain is never realized. Instead of realizing that the bargain is a bad deal, I think that if I just try harder it will be all right the next time. And it never gets better. I can be so preoccupied with what others are doing or not doing that I don't realize how my own attitudes and behaviors need to be examined.

My fear of autonomy is that I won't need anybody, although for me it is easier to adopt an extremely independent attitude rather than to face the devastation of disappointment when other people lie, let me down or embarrass me. But it is just an attitude. Inside I still want that close feeling, an attachment to other human beings. Through recovery I am learning how this disease impairs my judgment about other people. How often have I recognized someone's potential, but didn't acknowledge how far away from that potential their day-to-day behavior really was.

As I develop my own individuality, I am better able to help others do the same. The more responsibility I take for myself, the better my decisions will be. I don't have to wait for someone else to make my life okay – I can choose for myself. This is helpful in learning how to practice detachment.

As I become more real to myself, so does my perception of others. Instead of being totally dependent or totally independent, I look for interdependent relationships. Interdependency can be seen at meetings where we each do our part for the good of the group. A sense of self-worth develops. I have an opportunity to recognize my needs and abilities. I can share with other people and accept their sharing with me. We can see the program's integrity at work when everyone is treated by the same set of principles.

The good feelings invite me to make a commitment, not just to the program but to personal recovery. I begin to see that I can make decisions in my own best interests and that my personal recovery is the best thing for all. I can finally address the problem, not just treat the symptoms. Getting involved in the program strengthens that commitment. I get back to the degree that I give.

IN THIS Tradition I find balance – independence with consideration. In this Tradition it is important that we see the comma after the word autonomous; it is not a period, but a comma. We often hear immature people say, "I have a right to do whatever I want," without remembering that it is their decision only as long as it doesn't affect others. I once heard this idea expressed by an Al-Anon member as follows: "The right of your fist ends where my nose begins."

The rights of one person cannot supersede the rights of another. This is important in learning to work with others in a mature way. All of life is give and take. We learn in Al-Anon to drop our ironbound attitudes and pick up some flexibility. We learn to think a situation through and to examine our motives.

As one parent once explained to her son, "Yes, you do have a right to do in your room whatever you wish, except when it affects the rest of the household or members therein. If you decide to collect apple cores in your room, the bugs that would result would infiltrate my house, thus you would be infringing on my right to have a bug-free house."

Another thing I am learning in this Tradition is

LEARNING THE MEANING OF FREEDOM

that freedom and responsibility must go hand in hand. The more freedom I have, the more I must be willing to take responsibility for myself and my behavior and how it will affect others or the group as a whole.

The groups have many freedoms; there are no bosses. That is why it is so important that we understand our responsibility to obey the unenforceable.

As we look at our literature, we find the importance of sticking to Al-Anon Conference Approved Literature (CAL). Our literature contains a unified message, consistent in principle and language, and great care is taken to see that this literature adheres to our principles before it is Conference Approved. How do we know when something is Al-Anon Conference Approved? Look for the symbol: a triangle with a circle inside it. This symbol can be found in our Service Manual. When I first came to Al-Anon, I was told for the first year not to read anything but CAL. If I needed something more, I was told to find a good murder mystery or a good sex book. This was good advice for me, because I had read all kinds of self-help books with many theories; I was confused.

Then someone asks, "What about AA literature; is it Conference Approved?" Yes, it is approved by AA's General Service Conference for AA – but not for Al-Anon. At home I can read whatever I please, but when I come to meetings I leave those things outside. When I first read AA literature, I was trying to see if he was doing it right. After I was in the program for a while and I could keep the focus on me and remember that I am reading for me, not him, I found I could read some AA literature.

I have heard it said that Al-Anon is a selfish program. That doesn't mean that we become selfish people – the very opposite is true – but our program must come first. When I put my program first, I am putting God first, me first and my family first. My growth has been a result of Al-Anon and my growth in Al-Anon has benefited those around me.

In our groups we learn that while we are autonomous, we learn to think how any decision made would affect the group or the fellowship. In my home this Tradition has been very helpful. It reminds me that if I am to have freedom and independence, I must give that freedom to others around me. I need to have consideration for others but first I have to learn to have consideration for myself. I have learned that, in my group as well as in my home, what is in my best interest is often what is in the best interest of the group or my home as a whole, because I am a part of it.

I suppose that what I've learned best from Tradition Four is to use the slogan "Think" to examine any action before I take it. I might see, for example, that some momentary want I have will be in my best interest in the long run.

Working Tradition Four

Each group should be autonomous, except in matters affecting another group or Al-Anon or AA as a whole.

* How am I taking responsibility for my actions and thoughts? Is my group taking responsibility for its actions and thoughts? How?

* How am I allowing others the freedom to take responsibility for their own actions and thoughts?

* Am I accepting the consequences of my actions gracefully? Am I allowing others the same opportunity?

* Am I self-serving and selfish in the name of autonomy, or am I truly self-caring, asking for my Higher Power's guidance?

* How does my group consider the impact of its decisions on Al-Anon and Alateen as a whole? Has the group considered Lone Members, inmates, groups throughout the world? AA? Newcomers? Long-time members?

* What were my feelings as a new member? Did I feel welcomed? Can I share my thoughts with my group? Others?

* Do I remember Al-Anon's primary purpose – to help families and friends of alcoholics – in my service activities? How does this affect my actions?

* Am I dogmatic in my reasoning, or am I flexible in the interpretation of the suggested guidelines? How can I be more flexible?

* When visiting a new group, do I feel irritated if it's not just like my home group? Do I want to straighten them out? What can I learn from visiting other groups?

* In my personal life, how can I apply this Tradition to my family? Are we autonomous? Do our actions affect other families? Our community?

* Tradition Four asks us to be obedient to the unenforceable. What does this mean to me?

TRADITION FIVE defines Al-Anon's primary purpose. Helping families of alcoholics is the sole reason for Al-Anon's existence. This Tradition offers three guidelines to keep us on track and clear about why we are here: practicing our own Twelve Step program, encouraging and understanding our alcoholic loved ones and comforting people affected by another person's alcoholism.

Many of us were accustomed to blaming the alcoholic for all of our problems; many of us spent years trying to get someone else well while becoming progressively sicker ourselves. The idea of looking at our own lives, of practicing the Twelve Steps ourselves as a solution can be incomprehensible. Experienced members understand this and gently turn us again and again toward ourselves until we begin to get better and want Al-Anon recovery for ourselves. Working the Steps has the advantage of keeping us too busy to meddle with the alcoholic. Experience has shown that we actually help others best by taking care of ourselves first. It's like the safety instruction a flight attendant gives on an airplane: "Put your own oxygen mask on first and then help children or those having trouble." In an alcoholic situation, it is equally important to remember to take care of our own well-being first.

Perhaps the most challenging part of Tradition Five is "encouraging and understanding our alcoholic relatives." Though many of us come to Al-Anon to help an alcoholic, we often arrive filled with anger, disappointment and resentment. To extend compassion to the person who is the reason for our membership in Al-Anon requires us to refer again and again to our own practice of the Twelve Steps. Fortunately we are not alone. Other members, especially a sponsor, and our Higher Power help us to truly understand that alcoholism is a disease. We learn to detach with love, to hate the disease but not the person and to encourage the alcoholic in a new way. We may realize that in our desire to help an alcoholic get sober, our

Tradition Five

Each Al-Anon Family Group has but one purpose: to help families of alcoholics. We do this by practicing the Twelve Steps of AA OURSELVES, by encouraging and understanding our alcoholic relatives, and by welcoming and giving comfort to families of alcoholics.

"helping" actually hindered him or her from experiencing the consequences of drinking and, perhaps, from desiring sobriety enough to change self-destructive behavior. For those of us with a tendency to advise, direct and control, we must learn to help without enabling.

Once on our path to recovery, we have the experience, strength and hope to welcome and give comfort to those needing our help – other families and friends of alcoholics. Welcoming requires more than just a statement at the beginning of a meeting. We learn to make time for new members who might be too shy to share unless specifically invited. When we wonder what would help someone, we ask ourselves, "What helped me?" If we discuss this, perhaps using Tradition Five as a meeting topic, we find the variety of answers gives our group guidance and new ideas to try in our own lives.

Welcoming should not be reserved only for newcomers. All members of Al-Anon need to feel welcome and a part of the group. Some of us felt like outsiders for a long time, especially in groups where members seem to chat only with friends. Sharing the experience of feeling left out can help our meeting learn how to discourage such cliquish socializing, without stopping the much-needed warmth and friendly camaraderie that make Al-Anon a true fellowship. Sometimes we have to remind ourselves to focus on recovery and to include each person in the circle or to invite them for coffee after the meeting, if that is our group's style. A member may stray from attending meetings. A friendly call from someone in the group, saying that the member has been missed, can be encouraging. Common sense and the presence of our Higher Power help us welcome and give comfort without telling people what they ought to do. We usually find that such reaching out strengthens our own recovery.

We can also help make welcoming information

about Al-Anon available in the community. To do this, Al-Anon needs to be easily accessible whenever someone tries to find us. Information services, districts, areas and the World Service Office (WSO) are there to make Al-Anon available whenever and wherever the cry for help is heard. As groups and individuals, we support these services with donations and volunteer hours to assure that someone is there to pick up the phone and direct the person to the nearest meeting. Literature and news releases let people know help is available. Providing these services is part of welcoming the families and friends of alcoholics.

Welcoming families of alcoholics brings us back to our central purpose. Each newcomer who comes to our door reminds us vividly how much comfort we needed (and still need). To give comfort, we have to know comfort. We learn the meaning of kindness and the value of non-judgmental listening from those who gave it to us. Passing it on reinforces our own recovery. Listening to people who have felt the same feelings, and sometimes tried the same crazy things to cope with the insanity of alcoholism, helps us to develop acceptance of ourselves as well as others.

Al-Anon is not a cure-all for every human problem. Although practicing a spiritual program may help us in all areas of our lives, in Al-Anon we focus on just one purpose – helping families and friends of alcoholics. We help each other cope with the family disease of alcoholism and, in doing so, we usually help ourselves the most.

Members Share Experience, Strength and Hope

TRADITION FIVE offers me three challenges: to practice the Twelve Steps, to encourage and understand the alcoholic, to help families of alcoholics.

The Twelve Steps are the basic guidelines for life that I hear at every meeting. More than just repeating

THERE IS
COMFORT

them, I can refer to a specific Step when the need arises. Am I feeling helpless and wanting to control? If so, I can use Steps One, Two and Three. The other Steps offer guidance on actions that I can take, or maybe they will direct me not to take any action at all. If I continue to follow the Steps, I can experience serenity – maybe not as quickly as I would like – but the serenity will come.

Encouraging and understanding the alcoholic can be the most difficult part of Tradition Five for me. It helps if I keep in mind the basics about the disease. Yes, it is a disease. It is not a deliberate attack on me. Through Al-Anon meetings, I have found that I am not alone. Although I am an individual human being, other people's stories are a lot like mine. Often, the misery shared in the company of an Al-Anon meeting is more likely to end in laughter than in tears.

I am an individual. So is the alcoholic. I can honor both of us as valuable human beings. This does not mean I need to condone unacceptable behavior, but I have not walked along the alcoholic's path. I don't really know what that's like, and I'm thankful I don't. The alcoholics I know have not behaved the best or the worst. Can I treat them as I would like to be treated? What I would like to do is encourage and recognize their good deeds without overlooking the bad ones. If this is going to work, I need to be consistent. I need to be responsible for my own actions and I need to let the alcoholics be responsible for theirs.

In order to help families of alcoholics, I can offer a warm welcome and comfort. I can smile. I can let them know that I think it's okay for them to cry. I can relate to their confusion and bewilderment. I can empathize with them about their expectations that have failed. I can listen, listen, listen. I don't give advice. I don't promise a time deadline for improvement. I believe paradise is a state of mind that each of us might visit when we least expect it.

I can listen to people's pain. I can share my own

pain. My comfort comes from knowing that I'm not alone and that there are others who care and understand. I can pass on the comfort that someone else gave to me. By my words and actions, I can let others know that in Al-Anon we are safe and free to share our feelings. We need not fear criticism. Nothing that anyone says will ever be repeated to anyone else.

DOES STAYING true to our one purpose – helping families of alcoholics – have to limit our ability to welcome newcomers? I don't think so, but that's what happened to me. I called the Al-Anon information service (AIS) in my home town to request a schedule of Al-Anon meetings. I explained that my boss was using drugs and that I had gone to another fellowship about it. I heard Al-Anon had more long-term recovery than the other fellowship, so I wanted what Al-Anon had. The woman who answered the phone said I could not come to Al-Anon because it was for people who were concerned about somebody's alcohol use. She was polite, but adamant. I felt rejected, alienated and devastated.

Six months later I read in a book that my grandparents' alcoholism qualified me for Al-Anon. Although I had never met my grandparents, they raised my mother. My mother raised me and, boy, was I profoundly affected by the family disease of alcoholism. Coincidentally I found out that my boss was using alcohol in addition to drugs. I called the Al-Anon information service a second time to ask for a schedule of meetings. This time I got one.

Now I am a volunteer who answers the same AIS telephones. When someone calls who is not focused on someone's alcohol use, I let them know that Al-Anon is for people who feel they have been affected by someone's drinking. I also say that they are welcome to go to many different Al-Anon meetings before they decide whether they have been affected by the family disease of alcoholism. I know from

I DIDN'T
FEEL
WELCOME
AT FIRST

personal experience that ignorance and denial can run deep. Sometimes people focus on one thing while something else is their real problem. I briefly describe my own experience to the caller. I add that eventually my teetotaler dad admitted he had been a problem drinker when he met my mom. Since then I've been assured that my dad was a secret drinker throughout his marriage to my mother. After my mom's death, he remarried. His new wife says he is an active alcoholic.

Ultimately only the prospective members themselves can determine whether they are eligible for membership in Al-Anon. I try to keep my focus on welcoming the newcomers. I let them decide whether they belong in Al-Anon.

CARRYING THE MESSAGE

THIS TRADITION reminds us to set goals and not to be diverted by others or by our compulsion to fix others. Our one goal in Al-Anon is to help families of alcoholics to find the strength and hope for their own lives by sharing our own experience, strength and hope.

The Tradition points out that we help other families and friends of alcoholics by doing three things:

1. By practicing the Twelve Steps of AA ourselves. The Al-Anon Twelve Steps are the same as the AA Twelve Steps except for one word in Step Twelve. Before we can help others, we must help ourselves by practicing the Twelve Steps.

2. By encouraging and understanding our alcoholic relatives. As we attain more serenity through the spirituality of the Steps, we become more receptive to understanding that alcoholism is a disease, and learn to separate the person from the disease. As we become less angry and resentful, it is possible to learn more about the disease and have more understanding. For example, it may be necessary for the alcoholic to attend meetings frequently and to work with other alcoholics even when it is inconvenient for our plans. We learn that the alcoholic can't cure the disease any

more than we can. Understanding his or her confusion, guilt and defeat helps us to grow more compassionate.

3. By welcoming and giving comfort to families of alcoholics. Here we find that our Twelfth Step work is important to our continued growth.

I had learned from the beginning of my recovery to give newcomers to Al-Anon a warm greeting, so I thought I was practicing this Tradition until one day I realized that Tradition Five says, "welcoming and giving comfort to families of alcoholics." It doesn't say to welcome and give comfort just at Al-Anon meetings. Then I realized that every in-law and every relative I have is family of an alcoholic. After that I realized that since I have been affected by the disease of alcoholism, the people associated with me are also affected by the disease through me. This has helped me to be more understanding and patient with others. I also realized that I am the family of an alcoholic, and that I need to cease being so hard on myself, to allow myself to be good to me and to have more understanding of my mistakes and character defects. Learning to accept myself where I am at this time has helped me to learn to accept others as they are today.

I think this Tradition really helped my growth by changing my attitudes toward others around me. It has given me more understanding of their feelings and has made me more tolerant and better able to cope with our relationships in a more harmonious way.

Working Tradition Five

Each Al-Anon Family Group has but one purpose: to help families of alcoholics. We do this by practicing the Twelve Steps of AA ourselves, by encouraging and understanding our alcoholic relatives, and by welcoming and giving comfort to families of alcoholics.

* How do I describe our primary purpose in a meeting? To newcomers?

* Do I put my recovery first, ahead of others' needs? When? How?

* Do I realize that welcoming and giving comfort is not limited to newcomers? Why?

* Am I welcoming to all newcomers, no matter what their problems? How can I guide them to focus on the alcohol-related aspect of those problems?

* How can I be more "newcomer friendly"?

* How do I welcome members who have been in the program awhile or those who have returned after a long absence?

* How might my group give newcomers individual attention?

* Do I ever call newcomers or someone who has been missing from our meeting?

* As a group, how do we use the Steps and Traditions to help families of alcoholics?

* What can we as a group do to make our fellowship known to people outside Al-Anon?

* How can I help others understand that alcoholism is a disease?

* What does comfort mean to me? How can I extend that to another person?

* What does encouraging the alcoholic mean to me? How might I react differently if the diseased person I love had diabetes or cancer?

Tradition Six

Our Al-Anon Family Groups ought never endorse, finance or lend our name to any outside enterprise, lest problems of money, property and prestige divert us from our primary spiritual aim. Although a separate entity, we should always cooperate with Alcoholics Anonymous.

TRADITION SIX reemphasizes our primary spiritual aim as defined in Tradition Five – to help families and friends of alcoholics. Focusing on the activities of the groups, the Sixth Tradition reminds us of two of our slogans, "Keep it Simple" and "Easy Does it." We apply these slogans by working the Steps, Traditions and Concepts without diversion. Our groups stay on track by not endorsing, funding or lending our name to any outside enterprise, no matter how valuable and worthy it may be. Individuals are free to make personal choices in any issue but these choices are left outside the Al-Anon rooms.

A group's money is used to rent meeting space as needed, provide refreshments, share the costs of information services, purchase Conference Approved Literature (CAL) and to cover the expenses of trusted servants attending information service/intergroup, district or area functions. The use of group funds is fully explored in Tradition Seven. Some groups find it important to maintain a prudent reserve, such as the equivalent of one or two months' expenses. However, experience has shown that our primary spiritual aim can be diverted when excessive funds are retained. By keeping a spiritual focus, we are able to provide maximum access to Al-Anon with minimum diversion from our own recovery.

Should Al-Anon groups own property? Ownership of literature, coffee pots, baskets and other basic essentials is all that is required for an Al-Anon family group. Literature distribution centers (LDC), Al-Anon information services (AIS) and the World Service Office (WSO) own the office equipment they need to function. Our co-founders Lois W. and Anne B. found a simple typewriter essential in the early days of corresponding with the first groups who registered. Today our WSO uses the technology of the 21st century to communicate with the worldwide fellowship through computers, phone systems and fax machines.

Ownership of property by groups and service arms has been discussed many times over the years. As noted above, these entities do own property; as long as we do not "endorse, finance or lend our name to any outside enterprise," such transactions are consistent with our Traditions.*

An example of lending our name or diversion from our primary purpose could occur should we endorse films, outside recovery activities, political philosophies or religion. We cooperate with these entities in our Public Information and Cooperating with the Professional Community work. However, we do not recommend or otherwise endorse these things. For example, after long discussion, in 1995 the World Service Conference decided that, even though there are many fine films that depict our philosophy and that we might even become a resource for those desiring to make such films, making any recommendation lists would amount to endorsement.

Al-Anon is a spiritual program, and our primary spiritual aim is to help families and friends of alcoholics. Al-Anon is not affiliated with any religion. Many share in meetings how the reading of the Steps scared them when they heard the word God used. Newcomers are assured that the use of God does not imply or endorse any religion. For the purpose of recovery in Al-Anon, God implies a Power greater than ourselves – our Higher Power. For our trust and confidence in Al-Anon, we need to know that Al-Anon is a no strings attached spiritual program.

---

* In 1994, the World Service Conference (WSC) authorized the corporate entity, Al-Anon Family Group Headquarters, Inc., to purchase real estate for a trial period to house our World Service Office (WSO). Our trusted servants were guided in discussion of this decision by the spiritual principle of helping families and friends of alcoholics. The 15-year trial period on the property began in 1996.

An Al-Anon meeting is not a place where we endorse treatment programs or other facilities. Even though we may meet at an institution or church, we only rent space and make it clear that all families and friends of alcoholics are welcome, including those associated with that church, facility or treatment program. An exception may be an institutions meeting open only to residents for reasons of security or confidentiality. These Al-Anon groups are not affiliated in any way with the institution. There is no such thing as an Al-Anon clinic or Al-Anon hospital.

What about retreats or announcements and literature from other Twelve Step programs? These are "outside enterprises." Al-Anon does not sponsor such gatherings or affiliate itself with any therapy or religious organization, even if they use many of our principles and some of our members attend them. We want all our members to feel welcome and included. An agnostic or non-religious member could easily feel excluded from a religious retreat, however slight the overtones of the sponsoring church were, and announcing such gatherings at Al-Anon meetings could be taken as endorsement of them. Announcing AA events with Al-Anon participation would be an example of cooperating with Alcoholics Anonymous.

As individuals we may support, volunteer or endorse anything, anybody or any activity we like as long as we do not do it as Al-Anon members or as an Al-Anon group. Outside of meetings we are free to discuss anything that has helped us and we can champion any cause we care to. We just don't do it as representatives of Al-Anon.

Keeping Al-Anon a safe place where we can come for comfort and solutions means it must not be a place where we feel pressured or obligated to buy anything. Al-Anon Conference Approved Literature (CAL) is sold at meetings only to recoup the groups' out-of-pocket expenses to purchase it. Members are encouraged to subscribe to and to read *The Forum*, our monthly magazine, the "voice of the fellowship" in writing. Sale of trinkets and outside materials would create diversion from our primary purpose. For an in-depth understanding of these issues, members are encouraged to read the chapter in the digest of Al-Anon and Alateen policies from the *Al-Anon/ Alateen Service Manual* entitled, "Al-Anon As It Relates To Others."

Some of us belong to other Twelve Step programs that address specific needs we have outside the scope of Al-Anon. Having a grounding in the Twelve Steps makes crossover likely and even comfortable, but if we are to benefit fully from the experience Al-Anon has to offer, it is important that we leave our other hats outside the door and concentrate on Al-Anon solutions in Al-Anon meetings. An alcoholic who comes to Al-Anon for help related to someone else's drinking would find little help if the Al-Anon meeting turned into a discussion of how to stay sober.

It should not be forgotten that we are a fellowship separate from AA with a different focus, but we often cooperate to bring recovery to all in need of it. Al-Anon's Sixth Tradition recognizes the influence of AA on our recovery program and states that we "should always cooperate with Alcoholics Anonymous." Over the years groups, areas and even the WSO have cooperated with AA. An example of this spirit of cooperation on a worldwide scale is Al-Anon's participation with AA at our international conventions. In our districts and areas, large projects such as conventions and conferences are excellent examples of how cooperation can be in the interest of both AA and Al-Anon. Planning sessions can include members of both fellowships, although usually one group takes the lead while the other participates. Practical plans like meeting space, dates and basic ground rules either can be decided by the originating group or mutually agreed upon by both groups. Each group sets its own agenda and topics and is responsible for its own Twelfth Step work.

Another area of cooperation is sharing space or facilities to make recovery available in areas where groups are small and funds are limited. In these cases it is best to work toward full financial independence for both fellowships. Twelfth Step calls definitely should be fielded only by members of the appropriate group. Sometimes AA speakers are invited to address Al-Anon meetings, and Al-Anon members speak at AA meetings. The understanding of each fellowship of the many aspects of alcoholism and reactions to it can be expanded by such cooperation as long as both fellowships remain separate and available to their own members.

Our primary spiritual aim of helping families and friends of alcoholics is best accomplished when we stick to Al-Anon principles, focusing only on Al-Anon recovery.

Members Share Experience, Strength and Hope

OUR JAWS
DROPPED
OPEN

MY SATURDAY night home group decided to invite everyone to go for coffee after our meetings. It was a great idea. It let us get to know each other and it gave us a chance to share informally. It also gave newcomers a neutral setting, more familiar to them than an Al-Anon meeting might be, where they could talk to Al-Anon members.

The first time we announced our standing invitation in the meeting, we gave the name of the coffee shop so people would know where to go. After the meeting someone said, "I wonder if people will think we are endorsing that coffee shop or making it our official group coffee shop." Our jaws dropped open. That possibility had not occurred to us.

After a week's prayer, meditation and a group discussion, we rewrote our meeting script. We invited everyone to a "nearby coffee shop." If people wanted to know which coffee shop we were going to, they asked us after the meeting. This arrangement has worked very well for all of us.

Before Al-Anon I certainly endorsed, financed and lent my name, property and prestige to more than one person, whether or not they had a drinking problem. My primary aim was selfish, to say the least – ego gratification.

I NO LONGER HAVE TO BE OVERLY SUPPORTIVE

Our Sixth Tradition has taught me to preserve my own integrity and to protect my own identity. I no longer have to be overly supportive of anyone else – spiritually, emotionally, physically or financially. I've learned to give people the dignity to be themselves and to discover certain things on their own. My own primary purpose is to practice and to apply the principles of the Al-Anon program in all areas of my life. The Twelve Steps, Twelve Traditions and Twelve Concepts free me from despair and give me real hope. I no longer need to carry another person to prove that I am valuable.

The words cooperation and affiliation are defined in our *Al-Anon/Alateen Service Manual* as follows: "Cooperation: Joint operation or action (implies coming together of two or more people to work together for a common goal or benefit or a common problem)." "Affiliation: Association or close connection, a uniting (implies lending one's name, endorsement, legal or financial association)."

WHERE TO PUT MY FOCUS

It was important for me to understand this difference. Before Al-Anon I thought that cooperation meant that if I were to cooperate with you, then I would do it your way. If you were to cooperate with me, you would do it my way. Someone pointed out to me that co- means with. So to operate with another person is cooperating. It implies working together with some give and take on each side for our mutual benefit. The section "Al-Anon as it Relates to Others" in our Service Manual spells out various types of areas in which we can cooperate without affiliating.

Although there are many worthwhile causes in which we as individuals might be interested, we do not bring these things into our meetings. This includes other literature and its particular terminology. Using other literature could act as an endorsement. As a group or fellowship, we cannot finance anything or anybody other than Al-Anon. We do not lend our name to any outside enterprise. There is no such thing as an Al-Anon clubhouse any more than there is an AA clubhouse. I know that this term is often loosely used, but the clubhouses are owned by a group of individuals who may belong to the fellowship. Those who hold meetings there must pay rent to the facility. We cannot form combined AA and Al-Anon groups – groups must be either AA or Al-Anon, not both.

This Tradition reminds us to keep the focus on our spiritual growth. In my everyday life, I find this Tradition very helpful because it sums up "mind your own business." As a family we learn to cooperate – to work together for a common good. We learn that each of us can have our own outside interests and activities but these cannot be allowed to supersede the family as a whole. The Tradition points out that the spirituality of our program must come first, that we cannot allow outside things to sidetrack us from our real purpose.

Another part of the Tradition that has helped me in my home is the last part: "Although a separate entity, we should always cooperate with Alcoholics Anonymous." I can apply this by substituting the word alcoholic instead of Alcoholics Anonymous, now that I better understand the word cooperate. It reminds me that we can work together and still maintain our individuality.

Working Tradition Six

Our Al-Anon Family Groups ought never endorse, finance or lend our name to any outside enterprise, lest problems of money, property and prestige divert us from our primary spiritual aim. Although a separate entity, we should always cooperate with Alcoholics Anonymous.

* Why do we do not "endorse, finance or lend our name to any outside enterprise?" How is this principle used in our business meetings?

* Has my group ever had problems with money or property? How were these problems resolved?

* Have I or any member of my group allowed prestige to divert us from our primary spiritual aim? When? Why? What did we change?

* How does my group cooperate with AA? When?

* In planning a group fund-raising activity, has my group considered this Tradition?

* Does my group have CAL prominently displayed? Do I use CAL in my personal recovery?

* Does my group sell or promote outside literature? How does this violate Tradition Six? Do I have the courage to discuss the use of literature at a meeting?

* How do I consider cooperation with AA in my service work?

* Why should group funds support only Al-Anon programs?

* Has our group phone list ever been used for promotional purposes? How?

* How can I discourage members, without embarrassing them, from bringing outside enterprises into our meetings?

* Am I allowing material or financial concerns to gain priority over my personal spiritual needs and serenity?

* Am I allowing personal problems or successes to overwhelm me? Am I letting them get in the way of how I treat others?

* How can I apply our slogan, "Live and Let Live" to this Tradition?

* How can I apply our slogan, "Let Go and Let God"?

* How do I help my group to fulfill our primary spiritual aim?

* When participating at an AA convention or round-up, do Al-Anon members have Al-Anon logos or the name Al-Anon on their badges?

WE AS Al-Anon members provide the sole financial support of our Al-Anon groups. The only requirement for membership in Al-Anon is to have been affected by the disease of alcoholism in a friend or relative. The only requirement for any contributor to Al-Anon is to be a member. With sufficient membership contributions, Al-Anon will always be there for families and friends of alcoholics. This Tradition, although it speaks directly to individuals and the group, in fact, speaks to the entire fellowship.

Little is asked of us as newcomers. We are welcomed without obligation to a group with no dues or fees. When the group treasurer passes the basket, it is explained that contributions are voluntary. We are encouraged to take some time for ourselves before trying to take on part of the group function. Eventually we need to participate, to work the Steps and to add our voice and resources to the group in order to continue our recovery. As individuals we come to believe that, to keep Al-Anon functioning and available, our group has to take care of its own needs.

When we take care of our financial needs, we are free to run our fellowship exactly as we wish. There are no benefactors who can dictate or even influence our policies by threatening to withdraw resources. There are no dues or fees, but there are financial responsibilities. We choose to accept the responsibility to pay our own way with our voluntary contributions; thus Al-Anon's independence and continued availability depends on us.

Each group has expenses such as rent, group literature, refreshments, a post office box or the cost of sending its group representative (GR) to district and area meetings. Some of us believe that satisfying these group expenses means we are fully self-supporting. We are contributing to keeping one meeting available, and that is significant. However, as members of a worldwide fellowship, we eventually discover how vast our community really is and how important the

Tradition Seven

Every group ought to be fully self-supporting, declining outside contributions.

services are that we sometimes take for granted. The groups are the foundation of Al-Anon and have the final say in the fellowship, but a group can have no say unless it participates and sends a voice through an elected group representative.

As in any family, there is more to support than just bringing home the paycheck. There are dishes to be done and beds to be made. We support our groups by volunteering to serve as chairperson or secretary, by bringing coffee, by setting up chairs, by serving as group representative or by taking on any other job. We also carry the message by volunteering in our information service offices or by speaking about Al-Anon at other organizations or institutions. We sponsor other members and practice the Twelfth Step whenever an opportunity presents itself. If we don't have much money, there is still much we can contribute in time and energy. Groups can languish as quickly from unfilled service positions as from lack of money. Conversely, it is unhealthy for the group to let a few members do everything. The volunteers are likely to feel overwhelmed and unappreciated, while those not involved feel left out and discounted. When we volunteer, we enhance our own program, bond with the group and raise our self-esteem through useful labor. Balance is the key.

Groups benefit from the network of communication that holds our fellowship together. Information services/intergroups, literature distribution centers, districts and areas maintain phone lines so that those who still suffer can find a meeting. Our service centers also produce and distribute meeting lists, newsletters and fliers that help us find each other and learn of events of interest. District and area meetings keep our groups informed and also carry our voice to the World Service Conference (WSC). Without these resources, many of us would not have found Al-Anon or would miss events that aid our recovery. Our voluntary contributions and the purchase of our

Conference Approved Literature (CAL) are the only sources of support for these needed activities.

We are a worldwide fellowship rich in the experience of thousands of members. The World Service Office (WSO) is our central clearinghouse. We can travel worldwide and remain connected to Al-Anon because of its service structures. Our literature and our magazine, *The Forum*, are carefully designed and published to reflect the whole fellowship. We contribute our sharings. All that compiling, writing, editing, publishing and distributing work is done through the WSO. Area newsletters, weekends and conferences are created and planned at district and area levels.

Annually each area, on behalf of its groups, contributes to an equalized expense fund for sending their delegate to our World Service Conference (WSC). This annual meeting is a forum for the wide group conscience which unifies our fellowship. At the Conference, the groups have their say in how Al-Anon can best serve the fellowship with its resources. Conference members approve the annual budget for WSO activities. While the WSO administratively is responsible for meeting the annual budget, it is the responsibility of the members and groups to support the activities they have directed.

Day-to-day communications with the groups and with professionals interested in our groups are handled at the WSO. The WSO answers inquiries, registers groups, keeps up-to-date data about the fellowship and provides literature. Both local service arms and the WSO help spread the word of recovery in ever-expanding circles and are dependent on Al-Anon members for ideas, direction and resources.

Although many offers of outside contributions have been made to Al-Anon, we respectfully decline them. With all these expenses and needs, we might ask, "Why do we decline outside contributions? Couldn't we put that money to good use?" Certainly we could put lots of money to good use, but experience has taught us that there are two perils about money: having too much and being beholden for it. It would be tempting to cater to those who benefit us. We may laugh at the unlikely prospect of having too much money, but actually part of the value of our independence is that the WSO and areas are dependent on the groups and thus need to listen closely to the group conscience in order to truly serve our fellowship. Without group participation, it is possible that our service centers could get out of touch and go their own way until there was great dissension. Lengthy discussions on how to spend funds have, on occasion, diverted us from our primary spiritual aim. It is best to have enough, plus a prudent reserve, and not be worried about either creating or spending excess.

Even within Al-Anon, no one is allowed to contribute great sums. When any single person or a small group of people contribute too much, problems of jealousy and dominance are likely to arise. Our spiritual fellowship is based on equality and, though we may not all contribute exactly the same amount, by spreading responsibility widely, we assure ourselves of the mutuality of our self-help. When we did not contribute to the group, we found our participation was lessened, and in time, our own recovery was threatened. Tradition Seven keeps us self-sustaining.

Three times a year the World Service Office mails Seventh Tradition appeal letters to each registered group in the United States and Canada. This letter makes a personal appeal to individual Al-Anon members to make a special gratitude contribution. In this appeal group members, (rather than the group itself) are asked to help Al-Anon cover the expenses of our worldwide services, including sharing in the expense of the annual World Service Conference. Group representatives or group treasurers act as agents for the members by returning these special triannual appeal contributions to the WSO.

Al-Anon as a whole is self-supporting. This Tradition teaches us – as individuals, as groups and as part of the worldwide fellowship – the importance of the self-supporting concept. We can also use Tradition Seven as a model for healthy relationships in many other groups – families, jobs, community – just about anywhere. If we share the responsibility for the well-being of Al-Anon, we can be assured that Al-Anon will be there for anyone reaching out for help. Based on our spiritual principles, we place our ultimate security and the security of our groups in God's hands. As we learn to take care of ourselves materially and emotionally, Tradition Seven guides us.

Members Share Experience, Strength and Hope

TRADITION SIX points out that Al-Anon money can only be spent for Al-Anon purposes. Tradition Seven is very similar. Al-Anon cannot accept any funds from outside our fellowship. The WSO pays its own way because of generous Al-Anon groups and individual members who donate money. Another source is the sale of literature.

THERE ARE NO FREE RIDES

Al-Anon cannot accept money from someone who is not a member, even if the person donated the money as a memorial to one of us. As members we may make a donation in memory of anyone we choose. We may also bequeath money from our own estate. In our manual there are specified limits on the amounts that Al-Anon members can give.

As Lois W., our co-founder, said, "Purse strings can become ropes that can choke us." It is human nature that a person who gives someone money may have expectations about how it is spent. In Tradition Seven we learn that nothing in life is free. There are no free rides. When we are not self-supporting, we can easily become victims to those who support us. Inevitably, we would have to learn not to fight those who would control us. Once again it is not my job to work on them – I work on me. I must be able to stand on my own two feet and be self-supporting if I am to be independent.

Usually when we speak of being self-supporting, we think about money. Money is only part of the story. In my personal life I need to be self-supporting socially, spiritually, emotionally, mentally and physically. I cannot depend on another person for my happiness. I don't have to adopt the moods or attitudes of those around me. If someone else is angry, I don't need to be angry, sad or fearful. My moods and attitudes are something that only I can control. Just as I learned in Step One that I cannot control anyone else, neither can someone else control me – unless I give them the power to do so. Unless I rent them space in my head, they can't get in it.

As we learn to be self-supporting in our personal lives, we learn how to think for ourselves. When a question comes up, we know how to listen to others. We also know how to do our own research and how to make our own decisions.

PROTECTION FOR MY SPIRITUAL GROWTH

LATELY THE Tradition that has affected me the most is Seven. It seemed it was my turn to read that Tradition every week. I was getting very resentful of this. Was my Higher Power hinting at something? One week in July the topic was Tradition Seven. I volunteered to lead the meeting.

As I pored over the CAL, I began to see that Tradition Seven is more than balancing the budget and not depending on outside people for speakers or service work. This one-liner is in place to protect my spiritual growth. No one can buy or own the group with money, status or power. Outside influences necessarily are left at the door, willingly or not. They are not a part of the Al-Anon message.

To think of Tradition Seven as merely money irritates me. To think of Tradition Seven as a protection for my spiritual growth is humbling and freeing. This

Tradition was written with me and Al-Anon as a whole in mind. I now know that not only do I get to give my money and service, but I also get to receive miracles in abundance.

I CAME into Al-Anon completely dependent on outside contributions. Alcoholism had crippled me to the point where I wasn't responsible for myself and my life. I was a nineteen-year-old single parent on welfare, receiving financial aid for school. I was burning out my family members by having them constantly baby-sit my child and give me rides. I was rapidly using up everyone around me, especially those who loved me.

I BEGAN TO GRASP THE HOPE AND FAITH

Because I felt the world owed me, I filled myself with resentments and justifications. Alcoholism had stolen huge pieces of my life and I hated the pieces that remained. I tried to get even with the alcoholics by taking as much as I could. I sold my soul, gave up my independence and compromised my self-worth by depending too much on others. Eventually I began to feel I owed the world a debt I could never repay. I felt like I would never be worth anything. As a result I found myself in a constant state of submission.

As I kept coming back to Al-Anon, however, the Seventh Tradition sparked a hopeful challenge in me. I read the Tradition over and over. I practiced it in my meetings by contributing what I could when the basket was passed. I also practiced the Tradition by making commitments to do various things for my group. Eventually I tried applying Tradition Seven at home with my housework. I talked with my sponsor about it. Slowly I began to grasp the hope and faith that maybe I could become financially self-supporting, too.

I learned and grew by working the Twelve Steps of Al-Anon. My fear began to dissipate as I took action to become self-supporting. I began to realize that my need for outside contributions was lessening. I risked practicing the principles in all my affairs, and it worked. I found out that I have all I need to be exactly who God wants me to be. I heard in meetings that if I supply the willingness, God will grant me the strength. Finally I could start to see my way toward independence.

Today the only real ties or debts I have are to this program. I still owe a certain amount of money, but I have made arrangements to pay it back. I am bound by guilt to no one. I am useful today – a good Al-Anon member, mother, wife, daughter, sister and employee. I feel good about my life because I know I am doing my part. The Seventh Tradition has taught me to be a giver instead of a taker. I ask my Higher Power to show me where I can contribute to life each day. All of my needs are met. I am doing my part and I feel calm when that is my focus.

I have many alcoholics in my life. Sober or not, they don't have to worry about me evening the score. I leave the score-keeping to God. Just as I cannot live anyone's life for them, no one can live mine for me. The difference is now I don't want them to live my life for me. I want more of the good feelings that come from taking care of myself. Sometimes my sponsor and other Al-Anon friends remind me that I have made a commitment to Tradition Seven. That commitment calls for faith instead of looking frantically for other people to give me my answers.

My real answers have come from my Higher Power whom I found through Al-Anon. To think that when I first heard that the Twelve Traditions could apply to my personal and family life, I didn't get it. Tradition Seven hit me where I lived. The fear, shame and guilt that I constantly struggled with have been replaced with courage, acceptance and freedom that enable me to live rather than just to survive. I am so grateful to Al-Anon for showing me how to grow up. I am experiencing what it feels like to be a lady with dignity. I love the Steps and the Traditions. I love everything about Al-Anon, and today I love my life!

Working Tradition Seven

Every group ought to be fully self-supporting, declining outside contributions.

* What does fully self-supporting mean to me?

* How do I support my group?

* What can I do this week to contribute to my own support and to that of my group?

* Do I consider costs and what my group needs when I decide how much to contribute, or do I just keep tossing a dollar into the basket? Can I put a little more in the basket on behalf of the new person who can't?

* Do I personally contribute to the World Service Office triannual appeal?

* If members of my group do not understand the triannual appeal, am I willing to explain its purpose to them?

* Does my group pay a fair rate for rent, copying, refreshments and does it have enough literature?

* Do I encourage business meetings for my group?

* In what ways, other than financial, do I support my group?

* What benefits have I received when I have volunteered?

* How often do we rotate service positions? Do we expect a few people to hold up the rest of us?

* What could I do to encourage less-active members to become involved? Am I as active as I would like to be?

* Do we ever expect members in service positions to personally purchase coffee or to print lists at their offices?

* Do I support our service boards, such as district, information services, literature distribution center, intergroup, area, WSO? How? With money or time?

* What does my group do to support our service boards?

* How do we support our district?

* How do we support our area?

* How do we support the WSO?

* Do we contribute to the large group conscience by sending our group representative (GR) as our voice and vote at district or area meetings?

* What benefits do we get from being part of the worldwide fellowship?

* Do I subscribe to *The Forum*? Do I purchase gift subscriptions?

* Does my group have a group treasurer? Does the treasurer give regular reports?

* Has my group established a prudent reserve, or are we stockpiling moneys for no specific reason?

* Do I understand the spiritual aspects of contributing?

* Is my self-worth based on how much I'm needed by others?

* Am I afraid of letting go?

* Do I realize I can't have the respect of others if I can't stand on my own two feet?

* Do I contribute to my own well-being? Am I fully self supporting? Am I prepared to remain so?

* Can I accept and express my own feelings without feeling wrong or justifying them to others?

* Do I take responsibility for my own feelings or do I blame them on the actions of others?

* Is my happiness circumstance-dependent, or am I looking to myself for fulfillment? Explain.

Tradition Eight

Al-Anon Twelfth-Step work should remain forever nonprofessional, but our service centers may employ special workers.

TRADITION EIGHT reminds us who we are – a fellowship of equals sharing our mutual experience, strength and hope in order to recover and help each other along the way. Tradition Eight distinguishes Twelfth Step work from all other work in Al-Anon. Twelfth Step work takes many forms, including welcoming newcomers, sponsoring another member, sharing at a meeting, serving on a Public Information committee and volunteering time on a telephone answering service. Twelfth Step work is the special task of carrying the Al-Anon message to others.

We all come to Al-Anon in different circumstances, yet we are freely given all the gifts of experience, strength and hope that have been acquired by those who went before us. All that is asked of us is to pass them on. As members have done so, our fellowship has grown. There are nearly 30,000 groups sharing recovery all over the world.

Al-Anon membership is nonprofessional. We are a fellowship of mutual support, and we recover by using the Twelve Steps adapted from Alcoholics Anonymous and sharing our experiences with each other. We don't give professional guidance to each other in Al-Anon. Nor do we approach our Public Information and Cooperating with the Professional Community efforts as professionals.

Sharing our nonprofessional, personal experiences with each other provides our groups with a source of strength that grows as we grow. Twelfth Step work also works for us individually because recovery expands when we give it away. Many of us have answered a call from a newcomer only to find ourselves saying just what we needed to hear, but for the moment had forgotten to practice.

Because there are so many of us, the opportunities to learn and create new solutions are endless. Though many of us have sought professional help and found it useful, in Al-Anon we find something available nowhere else – a community of people who share many of the same life experiences we have had and who understand as perhaps no one else can. We also find people with whom we can identify who have solutions that worked for them which we can try. If they can do it, we feel we can too; we are encouraged. In the process, we experience loving relationships we may have never known before. This cannot be bought; it can only be shared. Our loving interchange through personal contact is invaluable, and it is possible only because of our commitment to doing Twelfth Step work and keeping it non-professional.

Another advantage of keeping Al-Anon non-professional is that it makes it possible for professionals in our communities who have difficulties with their own alcoholic relatives and friends to come to Al-Anon for their own recovery. In Al-Anon, professionals to whom others turn for help (clergy, counselors, doctors, social workers) can find the solace and support they need for themselves. When they share in a meeting, they do so as members of the group with their own recovery and experience their primary concern. Like each of us, they have many ideas and experiences that they bring with them. And like us, they are powerless over alcohol and alcoholics. Each of us holds some of the knowledge we all need, and our participation is necessary to our recovery. We learn together.

In the early years of Al-Anon, the practical office work of writing letters, helping groups contact each other and taking telephone calls was done by some wonderful volunteers – a most dedicated, hardworking and selfless group of people. They set a high standard of service to reach. They were so successful in getting the word out about Al-Anon that soon more than love and dedication from just volunteers was required to serve our growing fellowship. People needed to be hired to handle the increased workload.

Many local offices started as volunteer operations,

but found that there just were not enough people with enough time to spare to keep the offices open regular hours or to answer correspondence. Even dedicated volunteers can't always work for Al-Anon 40 hours a week without pay. How then, would Al-Anon offices be able to be self-supporting?

Anyone who has tried to order literature or find meetings through a telephone service that didn't return the call knows how frustrating that can be. We don't want to miss opportunities to help those who still suffer because we're too hard to reach. When we can afford it, we pay one of our members, or a non-member, to keep the doors open. In addition we volunteer in order to keep costs down and to be available when a Twelfth Step call comes in.

As we hire people to do the practical communication work of Al-Anon, it helps to remember Tradition Seven. If we are fully self-supporting, then we pay reasonable wages to those who serve us. Otherwise we are asking people to sacrifice their financial well-being, to give up taking care of themselves, in order to work for Al-Anon.

Today Al-Anon is a large fellowship with groups in more than 100 countries. Our WSO needs people with both clerical and professional skills. We need accounting and legal knowledge in order to keep abreast of current laws. We need editing, writing and publishing skills to see that our literature, while created by members, is quality work – both readable and translatable. Our special workers include paid management and support staff as well as specialists contracted for specific projects. Those in positions involved with decision-making that might affect our fellowship (such as the executive director and department heads) are required to be members of Al-Anon. Others might be selected for special skills (like accountants or secretaries) and need not be Al-Anon members. All of our operations are overseen by the Board of Trustees, an elected body of Al-Anon members, volunteers who are not paid, but are reimbursed for the expenses incurred in service (travel, phone calls, photocopying, etc.).

Tradition Eight guides us on how to carry the message of Al-Anon to others. Common sense dictates we hire the special workers needed to coordinate our efforts and keep regular hours so we can stay in touch with members and be available to newcomers. Most of the work of Al-Anon is done by member volunteers who understand that service deepens and enhances their own recovery and gives them an opportunity to put gratitude into action. Through voluntary service, our conferences, information services/intergroups, institution meetings and groups continue. Our paid employees and volunteers make possible a network of Public Information at the local and national levels as well as dissemination of meeting information and coordination of large endeavors such as area conventions, Regional Service Seminars and the World Service Conference (WSC).

When we volunteer we follow in the footsteps of those selfless, dedicated volunteers like Lois W. and Anne B., who started Al-Anon's first office, The Clearing House, in the sweltering New York City summer heat. Over the years, the combined efforts of volunteers and paid special workers have made Al-Anon what it is today.

Members Share Experience, Strength and Hope

I AM a volunteer in the local Al-Anon information service office and literature distribution center. I answer phones, pick up answering-machine messages, mail literature and handle any available clerical work, such as folding meeting schedules. No Al-Anon volunteer is paid for this work.

Our office manager, an Al-Anon member, receives a fair hourly wage. He has ultimate responsibility for

HE
MAINTAINS
A CLEAR
BOUNDARY

overseeing the volunteers, distributing literature and maintaining office procedures in the business end of this little operation. He often reminds us that the more volunteer hours we give to support our office, the fewer paid hours he must invest in clerical work. If no volunteer completes the clerical work that must be done, he does it. If no volunteer is available to ship the Conference Approved Literature (CAL) ordered by groups, he does it. In this way our literature distribution center fulfills its mission and keeps its reputation for reliable, prompt service.

Our office manager draws the line at handling Twelfth Step calls. He leaves them until the next volunteer is available. On the rare occasion when he has to handle a Twelfth Step call because it would otherwise go unanswered, he conscientiously clocks out as office manager and takes his role as an Al-Anon member. He maintains a clear boundary between carrying the message as an Al-Anon member and doing his job as office manager.

It is common sense to avoid having our paid employees carry the Twelfth Step message. All of us need to do this to maintain our own spiritual program. It is also common sense to have a smooth operation so that those who want to reach us are not frustrated into giving up. Tradition Eight addresses both aspects of Twelfth Step work with practical solutions. This model helps me in my everyday life to keep a balance between spiritual giving and taking care of business.

MY DESPAIR BEGAN TO LIFT

I NEVER paid much attention to Tradition Eight until I got in trouble with my own recovery. I developed an unconscious tendency to slip into my professional role. When I first came to Al-Anon, I was depressed, exhausted and despairing. I had tried to fix nearly every member of my family with dismal results. They let me do everything and then generally avoided me or faded away when I turned to them expecting a payback. I couldn't understand what was wrong. I was a trained alcohol-treatment therapist and I was sure I was right. Sometimes I was right, but that didn't matter.

Being a so-called expert in the field didn't help me deal with my alcoholic son. I was embarrassed to turn to my colleagues with the problem. I had forgotten the adage, "a doctor who treats himself has a fool for a patient." I was terrified that if I sought help I would meet my own clients coming through the door. I thought I would lose their confidence if they saw me. Eventually I felt desperate enough to go to an Al-Anon meeting in a neighboring town. Finally my despair began to lift.

After a while in Al-Anon, I began letting people know about my expertise. It felt good to be appreciated for my profession for a change. Soon I was engaged in therapy appointments all day and calls for advice all evening. My professional advice and my Al-Anon knowledge became hopelessly entangled. Soon neither one was very useful. I became more exhausted and desperate than ever. I began to feel that, if I was the expert, I couldn't call on those who called me for help. I isolated more and more.

Fortunately I had a wonderful sponsor who suggested a closer reading of Tradition Eight. I began to realize that being an expert jeopardized my sanity. I decided to take off my therapist's hat. I admitted to God, to myself and to my sponsor that I had exactly as much experience, strength and hope to share as the person sitting beside me in the meeting, perhaps less. What a relief it was to share compassion, love and spiritual seeking with no strings attached. I even let go of the temptation for ego gratification. Today I am no expert in recovery. I am a partner. As a result I feel a little less brilliant and far less lonely.

Working Tradition Eight

Al-Anon Twelfth-Step work should remain forever non-professional, but our service centers may employ special workers.

* Do I willingly share my experience, strength and hope with those who are suffering from the family disease of alcoholism?

* Do I ever have a tendency to be a know-it-all?

* How can I share with others without trying to fix them?

* At meetings do I speak as an expert or as a fellow member?

* What are the advantages of a fellowship of equals? Are there disadvantages?

* Do I ever regard other members as experts, perhaps because they are longtime members, very charismatic or professionals outside of Al-Anon?

* Do I ever hold back from sharing because I feel I don't know as much as others?

* What is the difference between Twelfth Step work and being a special worker?

* Am I committed to paying our special workers a fair wage, or do I expect them to give a lot for free because they are Al-Anon members?

* Do I understand what our local and WSO special workers do?

* Do I feel the need to look good or to be a perfect model of recovery? Does that stop me from being humble enough to get the help I need?

* Is someone else's opinion more important than my own? Why?

* Am I ever Mr. or Ms. Al-Anon?

* Am I ever judgmental?

* Do I take others' inventories? Is this ever appropriate?

Tradition Nine

Our groups, as such, ought never be organized; but we may create service boards or committees directly responsible to those they serve.

TRADITION NINE states that our fellowship, made up of the groups of families and friends of alcoholics who gather together in meetings to share their experience, strength and hope, is not organized. In our fellowship the Al-Anon group members are equals and no one member is viewed as an executive or in charge. In Al-Anon we have suggested guidelines, but no rules for conducting meetings and our service activities. The *Al-Anon/Alateen Service Manual* is written to further guide us in our service activities. Each member knows that their recovery is theirs and theirs alone and that Al-Anon does not have any rules or rulers.

"Wait a minute," some of us said. "Does this mean Al-Anon is supposed to be disorganized?" If we have total freedom, won't we become irresponsible, leaving our group rent unpaid, ignoring calls for help, and not being there for the newcomer? Fortunately, in the history of Al-Anon, common sense, experience and a loving Higher Power usually have managed to guide us back to Al-Anon principles before we did ourselves too much harm.

We do have a common structure and the groups as such are left to decide exactly what organization means to them. The experiences of other groups in our districts and areas can provide helpful suggestions. Keeping the structure simple and rotating leadership are the goals.

In each group the members decide how much organization is wanted. If what they decide doesn't work, they can change it. Most groups hold regular service or business meetings in which all members are encouraged to participate. At business meetings, group policies are established and members are informed of group, district, area and worldwide Al-Anon news. Such discussions help to maintain Al-Anon unity. Topics to be discussed are announced at the regular Al-Anon meeting so that all interested parties have the opportunity to attend the business meeting. Some groups use their business meetings to discuss recommendations and hold the group conscience vote at their regular meeting. This is a matter of group autonomy.

We all have voice and vote in Al-Anon. This is how the fellowship functions. If there is dissension, a group representative may take it to the district for discussion. If an issue is not resolved at a district level, it can be taken to the area trusted servants for discussion at an area world service committee meeting or assembly. Some ultimately choose to write to their regional trustee or the World Service Office (WSO) for recommendations. A usual response is not a directive or advice. Instead it may state, "our experience suggests," followed by examples of how a Tradition or Concept might be useful in creating an informed group conscience.

The second part of the Tradition says "we may create service boards or committees directly responsible to those they serve." Isn't that a contradiction? Don't be organized, yet organize service boards and committees.

Common sense tells us that if we want to accomplish something, like putting on a workshop or anniversary meeting, someone needs to find a place, rent it, set the dates, and call people to speak. So we organize a committee to do it. To spread the Al-Anon message to the public or to plan a convention, we organize Public Information and convention committees. These become our service boards and committees. They serve us well through planning and organization but final authority still rests with the groups.

How then, can a huge number of loosely organized groups govern these boards? The answer is in the committees and in the democratic voice of our elected representatives. For example, the groups choose a group representative to speak for them at the district meetings and area assemblies. Districts choose representatives to speak for them at the area committee meetings. Areas choose delegates to take their voice and vote to the World Service Conference (WSC), where policy decisions are made and the trustees are elected. Between Conferences the trustees oversee the operations at the WSO, which has executives and directors, who are Al-Anon members, to oversee day-to-day operations. At all levels – group representatives, district representatives, delegates, trustees or employees – we are all trusted servants with responsibilities and the right to use our best judgment after consulting a Power greater than ourselves.

Because one of our chief defects is a tendency to control in order to be safe, Tradition Nine is excellent counsel. Applying it allows us to trust our groups to a Higher Power and trust each other with a minimum of constraints and no ability to force compliance. We find that Tradition Nine is a wonderful way to expand our faith which began in Step Two when we "Came to believe that a Power greater than ourselves could restore us to sanity." Working Tradition Nine also helps us as a group to practice Step Three by deciding to turn our will and our lives over to the care of a God of our understanding who gently guides us without dictating our actions.

Although not organized in the usual sense of the word, Al-Anon does have a service structure. Our groups delegate responsibility to trusted servants who are responsible for their minimal obligations. Members of the groups are responsible to assure rotation in service and that the trusted servants answer to the groups. Al-Anon works with a minimum of services, united in a growing worldwide fellowship.

Members Share Experience, Strength and Hope

TRADITION NINE is very meaningful to me. From personal experience I have found that a group can't survive unless it follows the Traditions. My home group is a good example.

WE HAVE SURVIVED

Gradually our group had become organized. Monthly business meetings convened a half hour before the regular meeting. Members at the business meetings made decisions without the benefit of a full group conscience. The meetings produced minutes and kept names of those who attended. Five or six newer members seemed to take control of the group. Old-timers tried to be understanding because they realized the newcomers hadn't had time to develop a strong program. Eventually the old-timers had to put aside their desire to be understanding. They had to address the real concern for our whole group.

Old-timers who wanted to give the newer members the benefit of the doubt sought the advice of someone who had a very strong program, our delegate to the WSC. After an in-depth discussion, she gave her opinion that we indeed had a problem within the group. She made several suggestions. Among the suggestions was a study of Tradition Nine. When we did this, it became clear to us that our group's rigid organization adversely affected the group as a whole. We took a group conscience and decided to change our business meetings. Instead of holding a separate business meeting, we decided to have a brief period for business during the regular meeting. That way we could take a full group conscience on business matters. The members who did not like this decision left our group and started a new one. We have survived on our own, although we miss them. We feel very strongly that the Twelve Traditions are essential to the unity of our Al-Anon Family Group.

WE ARE a fellowship, not an organization. All of the members of our fellowship are equals. Organization implies that some members have power or authority over others. In Al-Anon each member is equal and everyone serves the group as a trusted servant. One reason that rotation of duties is so important is that it gives everyone an equal opportunity for responsibility. Rotation also helps to prevent a person from taking authority for a job. In rotation, each person will do the same job differently. In a group the various members can be responsible for those things necessary to make the group function. If one person does a task too long, others can come to expect this person to do the job and take him or her for granted.

As we grow in the program, we get more involved and get into more structured parts of the program. However, no matter how deeply we become involved in the program, Tradition Two still suggests that we have no bosses, that those who serve are our trusted servants.

In any group that we attend we need to do our part. How did the room get set up? Who set out the literature and put it away? It is not good for any one person to monopolize one or more responsibilities. In service we begin to learn to delegate responsibility to others. This is important because it helps us to get over our characteristic of feeling that "only I can do everything." By allowing everyone to help set out and put away the literature, more people become familiar with it. It is important that the treasurer be permitted to give a report of the group funds. A group can become active in many ways, such as doing Public Information work, and can form committees to do these things.

A group can have an active secretary who makes all the announcements. The more people involved in each meeting, the better the meeting. A group that is busy and involved is more enthusiastic. Each person needs to know how to chair, how to find the literature, how to set up the room, how to clean up the room after the meeting, how to greet newcomers and how to perform all the other functions. Then if someone is absent the meeting doesn't fall apart. We never know when our Higher Power is going to put us in a position of responsibility.

I find that this Tradition is very helpful at home. At first I thought that things should be structured and that we always do specific jobs, but I learned that this isn't true.

I also learned that I am not in charge of determining what jobs others have. I may want my husband to be in charge of washing the dishes but he may decide to run the sweeper. I had to learn that he lives here too, and that we are equals. I can ask another person if he or she would take a certain responsibility but that doesn't mean that they must do it.

Tradition Nine helps me learn to balance responsibility, to define my own and others' responsibilities and to follow up on my part in any task.

Working Tradition Nine

Our groups, as such, ought never be organized; but we may create service boards or committees directly responsible to those they serve.

* How often does my group rotate our leadership positions? Is everyone encouraged to participate?

* Does our group have unnecessary extra rules for its servants or members?

* Do I try to control my group by organizing it? Why?

* How flexible am I? How flexible is my group? How might we encourage flexibility at our meeting without creating chaos?

* How do I resist suggestions for changes in structure? Why?

* How does my group support our service boards and committees (literature distribution center, information service, Public Information, etc.)?

* How do I support our service boards and committees? Do I donate money? Do I volunteer?

* How can I benefit from being a trusted servant?

* How have I gained any patience or humility by serving the group?

* How do I treat those who serve us? Do I appreciate them and support them or criticize and second-guess them?

* How do I acknowledge my trusted servants' need to report back to my group and support them?

* Has my group invited any district or area trusted servants to our meeting to share their experiences?

* When my service term is over, have I encouraged new servants by passing on my records and experiences? Have I ever tried to interfere with a trusted servant's way of doing things, or do I practice "Let Go and Let God"?

* Has my group discussed our role in the entire Al-Anon structure? Do we tend to think that the only thing that matters is our home group?

* What can we do to connect with the worldwide fellowship that will enhance our own recovery?

* Have I ever considered that service rotation keeps me humble?

* How am I taking on my share of responsibilities?

* How am I taking responsibility for my own actions?

* Do I speak up when others' actions are unacceptable, or am I so fearful of confrontation that I am willing to have peace at any price – even the loss of my own serenity?

* How am I putting my abilities to their best use?

* Am I taking on more that I can handle?

* Do I understand Al-Anon's service structure?

* Have I ever considered being a service sponsor?

Tradition Ten

The Al-Anon Family Groups have no opinion on outside issues; hence our name ought never be drawn into public controversy.

ALL OF Al-Anon's Traditions, including Tradition Ten, keep us unified in one purpose – helping families and friends of alcoholics. Tradition Ten specifically reminds us that, no matter what the cause, Al-Anon's name "ought never be drawn into public controversy." The reason is simple: outside issues can divert us from our primary spiritual aim. Members are always free to act as individuals in favor of their own personal causes, as long as they keep Al-Anon's name out of it.

Our fellowship could be severely damaged without our willing adherence to Tradition Ten. The spiritual principle underlying it is "Live and Let Live." Realizing how important and vital our main aim is to the millions who still suffer, we guard it by voluntarily not taking group stands on public causes, other beliefs or outside issues, no matter how worthy.

We might ask how we determine whether something is an outside issue. Al-Anon does not prepare lists of controversies to avoid. It would be impossible, for they arise daily and range from issues of national or international concern to timely local topics. If we are unsure whether or not something is an outside issue, we might apply the following questions to it: Does it fall within Al-Anon's single purpose – to help families and friends of alcoholics? Does my group, as a group, have a stake in this issue? Might discussion of this matter result in involvement in public controversy?

There are many issues and problems in our society related to alcoholism. Al-Anon takes part in healing social problems by helping people help themselves to find their own solutions and by giving them the emotional support and spiritual strengths they need to solve their problems. To do this for the largest number of people, we need to avoid taking stands on specific programs, institutions, legal remedies or religious beliefs. Working for specific outcomes on outside issues is fine for us as individuals. As Al-Anon groups, we have no opinion on them and we leave discussions of them outside the door. The best solution for one situation might be very different from the best for another. By sharing our experience, strength and hope, we demonstrate how bad situations can be made better.

When a member is in an extreme situation, we need to distinguish between helping them apply the Al-Anon principles to take care of themselves and taking a group stand on a social issue. Groups can get involved in outside issues quite innocently. A member may share an experience that outrages the group. Carried away by emotion, discussion can center on what happened rather than maintain the focus on Al-Anon principles. Asking a question such as, "How will our taking a position on this issue help families and friends of alcoholics?" may bring the group back in focus. Long-term solutions that fit the individual, as well as the strength to carry them out, come from practicing the spiritual principles of Al-Anon. Groups can encourage such members to work closely with a sponsor for assistance in finding solutions.

One reason not to get involved in societal solutions is that there are so many related causes, it would be difficult to choose among them and the choice itself could tear a group apart. Another reason for not taking a public stand, even in an extreme case, is that some of our members live with alcoholics whose behavior is different from these extremes, and some no longer live with active alcoholics. If we focused on the most startling among us, it would be possible for the others to feel alienated from the group. Alcoholism affects many people in many different ways but we all belong. Not taking stands supports inclusiveness.

On rare occasions our fellowship itself has become the center of a controversy despite our best efforts to avoid it. What is our approach if we are unfavorably spoken of in a public forum like the press? Surely we can't reach those still in need if we are being maligned.

If we have been adhering to the Traditions, we know our own house is in order. Responding to accusations can only result in drawing Al-Anon further into controversy. In these situations, we have found that Tradition Ten's guidance to avoid opinions on outside issues works best.

It may seem to some that having no opinion and not responding to provocation means that we are either doormats or some great, happy family that never quarrels. As individuals we have plenty of opinions and passions. We discuss them outside the group and we sometimes argue among ourselves over business matters within the fellowship. However, as we practice together the spiritual principle of Tradition Ten, we learn that each member can have his or her own opinion on any issue but our group, as a group, cannot. We learn to apply "Live and Let Live" in our groups.

Coming from homes affected by alcoholism, many of us have a great fear of conflict. Practicing the Traditions among ourselves helps us learn how to work through disagreements to a mutually satisfying solution as well as how to stay out of situations that are not our business. Conflict is minimized when we focus on our common problems and solutions and avoid divisive struggles over outside issues. This reinforces our primary purpose and gives us time to take care of ourselves.

Having no opinion on outside issues also means not promoting our businesses in the group or making private social plans in the meeting. What a relief it is to go to a meeting we know is exclusively for us and our recovery without worrying if we might be recruited for a good cause or solicited to buy a product.

Members are free to get involved with issues and causes that are near to their hearts – outside the rooms of Al-Anon. Al-Anon has only one purpose: to help families and friends of alcoholics. Tradition Ten keeps us focused on that primary purpose.

Members Share Experience, Strength and Hope

I HAVE opinions on lots of issues but in my recovery I try to keep the focus on Al-Anon. I do that even in sponsorship. My Al-Anon sponsor's political and religious beliefs are very different from mine but the details have nothing to do with Al-Anon. When I'm feeling upset about world events or religious matters, we discuss my feelings, reactions, insecurities and fears. It would be inappropriate to talk a lot with my sponsor about the events that triggered my inner reactions. My sponsor's job is not to discuss world affairs with me but to help me gain perspective on my inner reactions. My group deserves the same consideration. They don't need to hear me discussing my beliefs and my political convictions. It's important for me to share my inner state, however, and my willingness or resistance to using the Al-Anon tools. For example, admitting my powerlessness and taking my own inventory might lead me to a decision to practice detachment.

During a time of political upheaval in the nation where I live, I went to Al-Anon meetings where many people shared their feelings about what was going on. I happened to feel the opposite way from many of them, which made it even more painful for me to sit while they vented their outrage. I, too, had feelings about what was happening in our country but I came to Al-Anon to focus on spiritual recovery from the family disease of alcoholism. When I approached some of them after meetings, I requested that they focus on their feelings without identifying their political stance. Most were surprised and many said they were just expressing their feelings.

I began to realize that people who are upset may have a hard time expressing their feelings without exposing their political affiliations. This provided me with the opportunity to change the things that I

RESPECT
TAKES
EXTRA
CARE

could. For me that meant speaking up again and again and accepting that I would probably hear politics in Al-Anon meetings for a while because it was stirring up a lot of feelings. It was a painful period for me but I stuck it out. The recovery that comes even in painful periods is worth it. I do hope people will take extra care to respect Tradition Ten during times of public stress and upheaval.

MY SPONSOR
TAUGHT ME

WHEN SOMETHING controversial came up in my discussions with my sponsor, he asked me how I felt about it. Specifically he wanted to know what I was feeling. Did the controversy bring up feelings of vulnerability or shame? Did I feel angry or guilty or embarrassed? Did I feel hopeless or depressed? Sometimes he went through a process of elimination to help me get to the bottom of my true feelings.

The one specific controversy that always grabbed me by the heart was child abuse. In my first few years in Al-Anon, it seemed like child abuse occupied the front page of every newspaper and appeared regularly on TV. I discovered that I couldn't stand news reports about women who failed to protect their children from abusers.

My sponsor encouraged me to recognize when I was having strong feelings. Then he taught me how to explore different possibilities until I could discover what those feelings were. For some reason, when I finally put a name on my feelings I always felt better – more centered, less scattered and more sane.

My sponsor also taught me that controversy can be a trap. If I got all caught up in the details of the controversy, I tended to get lost. I lost track of the fact that this, too, might be an opportunity for me to get to know myself better. If I spent all of my energy on the controversy itself, that was my choice; but it only had to do with my Al-Anon program if my purpose was to learn more about me.

I have heard all kinds of controversial subjects referred to at Al-Anon meetings. Alcoholism itself is very controversial for many people. The fact that Al-Anon groups have no opinion on outside issues is what gives us permission to talk about our experiences. Criticism and advice-giving, however, don't belong in Al-Anon or Alateen meetings. The fact that so many of us have survived our controversial experiences is what turns our stories into expressions of strength and hope.

At various times in my life I have played three distinct roles. I have played victim, I have played villain and I have played rescuer. Because Al-Anon has no opinion on outside issues, I feel free to explore my feelings about any of the controversial subjects that have affected me, no matter what role I have played in them. I try to limit my sharing in meetings so I don't monopolize our time and I save the majority of my self-exploration for conversations with my sponsor. As long as I am using Al-Anon's tools to help make me better, I'm on the right track. When I'm using Al-Anon to try to change other people, whether they're inside or outside the program, then I need to remember my sponsor's words: "That's too bad about them – but how do you feel?"

Working Tradition Ten

The Al-Anon Family Groups have no opinion on outside issues; hence our name ought never be drawn into public controversy.

* How do I concentrate on our common bonds rather than on our differences?

* Do I remember that there is no official Al Anon opinion?

* Have I ever asked my Al-Anon group to further a cause or business venture?

* If someone does bring up what I think is an outside issue, how can I gently bring discussion back to our Al-Anon approach?

* Have I called my sponsor to air out my anger or resentment?

* How do I let myself react to emotions rather than thinking about what I want to say and how I want to say it?

* Can I find ways to say what I mean without being mean when I say it? How?

* Am I defensive because someone doesn't agree with me? How do I respond?

* Even though I have a right to my feelings and opinions, can I admit that I am sorry for letting my anger control my emotions?

* Do I ever give the impression that there is an Al-Anon opinion on a subject?

* What would Al-Anon be like without this Tradition?

* How can I use this Tradition in my personal life?

TRADITION ELEVEN defines our public relations policy, giving us guidelines for use in making the public aware of Al-Anon and attracting families and friends of alcoholics, while maintaining personal anonymity and protecting the anonymity of AA members.

From the earliest days of Al-Anon, we have sought to make recovery available to the widest possible audience through the many avenues of press, radio, television, educational and community institutions and the helping professions. We have benefited greatly from the exposure that the media has provided. Informing the public about our availability and the recovery we have to offer is an essential ingredient of carrying the Al-Anon message to families and friends of alcoholics. How we can best approach these opportunities for Twelfth Step work is addressed in Tradition Eleven.

Defining the difference between attraction and promotion can be difficult. Many members attend their first Al-Anon meeting without the knowledge of family members. They are fearful, embarrassed, unsure if they belong or if Al-Anon can help. Anonymity assures newcomers that Al-Anon meetings are a safe place.

In addition, newcomers arriving at the doors of Al-Anon can't help but notice the calmness and serenity of Al-Anon members. We are people who are coping with the effects of alcoholism by practicing the Al-Anon principles. If a newcomer feels safe and wants what we have – that's attraction.

As we begin to feel the peace and serenity in our own lives, we may become eager to share the program with others: family, friends, the public. The problem is that those who need it don't always want it. We can share our experience, strength and hope with them and be a good example of Al-Anon recovery by practicing its principles in all our affairs.

In maintaining personal anonymity at the public level, we ensure that no individual represents

Tradition Eleven

Our public relations policy is based on attraction rather than promotion; we need always maintain personal anonymity at the level of press, radio, TV and films. We need guard with special care the anonymity of all AA members.

Al-Anon. We remember that, in our fellowship of equals, we each speak for ourselves, but none of us speaks for all Al-Anon members or for Al-Anon as a whole. Equality allows the most long-term, service-oriented person among us to go to a meeting and ask for help. Equality keeps us humble enough to continue to be teachable and focus on our personal recovery. Tradition Eleven encourages us to lead by example.

We frequently hear stories of people who heard about Al-Anon here and there, over and over, before one particular circumstance finally brought them to the door. It is our job to see that those messages will be there to be heard, seen and read again and again if necessary until someone who needs us is ready to respond to them. We do this with a wide variety of Public Information services. When we as members participate in providing the information, we request personal anonymity. This not only assures that Al-Anon will not be associated with a particular person or personality, but just as importantly, it demonstrates to potential members that we are serious about protecting their anonymity should they become members. If they saw us clearly on TV and knew our names, they might well wonder just how they could avoid exposure themselves.

Celebrity endorsements are a common promotional technique and there certainly are celebrities in Al-Anon. While using their names or faces might bring a few more people to our doors, it could do far more harm than good. Al-Anon could be linked in people's minds to the particular personality, activities and fortunes of a celebrity. It could also discourage other well-known people from seeking the help we offer, for fear of being revealed. Anonymity is very important to those in the public eye, for there are few safe places a famous person can go to be themselves while wrestling with a difficult problem like alcoholism in a family member.

Anonymity is crucial to all of us. It allows us to share honestly at meetings to get the full benefits of recovery. Just how anonymous each of us wishes to be within the fellowship is a matter of personal choice. Confident that our names will not be taken outside of Al-Anon, some of us use our full names when we speak or do our service work. Some of us prefer to use a first name or even a pseudonym in meetings. The decision is up to us. However, when we go to the level of press, radio, TV or film, we are particularly careful to explain anonymity because that may be the first contact an outsider has with Al-Anon. We ask that our faces not be shown and that only our first names or a pseudonym be used. This assures the potential newcomer that Al-Anon is a safe place to go with a problem connected with alcoholism; a place where they, too, can remain anonymous.

Revealing our identities can also reveal the identities of our families and friends, possibly putting them in jeopardy. Tradition Eleven reminds us to guard with special care the anonymity of AA members. Though we have come a long way in understanding the disease of alcoholism, there is still a great deal of misconception about it for both alcoholics and their family members.

Personal anonymity and the caution against promotion have sometimes confused members into thinking they should never mention Al-Anon. Some have thought any form of public announcement was promoting. The intent of Tradition Eleven is to keep us anonymous as individuals, not to keep the Al-Anon program anonymous. We can let people know about our program without breaking our personal anonymity.

Though no one is required or expected to reveal himself or herself in any public forum, some of us do choose to use our full names in interaction with outside agencies and the media to keep accurate information flowing and to be a credible resource to them.

When we interact with the media, we are responsible for informing them about Tradition Eleven and soliciting their cooperation in maintaining our personal anonymity in published or broadcast reports. Deciding to participate in Public Information service is up to each of us. In all cases we refrain from revealing the identities of other Al-Anon and AA members.

The principle of anonymity serves us on our personal spiritual journey and also works well for those we might attract. As one member humorously expressed it, "A man noticed another man pulling a chain down the road. 'Why are you pulling that chain?' he asked. The other man replied, 'Have you ever tried to push one?'" We can lead people to Al-Anon but we cannot push them. Many of us may have heard of Al-Anon, or even attended a few meetings, before we were ready to hear the message. Perhaps prompted by the example of another's recovery, we returned when we were ready. Promoting our cause with excessive zeal in a hard sell manner is like trying to push that chain. However, each of us is an Al-Anon ambassador in everyday life when we live recovery and gently invite others to join us.

Al-Anon is not a secret society. We want people to be able to find us and feel personally safe in their anonymity. Practicing Tradition Eleven means doing all we can to make honest, humble, straightforward information about Al-Anon available to those who still suffer. We sometimes print announcements, participate in discussions in the media, write, publish and make available Conference Approved Literature (CAL) in bookstores and our own meetings, publish articles, attend health fairs, speak in classes, cooperate with the helping professionals and engage in a wide array of Public Information work. Tradition Eleven guides us to maintain Al-Anon's spiritual foundation of anonymity while attracting those who need recovery to our doors.

JUST WHEN I thought I had everything taken care of, the God of my understanding helped me experience something new. In spite of all my Al-Anon service footwork, a radio announcer broke my anonymity by citing my full name on the air. Ultimately it turned out to be an excellent lesson in letting go and letting God. No matter how much planning I did, there was always the potential for human error. In the great scheme of things, it was just another reminder of who is really in charge.

It was relatively easy to get Al-Anon members to volunteer to do the interview because we would be so anonymous on the radio. It seemed perfect. All the announcer had to do was introduce us by our first names. I met with the announcer and the two volunteers several days before. We went over all the materials in the Media Kit. I specifically covered Al-Anon's purpose, the principle of anonymity, avoiding public controversy and outside issues and the importance of keeping the interview focused on us as family members.

What I hadn't planned was another announcer informing the audience ahead of time about our upcoming interview. Although I said, "Oh, no!" when I heard my last name on the air, there was nothing I could do to stop it. I had to forgive myself and to realize how impossible it was to speak with the entire radio station staff.

As it turned out, no one called me or the radio station to say they had heard my full name. I worried that people who heard my last name would know my ex-husband was an alcoholic. I thought maybe my ex-husband would be angry at me. It crossed my mind that other Al-Anon members might think I was trying to be Mrs. Al-Anon. The real truth, however, is that some of my character defects were working overtime. Self-doubt and self-criticism filled my head. I thought it over and decided to tell my group what had happened. They were very understanding about everything. They accepted my good intentions and agreed that making arrangements with the media involved a certain amount of unpredictability.

Now when I look back on that experience, I focus on the good things that we accomplished. We informed people about Al-Anon. We shared with the radio audience how Al-Anon has helped us immensely in our daily lives. Most importantly we told them how they could find an Al-Anon meeting right here in our community.

WE READ
AND TALK
BEFORE WE
DECIDE

OUR GROUP believes that the Traditions are as important as the Steps but sometimes our well-meaning adherence carries us too far in one direction or the other. Fortunately having a variety of members to consult before we take a group conscience usually sets us right. I am always a little amazed when this happens, but it never fails to increase my faith in our program and our own good will. Two examples of this come to mind when I think about Tradition Eleven.

How do we attract the people who might be helped by Al-Anon? I remember when our group representative (GR) came to us with the idea of placing an advertisement in the personal column of our local newspaper with a phone number where they could reach Al-Anon. "No way!" we said, "Advertising is promotion!" We were quite sure we were right.

Our group representative (GR) smiled and invited us all to read the simple guidelines about public relations in our *Al-Anon/Alateen Service Manual*. Were we shocked to discover that advertising Al-Anon is fine, as long as we maintain personal anonymity and stay away from a hard sell approach.

At another meeting, we wondered why Tradition Eleven speaks of guarding AA members' anonymity with special care, rather than with equal care. Was this an example of our treating others better than we treat ourselves? At first we thought it was and we prepared a memo asking our district's groups to consider whether we might want to request that the word be changed to equal.

During the discussion, a member said he found it easy to remember to keep his own anonymity and ours, but he sometimes caught himself unconsciously saying things that might reveal that his son was a member of AA. He said that for him it did indeed require special effort to guard the anonymity of his favorite member of AA – his own son. Someone else pointed out that when she was livid with the alcoholic, she was tempted to complain to anyone who would listen about how he worked or did not work his program, but the special care sometimes stopped her in her tracks and made her return the focus to herself and what she could do to retrieve her own serenity. We thanked them and filed our unused memo with the group archives.

Working Tradition Eleven

Our public relations policy is based on attraction rather than promotion; we need always maintain personal anonymity at the level of press, radio, TV and films. We need guard with special care the anonymity of all AA members.

* What can my group do to inform people of its existence?

* What can I do as an individual?

* Am I careful to keep the confidences of other members?

* How do I support our information services?

- When I talk to the media or write about Al-Anon, do I request that my face and name be left out of the story?

- When I write about myself and use my name, do I avoid implying that I am a member of Al-Anon?

- How can I talk about my recovery without revealing the identity of the alcoholics in my life?

- How can I share Al-Anon with friends and colleagues who might be interested while keeping the spirit of anonymity alive?

- Am I attracting others to my new way of life or trying to convince them to change? How?

- Am I the man or woman I want to be? Why or why not?

- Do I ever over-promote Al-Anon, making it unattractive?

- How am I practicing the Steps and Traditions in all phases of my life?

- How am I grateful for the people in my life?

- Am I trying to force someone into living the way I think is right? How?

- What is the value of anonymity to me?

- What does it mean to me to carry the message while remaining personally anonymous at the public level?

- Is my recovery attractive to others?

THE KEY phrases in Tradition Twelve are anonymity, spiritual foundation and principles above personalities. Tied together, these words and phrases embody basic principles of our program. Whenever and wherever a potential member reaches to Al-Anon for help, we want to be assured that Al-Anon is there. It is in learning about Tradition Twelve that we learn the spiritual guidance anonymity offers, its intent and how we can humbly apply the program to our daily lives.

When we first came to Al-Anon, the fear of knowing someone in the meeting was immense. Many of us were afraid someone, possibly the alcoholic, would know of our attendance and not approve. Although many were familiar with the principle behind anonymity, few of us truly realized the power it provides to each and every one of us. As a new member, we heard these words read at the opening of a meeting: Al-Anon is an anonymous fellowship. Everything that is said here, in the group meeting and member-to-member, must be held in confidence. Only in this way can we feel free to say what is in our minds and hearts, for this is how we help one another in Al-Anon.

In meetings we also heard it said or saw the table card which states, "Whom you see here, What you hear here, When you leave here, Let it stay here." This meant that members, for many reasons, depended on anonymity for their personal recovery and safety. It is anonymity that helped many of us open up and become willing to share, to ask questions. New members learn, by listening to others, that Al-Anon provides a place where they can talk about the effects of living with the disease of alcoholism and its impact on them. We can also talk about how we are feeling about the alcoholics in our lives. In meetings members talk about their confusion, anger, concern and resentment as well as their first steps to recovery and their personal successes. We learn that, by sharing our

Tradition Twelve

Anonymity is the spiritual foundation of all our Traditions, ever reminding us to place principles above personalities.

experience, strength and hope, our sharing is safe and that no one will repeat it.

Understanding that anonymity goes beyond the identity of individual members is a portion of the spiritual foundation of Al-Anon. Anonymity embodies each Step, Tradition and Concept by stating that what we learn in Al-Anon is far more important than the member of the group who is sharing or getting help. Anonymity implies that, no matter who we are, where we live, what car we drive or what book we have read, the basic premise is humility. By practicing humility in recovery by remaining anonymous, we can be assured that Al-Anon will always be here and that its legacy is sound and maintained.

As we attend more and more meetings, we understand how the principle of anonymity works. As newcomers many of us were handed a phone list containing the names and phone numbers of the regular members. All of us are encouraged to call another Al-Anon member if we need to talk with someone. Not knowing who might hear a telephone message, we learn to leave a name, phone number and brief message, not mentioning Al-Anon, on an answering machine or when someone else answers. Conversely many a member in service has been challenged in not knowing how to contact another Al-Anon member by phone because they didn't have a last name. Others have wanted to visit a member in a hospital only to find themselves not being able to identify their good friend. We can know each other. We just don't tell others about each other. This protects the anonymity of all.

Why is anonymity the spiritual foundation of our whole program? There are many significant spiritual concepts embodied in the practice of anonymity. Among them are safety and respect for our fellow members, humility and the willingness to trust a Power greater than ourselves, acceptance of each other and the willingness to live by principles we value rather than always reacting to the personalities of those around us. Anonymity unifies our fellowship by removing individual status so we can listen to the message rather than the messenger.

As we begin to serve our groups, we are called upon to expand our understanding of anonymity to include humility and trust in a Higher Power. Our job as a trusted servant is not to govern, but to serve and to carry out our assigned tasks. We have to listen and forgo the temptation to take charge. Performing the job becomes the principle and who is doing the job – the personality – becomes unimportant. Instead we need to keep the guidance of a Power greater than ourselves always foremost in our considerations.

Our recovery and the health of our groups is assured when we place principles above personalities. Many a squabble over who is right can be avoided by focusing on principles. Even if we argue about what they mean, placing principles above personalities helps us reconnect after we have had a big discussion. Sometimes we tend to discount a message just because we don't like the messenger. Remembering to focus on principles helps us to listen to the message and not judge its content by the personality of the one delivering it. In the process many of us are surprised to discover that we even come to appreciate the messenger – we grow in tolerance. We don't have to like each other to respect each other, offer courtesy and love each other in a very special way.

It isn't always easy. Many of us are used to getting credit for what we contribute. In meetings we learn how to share our recovery with humility. We learn to surrender the satisfaction of being somebody special to the common good – we are all special. We come to know that our personal good is being served by furthering the common good.

The spiritual principle of humility through anonymity also helps us recognize that, while it is tempting to be the object of our group's admiration, it is dangerous to our own recovery. Being put above others leaves us vulnerable to envy, criticism and loneliness when we have challenges of our own and need supportive friends. It isn't worth it. The humility required to refuse to be put on a pedestal comes hard for many of us. However, we learn that when we try to elevate ourselves by forcing our will or insisting we know best, or even just by doing everything for everyone else, we reap hostility, isolation and a good deal of misery. Practicing anonymity with humility within the group protects our recovery.

The Twelfth Tradition calls upon us to integrate all the Al-Anon principles. It is worth the effort. By attending meetings, our lives and relationships measurably improve. Our understanding of the spiritual foundation that anonymity provides grows as we grow.

Members Share Experience, Strength and Hope

IT DOESN'T
MATTER

MY FAVORITE Tradition is the Twelfth. I feel that anonymity in an Al-Anon group means that we attend meetings without mentioning our professions or our status in life. A professional may sit next to someone on welfare and it doesn't matter. I feel that too many Al-Anon members have the wrong impression of what anonymity is. They seem to think it means keeping others in the group from knowing their last name.

We become members of the worldwide fellowship of Al-Anon. We strive for recovery completely unconcerned about what we do outside of Al-Anon or what other members may do. We share a common problem, alcoholism. That's the important issue. By keeping the focus on the program, no one person can ever become the voice of Al-Anon. If they have forceful personalities or prestige in the world, that doesn't matter in Al-Anon.

I THOUGHT I understood anonymity, but "principles above personalities" puzzled me for a long time. Now several years into my program, I'm grateful for all that Tradition Twelve has taught me. Because of it, I have received the gift of freedom to speak my deepest thoughts at meetings.

In my town several Al-Anon groups have members from different countries, cultures and languages. Our different life styles and beliefs do not interfere with our respect for one another. At these meetings I appreciate insights from people whose paths would never have crossed mine if all of us didn't practice Al-Anon's "principles above personalities."

Anonymity means that I respect the challenge of "principles above personalities." When I meet a colleague or an employee at their first meeting, I say to myself, "We're all growing. We are all human and deserve respect. All of us deserve a chance to grow using the Twelve Steps and the Twelve Traditions."

Working Tradition Twelve

Anonymity is the spiritual foundation of all our Traditions, ever reminding us to place principles above personalities.

* Do I practice this Tradition in all of my affairs? How?

* Am I able to listen to others with an open mind, or am I discounting them because they are not agreeing with me?

* Do I understand the spiritual foundation of my personal anonymity? My group's? My area's?

* Am I able to see the good in others or just notice their faults?

* How do I remember not to identify anyone or tell an identifiable story even if I'm speaking to a group member?

* What is the relationship between anonymity and confidentiality?

* Do I put anyone in our group on a pedestal, expecting more of them than I do of myself?

* If a well-known member of my community comes into my group, do I resist letting people know I have seen them in Al-Anon?

* How do I let Al-Anon be known without breaking anyone's anonymity?

* What does it mean to understand that it is up to each of us to decide just how anonymous we want to be?

* Do I ever use Al-Anon to promote my personal agenda? Products? Ideologies?

* Do I respect Al-Anon's trusted servants and thank them for their service?

* Is Al-Anon a secret in my community?

* How does Tradition Twelve relates to Tradition Ten? To Tradition Eleven?

* When I meet people I know from Al-Anon outside of a meeting, how can I acknowledge them while protecting their anonymity?

* How does my group inform all members about our principle of anonymity? Do we do this on a regular basis?

* How does this Tradition impact Al-Anon's primary purpose?

* What is the importance of my membership in the

Al-Anon fellowship to the worldwide fellowship?

* How has study of the Traditions improved my understanding of my role in my group?

* How has study of the Traditions improved my understanding of my group's role in our district? In our area? In worldwide Al-Anon?

* How can I apply the Traditions to my personal life? To my work life?

The Twelve Concepts

Al-Anon's Twelve Concepts of Service

1. The ultimate responsibility and authority for Al-Anon world services belongs to the Al-Anon groups.

2. The Al-Anon Family Groups have delegated complete administrative and operational authority to their Conference and its service arms.

3. The Right of Decision makes effective leadership possible.

4. Participation is the key to harmony.

5. The Rights of Appeal and Petition protect minorities and assure that they be heard.

6. The Conference acknowledges the primary administrative responsibility of the trustees.

7. The trustees have legal rights while the rights of the Conference are traditional.

8. The Board of Trustees delegates full authority for routine management of the Al-Anon Headquarters to its executive committees.

9. Good personal leadership at all service levels is a necessity. In the field of world service the Board of Trustees assumes the primary leadership.

10. Service responsibility is balanced by carefully defined service authority and double-headed management is avoided.

11. The World Service Office is composed of standing committees, executives and staff members.

12. The spiritual foundation for Al-Anon's world services is contained in the General Warranties of the Conference, Article 12 of the Charter.

The General Warranties

IN ALL its proceedings the World Service Conference of Al-Anon shall observe the spirit of the Traditions:

1. that only sufficient operating funds, including an ample reserve, be its prudent financial principle;

2. that no Conference member shall be placed in unqualified authority over other members;

3. that all decisions be reached by discussion, vote and, whenever possible, by unanimity;

4. that no Conference action ever be personally punitive or an incitement to public controversy;

5. that though the Conference serves Al-Anon, it shall never perform any act of government; and that, like the fellowship of Al-Anon Family Groups which it serves, it shall always remain democratic in thought and action.

Introduction to the Twelve Concepts

AL-ANON's best kept secret for many years is no longer a secret. Many members of our fellowship have studied and now cherish the wisdom found in our third legacy. The powerful words contained in these Concepts were written by our co-founder Lois W., with the assistance of the 1968-70 World Service Conference (WSC) members. In 1984, the Conference voted that the Twelve Concepts be given the same stature as the Twelve Steps and Traditions, thus completing Al-Anon's three legacies.

Unlike the Twelve Steps and Twelve Traditions which are direct adaptations of AA's Twelve Steps and Traditions, Al-Anon's Twelve Concepts were first drafted by a committee, chaired by Lois, using the AA Twelve Concepts as a resource. The version we value today is the fourth and final draft.

The Twelve Steps provide Al-Anon members with spiritual guidance for personal recovery. The Twelve Traditions provide direction for group unity. The Twelve Concepts provide guidance in serving each other in our business matters. The Concepts were first presented in a booklet titled *Al-Anon's Twelve Concepts of Service* and are now included in the *Al-Anon/Alateen Service Manual.* Additionally, "The Concepts show how Twelfth Step work can be done on a broad scale; how members of a World Service Office can relate to each other and to the groups to spread Al-Anon's message across the world; and how a conference of delegates from all parts of the continent can supervise such a world service, so it will always conform to the Traditions." (*Al-Anon/Alateen Service Manual*).

The Concepts of Service show how Al-Anon members can apply the spiritual principles of our program to working relationships in our service structure. Whenever we participate, we expand our own recovery. We are individuals and have different ideas about solutions to our common problems. Sharing ideas, exploring alternatives, seeking spiritual guidance and using the Concepts helps us reach decisions we all can live with. The Concepts show us practical, healthy ways to arrive at decisions that involve others. We become more comfortable with the process of deciding and able to accept the effects of the decisions. Many Al-Anon members have also found that the Concepts are applicable to home and work situations.

Ultimate responsibility, delegated authority, leadership, participation, acknowledgment, rights, delegation, balance, and spirituality are all key principles found in the Concepts. They bring these principles down to practical terms – actions we can take in our everyday lives, in all of our affairs, One Day at a Time.

"AL-ANON has grown so fast and so far, it takes my breath away! The more it grows, the greater the contrast between the early days and now." These words were written by Al-Anon's co-founder Lois W. in 1979. Looking back at the early days of our fellowship provides some background that will help us to understand and to apply Concept One today.

In the early days of AA, numerous family groups developed around the United States through the efforts of AA members' wives. In 1951, the AA office turned the names of 87 of these groups over to Lois and her Al-Anon co-founder, Anne B., who began the project of registering them. Al-Anon's first office, the Clearing House, was soon opened with 50 registered groups. By polling the groups, the name, purpose and method of support for the fellowship were determined. Modified versions of AA's Twelve Steps and Twelve Traditions were also adopted by this method.

This procedure worked well in the early years when the quantity of groups was small and manageable. By 1960, there were more than 1500 groups (in 1997, there are nearly 30,000), and many did not respond to polls. Our founders realized keeping close connection with the groups was essential to our fellowship. Something needed to be done to see that the group conscience accurately reflected our membership and was available to all those who served us. In 1961, the Al-Anon World Service Conference (WSC) was begun on a trial basis. In 1963, it became a permanent annual feature of Al-Anon's. With participation from 67 area delegates, 18 trustees, members of the Executive Committee and staff, it is the largest group conscience of our fellowship.

Al-Anon's structure is often described as an upside-down triangle, with the Al-Anon groups at the top. Members volunteer service and act as representatives from the groups to our districts and areas and from the areas to the WSC. At the narrow point at the bottom of the triangle are our trustees and staff at the

Concept One

The ultimate responsibility and authority for Al-Anon world services belongs to the Al-Anon groups.

World Service Office (WSO). Many people marvel that this structure – a volunteer organization with a few paid workers – could work at all.

We do not depend solely on our own wisdom. Tradition Two reminds us, "For our group purpose there is but one authority – a loving God as He may express Himself in our group conscience. Our leaders are but trusted servants; they do not govern." Our leaders are there to serve us. In our groups a Higher Power guides our group conscience. Concept One tells us that this group conscience has the ultimate authority for Al-Anon world services. Thus we follow the guidance of a Higher Power at every level of Al-Anon. In offering guidance to our service arms, our groups have ultimate responsibility.

What does "Al-Anon world services" mean? These are the services provided to groups all over the world by the Al-Anon Family Group Headquarters WSO, and by general service offices (GSOs) outside the United States and Canada. Services are channeled through the area world service committees (AWSCs) and the general service committees in other countries. Thus our "links of service": Group representatives (GRs) represent their groups at district meetings and area assemblies; district representatives (DRs) represent the groups in their districts at AWSC meetings; area delegates represent the groups in their assembly areas at the annual WSC.

No organization can survive without clear definitions of responsibility and authority to decide policies and procedures and to act on decisions once they are made. Ultimately the primary unit of Al-Anon – the group – is responsible for becoming informed, discussing the matters at hand and relaying its decisions through its representatives. An informed group conscience is essential. As members of a group, we participate by becoming informed ourselves, listening to others and adding our voice and vote to the matters being considered. Together the groups, through their representatives, decide matters that affect their district, area and the fellowship as a whole. Together the groups share responsibility for the survival of Al-Anon. They contribute their experience, strength and hope as well as their time, effort and money.

Concept One is about ultimate responsibility and authority – the right to have the final say. There are two types of authority and responsibility explained in the Concepts – ultimate and delegated. The other eleven Concepts address delegated responsibility and authority. The groups exercise their ultimate authority by wisely electing people to speak for them, keeping these representatives informed through the group conscience, and then trusting them to do their jobs. In Al-Anon ultimate responsibility is exercised with loving care and wisdom.

Members Share Experience, Strength and Hope

RECENTLY I visited an Al-Anon group while on vacation. This group was reviewing the results of their written group inventory. One member shared that some things were going on in the meeting that he didn't like. He kept looking around for the person in charge so he could complain to the authorities, but there didn't seem to be such a person. He eventually figured out that if he had a problem, it was his own responsibility to explain his opinion to the group. When he did this, the group discussed the issue and resolved it in a way he couldn't have imagined, and he could accept the decision. This experience illustrated to me how many of us find the God of our understanding: through discussion among ourselves, by listening to others, by making a decision only after the discussion is complete and by accepting the group's informed decision.

This Concept reminds me that it is the responsibility of my group to let the public know where and

WHERE THE
RESPONSIBILITY
LIES

when we meet. We can place information in the local newspaper or allocate funds to list a local phone number in the phone book. We can provide speakers at various events perhaps, at a health fair or at school health classes. We can provide literature to our employers' human resources departments or speak to our physicians about the recovery we receive from Al-Anon.

The groups are responsible to Al-Anon as a whole and have the ultimate authority for Al-Anon's world service. How my group attracts the newcomer, how it welcomes the newcomer and acts to keep the newcomer coming back are very important factors in the growth of Al-Anon as a whole, as well as the growth of my group. Without the constant infusion of newcomers, the program can become stale and repetitious. This may cause regular members to abandon the group and possibly Al-Anon altogether.

Consider the group that ignores the newcomer who walks in the door. Would I have come back if no one welcomed me? As a newcomer I prefer not to be the focus of the meeting. But I can say that the welcome I received as I entered helped me to realize the effect that alcoholism had on my own life.

Where is the middle ground? A group that establishes a policy on how to greet a newcomer, how not to let the focus of the meeting be on answering all the newcomer's questions as though this is the person's only contact with Al-Anon, is one that will gain the most serenity. When the group reaches out, the members find help for themselves, even if the newcomer does not return.

Concept One shows me where my responsibility is. It is mine to take. No intergroup, information service, district, area or WSO suggestion or directive can take the place of my responsibility as a member of my group or of the authority of my group in relationship to its conduct.

I LOVE Al-Anon, owe my life and health to Al-Anon and want it to be there for those still suffering. Therefore, I selfishly serve Al-Anon. My service is important, but I could never do all that needs to be done to protect and assure Al-Anon's continued availability. I can't write the books alone. I can't answer all the calls. I can't send out all the information needed. But I can take responsibility for the pages I can write, the calls I can take and the literature and information I can pass on. I am also responsible and have the authority to join with others in my small little corner of the world to see that jobs are done by those able to do that.

Personally, I interpret this Concept as an additional tool for my recovery. It reaffirms that I am responsible for my life. I can't expect others to do for me what I can do for myself, nor do I assume responsibility for them. I have responsibility for my life and can choose when to welcome others into it. We share together, work together and grow individually.

Working Concept One

The ultimate responsibility and authority for Al-Anon world services belongs to the Al-Anon groups.

* What does Al-Anon world service do for us?

* Does my group take responsibility for supporting Al-Anon world services? In what ways?

* Do we support our district? Area? WSO?

* Do we participate in district and assembly meetings? How?

* How do we keep ourselves informed?

* Does information from the delegate get passed on to the district representative? Group representative? Group?

* Do I trust in the process?

* How well do I accept decisions of my district? My area assembly? The World Service Conference?

* Do we hold regular business meetings?

* Do we welcome newcomers?

* For what part of my life am I ultimately responsible? What responsibilities might I share or delegate?

* How do I contribute to the group conscience?

* Referring to Tradition Two and Concept One, can I accept and support the group conscience when I don't agree with the outcome?

* Do I express my gratitude for service work?

IT IS with Concept Two that we begin to understand the immensity of the worldwide fellowship of Al-Anon and how such an organization can operate effectively. Each Al-Anon Family Group meets at a set time and location fulfilling our primary purpose: to help families and friends of alcoholics. At these meetings Al-Anon Conference Approved Literature (CAL) is available, and the common language of love is spoken. How can each group be so similar and yet be in so many different places? It is in Concept Two that we learn how each group has a say in a common experience through its participation in the process of the World Service Conference (WSC) and the many service activities that support it.

Within each Al-Anon Family Group, members elect a single person, a group representative (GR), to represent them for a three-year term at district and area Al-Anon business meetings. A district contains groups in a designated geographic area. Every three years the GRs select a district representative (DR) to lead district meetings and represent their district at area business meetings. Throughout the United States and Canada each area is autonomous in how they structure their districts.

A number of districts make-up an area. As of 1997, there are 67 areas in the United States and Canada. (most areas are an entire state or province, some have divided into two because of the number of groups.) Every three years each area elects a delegate from the eligible members to represent their groups at the World Service Conference. Within the United States and Canada, the areas are grouped into regions, which select a regional trustee candidate. As of 1997, there are nine regions.

Additionally, the members of the Board elect trustees-at-large who, along with the regional trustees, attend the WSC and quarterly Board meetings. All of these trusted servants: delegates, regional trustees and trustees-at-large, attend the annual WSC (for a

Concept Two

The Al-Anon Family Groups have delegated complete administrative and operational authority to their Conference and its service arms.

complete explanation of Al-Anon's service structure, please refer to the *Al-Anon/Alateen Service Manual*).

The World Service Conference members, which also include designated WSO staff, volunteer committee chairpersons (Al-Anon members) and Executive Committee members (see Concept Eight), meet to make decisions that affect the fellowship as a whole. This worldwide group conscience helps make the administrative and operational decisions needed for Al-Anon to function. Every voting member of the World Service Conference is first and foremost an Al-Anon member. Each Conference member is working a program of personal recovery combined with his or her service or professional expertise. The groups, individually and collectively, trust the World Service Conference members to speak for them and rely on all the service arms to faithfully carry out the Conference's decisions.

What are service arms? The World Service Conference structure explained above details a number of service arms including districts, areas and regions. Other service arms include the committees that exist within the WSC, literature distribution centers, Al-Anon information services/intergroups and other committees in the groups, districts, and areas.

An example of the links among the service arms is the literature process. The idea or need for a new brochure or booklet goes through the service structure to the Literature Committee. After consideration and referral to the World Service Conference, conceptual approval may be given and the literature developed. Such new literature may help potential members find Al-Anon with the help of the outreach activities generated by a Public Information committee. Through the service activities of Public Information Coordinators or Al-Anon information service volunteers, new members who pick up that new brochure or booklet may be attracted to the message of hope we offer. Our service arms reach out worldwide to lovingly welcome

us into our fellowship of families and friends of alcoholics.

In our groups, service authority is delegated to our
groups' trusted servants. Encouraging Al-Anon members to get involved in Al-Anon service can be done
with love and enthusiasm. This is the time to implement our program of attraction in a new way. We can
first encourage them and include them in small tasks.
We can set the example by being a trusted servant
ourselves. It is through the energy of trusted servants
who share the joy of service and their service experience, strength and hope that newer members can find
loving service sponsors.

A service sponsor is someone who has had experience in service work and can help us understand the
Twelve Concepts of Service, the links of the service
arms and the *Al-Anon/Alateen Service Manual*. Many
find that their recovery sponsor serves as a service
sponsor, while others seek the guidance of another
member for their service work. In service the principle of giving back that which you have been given
comes to life. Many a service sponsor has been known
to say as they make plans to attend a district or area
function, "Get in the car and come with us to see how
Al-Anon works." As we expand our experiences in
service we begin to see the bigger picture. We understand that decisions do have to be made. We learn
about the interlinked work done by our World Service Office, the World Service Conference, our area
assembly, districts and group business meetings.

Most service sponsors say that once we become
comfortable, it is time to move on to the next position or to move over and let someone else experience
the joys we have had in service. By delegating authority, no one volunteer becomes overly burdened or
responsible. Elected members in areas, districts or
groups and elected members of the Conference each
serve three year terms. (Trustees may serve two three-
year terms). Democratic in thought and action, the

Conference assures us that Al-Anon's work will continue. Humbly, each outgoing trusted servant relies on the groups to find the next servant to follow in his or her footsteps, thus assuring us that rotation of service continues.

Members Share Experience, Strength and Hope

ANSWERS
DO NOT
COME FROM
THE TOP

IT IS the responsibility of the Al-Anon groups to provide for Al-Anon's world services, but there are certain world services that cannot be provided by an individual group. Those services include the development of printed literature, Al-Anon films, videos and advertising material, as well as attendance at national and regional seminars, conventions and other forums where the public learns about the disease of alcoholism.

The early Al-Anon groups voted to entrust some functions to a Conference of delegates, trustees and their service arms, especially the World Service Office (WSO).

The key here is to recognize that the responsibility of the WSO is to carry out the directives of the Conference. Concept Two does not give the WSO the responsibility to solve all the groups' problems nor do the groups have to refer all questions to the WSO. While all decisions of importance must be decided through thorough discussion of the Steps, Traditions and Concepts, there is no need to go to the top for every problem that occurs. The World Service Conference (WSC) and the WSO have only been delegated administrative responsibility for the management of Al-Anon's services. Answers to questions come from each of us as we discuss, research and study the problem we have and look for solutions at the group level.

Many times groups will ask members experienced in service at the district or area level for their opinions. With this experience, the servants will often suggest avenues of discussion instead of providing an answer.

Another application of this Concept is from the view of the trusted servant who is performing administrative roles. Many of us have an opinion as to what the trusted servant should do, perhaps because we have done it ourselves. On the other hand, the trusted servant may be fearful of doing the job, because he or she thinks all the decisions need to be made by the group.

For example, since my group had previously decided that rent, coffee, refreshments and donations to our intergroup, district, area and the WSO were acceptable expenses, I felt it was my obligation as group treasurer to pay these expenses as they occurred. I observed that the treasurer of another group continually asked his group if it was okay to pay these same expenses. My understanding of Concept Two is that, once the group delegates the function of paying expenses to the treasurer, then it becomes the treasurer's responsibility to do so. Of course a good treasurer also makes periodic reports of both income and expenses. In this way, the members of the group have some knowledge and understanding of what happens to their donated funds.

This principle is at work at the WSO. It is the function of the WSC to decide on policy, but once the policy has been decided, then it is the responsibility of the office employees to implement it. The members in a group are the policy makers for that group, the group representatives in my area are the policy makers for my area, and the Conference members, which include delegates, trustees and a few WSO staff, are the policy makers for worldwide Al-Anon. The group officers, the area officers and the WSO staff are responsible for implementing their respective policies.

CONCEPT TWO taught me reliance. Even though the individual group is the heart of Al-Anon, as we saw in Concept One, the individual group cannot do many things. How does a new edition of *One Day at a Time in Al-Anon* get published? Who produces a television spot that can be shown by our local stations? Who publishes our *Blueprint for Progress* inventory booklet? Who revises the pamphlets? In our district, who writes and publishes the newsletters? In our area, who makes decisions about when and where our next convention or assembly will be held? These are all very important; they are things our individual groups cannot do. Therefore we have delegated to others not only the authority but also the responsibility to do these things. Each group realizes that it has to rely on others to get this work done.

In my personal life, I have finally realized that I cannot do everything; indeed I do not even want to. Therefore I must learn to rely on other people. At one time I did not want to ask anybody to do anything. I tried to do everything that pertained to my own being and welfare. I thought this was recovery, but it was actually still a desperate attempt to control my life, because I didn't believe I could rely on anyone else. I had to learn to feel the loneliness and difficulty of this attitude deep within my heart until, at last, I could say, "Yes! Please do this for me. I cannot."

I began by relying on my Higher Power and I also learned to ask people for help. I had to sort out my own responsibilities from the things I could not possibly do alone, and then I had to rely on others to do those things. I finally understood that we are meant to be interdependent. In many things I am quite independent, but in some things I am actually dependent. Knowing that I can rely on other people has brought me great relief.

In order to rely on others, I had to practice humility and willingly give up some tasks. More difficult, in order to elicit another's willingness to help I had to give up insisting that my way was the only way a task could be done. I realize more than ever that I am not God, that tasks will get done and that I don't have to do them all myself. When I have done what I can, I am now able to say to another, "I need you. Will you help me?" Life has become much richer since I have learned the concept of reliance and trust in my fellow human beings.

Working Concept Two

The Al-Anon Family Groups have delegated complete administrative and operational authority to their Conference and its service arms.

* How does my group encourage newer members to become involved in service?

* Do I attend an Al-Anon meeting that I call my home group?

* Does my group hold business meetings?

* Does my group have a group representative? Does that trusted servant attend district meetings? Area meetings?

* Does my group participate in decisions made at area assemblies? Do we know who our trusted servants are? Have we asked one of our trusted servants to attend our meetings?

* Have I ever attended our area's delegate report after the World Service Conference (WSC)?

* Has our group ever sent our delegate a loving card of support when he/she attends the WSC each year?

* When our group gets a copy of the annual Conference Summary, do we read and/or discuss it?

* Do I have a service sponsor? Do I know someone I can ask?

* What service characteristics do I want that others have?

* Am I willing to be a service sponsor?

* Do I thank our trusted servant for representing us at the district and area business meetings?

* Do I understand the function of some of the many service arms?

* Does my area invite our regional trustee to attend our assembly on a regular basis?

* Why is it important to delegate both responsibility and authority in general? In Al-Anon?

* Am I able to share responsibility? What responsibility? Am I willing to offer my assistance to others?

* When do I rely on others? Can I ask for help?

* What responsibilities in my life could I delegate to someone else?

* Whom can I trust to be reliable?

* Am I reliable and trustworthy? In what ways?

* How willing am I to work with others and to consider their ideas? How often do I trust the knowledge and experience of another person? Do I support and encourage others?

* For what am I responsible?

* How willing am I to try something new?

IN OUR service structure, the Right of Decision belongs to the trusted servants at every level of leadership – from the individual groups, districts, Al-Anon information services (AISs), intergroups, literature distribution centers (LDCs), and area assemblies, to the World Service Conference (WSC), trustees and WSO. Without the freedom to decide when and how to proceed, nothing could be done; everything, no matter how great or trivial it might be, would have to be referred to the groups. Our trustees, employees and delegates would not be trusted servants, but merely messengers, continually soliciting the input of thousands of groups.

For all levels of Al-Anon service, from the group to the Conference, the authority and ability to make decisions for the good of Al-Anon as a whole is found in Concept Three. Decision-making authority is important for our leaders to be able to serve us effectively. At each level of service, we remember that Tradition Two refers to trusted servants who do not govern. We trust our group leaders to decide how to handle group affairs and when to bring an issue to the whole group for its consideration. We trust our Conference to decide which matters to dispose of and which to refer to the groups. We trust our trustees to know how to direct our World Service Office (WSO) and when to consult with the Conference. We trust our staff members at the WSO to do their jobs and to know when to ask for guidance. This leadership empowerment makes an efficient business, Al-Anon Family Group Headquarters, Inc., possible within our unique structure.

When given a new responsibility in Al-Anon, many members express joy at being asked, are humbled by the responsibility and learn a new sense of trust. When we choose leaders, we trust them to serve in our best interest and in the interest of the group. We choose our leaders because they are knowledgeable, responsible and able to lead and we urge

Concept Three

The Right of Decision makes effective leadership possible.

them to put those traits into action as they serve. We also trust that, when provided with new information, they will act in a responsible way, changing their opinion or vote if necessary. This makes effective leadership possible.

Sharing the decision-making power is also an important part of Concept Three. When matters of great importance need to be decided, it is wise to consult others as well as Al-Anon literature to get the best possible solutions on the table before a final decision is reached. Many a service sponsor has said that, with research and prayer, almost all of the answers are already in our literature and are more than likely found in the wisdom of our *Al-Anon/Alateen Service Manual* – we just have to look. The leadership of these trusted servants is never more apparent than when they seek the counsel of others, research previous similar decisions, delay or postpone decisions and seek spiritual guidance.

Even carefully drawn-up charters and bylaws such as Al-Anon's cannot anticipate everything that will come up in the day-to-day operations of a large fellowship. Similarly, in our personal lives, it would be restrictive to have to operate our families and work situations by a book of detailed instructions. Where would be the room for changing our minds or allowing for new information that becomes available? Where would be the possibility of creativity in changing circumstances? When we grant our trusted servants the Right of Decision, we put our faith in a Power greater than ourselves and trust in the integrity of others. At the Conference or area meeting, at the committee meeting at work or in planning a family holiday, we learn to develop guidelines, offer our best ideas for consideration and trust each other to do the best we can. With dignity and confidence, we are more likely to rise to the occasion, be willing to lead and together create workable solutions for whatever task is at hand.

In our own lives, the Right of Decision means we have the right to proceed in the best way we know and to ask for help when it is needed. It also means that, when we delegate responsibility for some task, we might set general guidelines, but we allow the person doing it to decide on the details. We don't impose our constant oversight or our suggestions without being asked. Our trust and confidence support that person's competence, autonomy and personal dignity.

Most of us can easily recognize the usefulness of granting the Right of Decision to others when we consider how we would feel if we were asked to do a job and then were closely supervised and criticized as we went about trying to do it. For example, many a parent has worked with a child trying to teach him or her how to tie shoelaces for the first time. The child wants to do it, but often makes mistakes. In the interest of time, it is difficult for a parent not to want to show the child how to do it one more time. By allowing the child to struggle and hopefully do it on his or her own, the child feels a sense of success, independence and self-worth. A typical child will show the product of his or her success to the other parent or a sibling. This scenario is repeated throughout our growing-up years and in our employment. Concept Three shows us how to be both willing employees and effective employers. Is this not letting go and letting God? Is this not trust? Is this not effective leadership?

As leaders we are responsible for asking for help when it is needed. Similarly with all other trusted servants, we give them the dignity to make informed decisions, the power to change the decision of the group with new information and the trust that they will do the job we have asked them to do. Except for the paid workers at the World Service Office or at Al-Anon information service/literature distribution center offices, most trusted servants are volunteers. These entrusted servants gain confidence, set examples and, more often than not, are ready to take on new leadership roles when asked. In Concept Three, the Right of Decision demonstrates our active faith in our leadership and its knowledge in making the decisions which are right for Al-Anon worldwide.

Members Share Experience, Strength and Hope

I GREW up in an alcoholic home with many strict rules. The rules did not flex, were always understood and enforced with quick and sure consequences for infractions. Mother was the ultimate authority and chief enforcer. There were no allowances for discussion or appeal.

This Concept has helped me to understand my own attitudes and where I got them. Though instructions and directions at home told me to think for myself, I was not allowed to do so.

I can trace a good number of my character defects and warped self-worth to my experiences in a system where I was not trusted. It bred in me the demoralization referred to in the discussion of this Concept found in our *Al-Anon/Alateen Service Manual.* I did not know that my submitting and smoldering, and eventually my hateful rebellion toward my mom, stemmed from not having any rights of decision in my family. How grateful I am that my service in Al-Anon and my thirst for learning about it and how it works led me to this personal revelation.

Bless her, Mother still considers herself and conducts herself as our family's ultimate authority. A further bonus was mine (after I finally let go of a strong need to have Mother understand me) when she instigated a real sharing recently. Mother asked me why I supposed she didn't allow me to do thus and so when I was a kid. At 50 years old I felt scared! I instantly saw that door open for taking her inventory and laying my resentments at her feet. I knew better than to harm this person with all that. God gave me the strength and courage and the simple response, "Well Mother, I've always felt you didn't trust me." We had our first real talk on an equal and adult level.

Who would have guessed? Doing the personal footwork to serve and carry the message of Al-Anon gave me the dignity, freedom and maturity to be honest, real, loving and even compassionate with the one person I resented the most.

As ALTERNATE district representative (DR), I became the DR when our DR moved to another state just six months after our elections. I had planned on spending three years learning the jobs of alternate DR and DR, but that was not the way it was going to happen.

All went well for a few months until a group representative (GR) at one of our district meetings challenged everything that came up for a group conscience by saying that it should be taken back to the groups. It seemed awkward to take everything back to the groups. After all, they did elect us for the task of getting work done.

I left the meeting angry and ready to throw in the towel. My Higher Power was not going to let me off the hook so easily. When I arrived home, my phone was ringing. It was a longtime Al-Anon member calling about another matter. I told him what had happened at the district meeting and how discouraged I was. He encouraged me not to quit, but to do a group inventory or to hold a meeting on how to have a district meeting. I liked the last idea best. But did I know how to have a district meeting?

I thought maybe the *Al-Anon/Alateen Service Manual* could help. All the way home, the words trusted servant and ultimate authority ran through my head. I found trusted servant mentioned in the Second Tradition, but Concept Three seemed to explain it more fully: "...it should be traditional for all world service boards, committees, and executives to decide which matters they may properly dispose of

WE ALL
LEARNED
TO READ
AND USE
OUR
SERVICE
MANUAL

and upon which they will report, consult, or ask specific directions. Our world servants should be trusted with these discretions, otherwise no effective leadership is possible…. Nevertheless, the 'instructed' delegate who cannot act according to his own conscience…would not be a 'trusted servant' at all but a messenger."

The next day I called all the GRs and asked them to please read Concept Three in the Service Manual before the next district meeting. Needless to say, things went much better after that, and we all learned to read and use our Service Manual.

A LOVING
GOD AS HE
MAY EXPRESS
HIMSELF

THERE IS always a debate within Al-Anon about how our members and elected leaders should vote at Al-Anon business meetings. There are two basic Al-Anon principles at work in this debate.

By studying Tradition Two and Concept Three together, I have come to understand the balance that has been built into our program. Tradition Two reminds me that, as a leader, I must be willing to listen to the thoughts of the members rather than to impose my will on the group. On the other hand, Concept Three reminds the group to trust the leader to participate and vote rather than to force the representative to return to the group for voting permissions.

In summary, it appears that there needs to be trust all around. I must trust that the group has the responsibility to voice its collective opinion. The group must trust its leaders to exercise good judgment at Al-Anon business meetings. As stated in Concept Three, "We trust God, we trust Al-Anon and we trust one another."

The Right of Decision makes effective leadership possible.

* Do I ever ask someone to do a task and then try to direct the details of how it should be done? If so, how can I change this pattern?

* What would give me confidence to decide when to take charge of a job and when to consult with those who might be affected?

* In what ways am I willing to be responsible for the outcome of my decisions?

* Do we, as a group, trust our trusted servants?

* What do we need to do to help our trusted servants?

* Have I shared with my group the process I used as a trusted servant in making an informed decision?

* Do I use the *Al-Anon/Alateen Service Manual* as a tool to make my decision? My service sponsor? Those who have served before me?

* What leadership qualities do our leaders possess that I aspire to have?

* Can I make a decision and be comfortable with it? If not, why not?

Concept

Four

*Participation
is the key to
harmony.*

THE PRINCIPLE of participation is applicable at all levels of our service structure. We know that the groups have the ultimate authority in Al-Anon (Concept One), but the groups delegate responsibility to the Conference and its service arms (Concept Two). Our leaders are but trusted servants (Tradition Two) and have the Right of Decision (Concept Three). With the principle of participation, all of these seemingly contradictory ideas work together. When we take part in a decision, we feel that we are a part of the group and can support the decision it has made. Because we have contributed to the group, we feel included, heard and valued. Participation makes us a part of the group rather than apart from it. Belonging is a deep spiritual need. The harmony created by our active, willing participation encourages others to participate.

Assigning the authority to one group and the responsibility to another group could seriously handicap harmony and efficiency. Al-Anon's Concepts provide specifically for participation among all levels of the service structure. All of the various groups involved in world service – trustees, Executive Committee, World Service Office (WSO) staff and the delegates from each area – have voice and vote at the annual World Service Conference (WSC), which is the broadest group conscience in Al-Anon. This way those who make the policies and those charged with carrying them out on a day-to-day basis meet and make decisions together.

Some members question whether it is wise to allow our service workers and trustees to vote on matters concerning their own activities. Those members suggest it might be better if other Conference members made the decisions, let our paid and volunteer staff carry them out and examined the results. Our *Al-Anon/Alateen Service Manual* explains why including trustees, Executive Committee and staff in the decision-making process works better for us than a more traditional corporate way of doing business.

The current activities of the WSO staff and volunteers are a very small part of the World Service Conference agenda. Most of the job of the Conference is to plan policy and action for the future and to create guidelines for the service work still to be accomplished. Our service workers have intimate familiarity, experience and knowledge of many matters precisely because they deal with these issues on a daily basis. They can help to troubleshoot plans or give valuable, practical insights into ideas being discussed. Thus their voice and vote are an important contribution to Conference decisions. In the same way, an employee of an Al-Anon information service (AIS) office might serve on the AIS steering committee or board.

The concern is sometimes raised that the combined votes of trustees and service workers could overrule delegates' votes and thus decide questions that might be closely debated. The World Service Conference is structured so that there is always at least a two-thirds majority of delegates to WSO members when voting occurs. This voting structure assures participation from all service arms and that the delegates, representing the groups, will always be able to express the conscience of the groups (Concept One).

The Conference meets annually; the Board of Trustees meets quarterly. Month-to-month oversight of the WSO is delegated to the Executive Committee. The Board is mindful of the principle of participation when appointing members to positions on this committee. Though conceivably the Board could appoint its own members to all the positions, thereby monopolizing decision-making, it does not do so because that would lessen participation and contribute to disharmony. Experience shows us that work at every level of service is best accomplished by ensuring wide participation.

In our groups we participate in group conscience

decisions. Our group will be harmonious if our group conscience is an informed one, with many members participating. Our groups participate in district, area and world service decisions through elected representatives. We delegate authority to these members and, because we are a part of the process, trust that they will fulfill their duties in our groups' best interest and will come to us if they need more direction.

In Al-Anon, working together harmoniously requires that we have respect for one another. This is not the forced respect we might have given an authority figure who had power over us. We respect each other as we ourselves want to be respected – as equals and partners in a spiritual enterprise.

Respecting each other and inviting participation works in our families and other relationships as well. When we fully participate and invite others to do so, we are practicing the Golden Rule of treating others as we want them to treat us. We act as caring and understanding adults and partners. As we invite others to do the same, the likelihood of them being responsible, willing participants increases.

We might think of it as if we were playing the instruments in an orchestra. There is a conductor whom we willingly follow in order to coordinate our music. Each of us has a different instrument and plays a different set of notes. All participants know that in order to make music, rather than noise, following the conductor's leadership is necessary. Similarly, in Al-Anon each trusted servant has a job to fulfill and accepts guidance when it is appropriate.

There are two sides to participation – giving of ourselves and including others. We give of ourselves, our opinions and our time, we become participants. Those in leadership positions include others by consulting members for discussion before taking action. Full participation leads to harmony because there is less opposition and alienation when all of us have a chance to contribute our voice and our vote.

Respect for ourselves and others, combined with full participation, help us to serve Al-Anon as trusted servants. We come to realize we really are being trusted, not only to do the work, but to decide what work is important and how to go about doing it. As each service body and the membership at large practice the principle of participation, our deep desire to belong is satisfied in a fellowship of caring equals. We are spiritually nourished when we participate.

Members Share Experience, Strength and Hope

Lois W., Al-Anon's co-founder, said, "Anyone can start something, but it takes many people to keep it going." To me that's the essence of Concept Four. I began my Al-Anon recovery as a desperately sick, suicidal person and was truly grateful to the members who were at the meetings and shared with me. Slowly I became a little more sane and I heard at meetings words like group representative, district meeting, and delegate. As members shared their personal recovery with me, they also shared their service recovery with me. It didn't take long for me to see that the members who participated within the group, district and area seemed to have a little extra spiritual strength and serenity. I discovered it's really true that in order to keep it, we have to give it away. It amazes me that such a diverse group of people can gather, share, disagree, agree and reason things out all for the common good of the Al-Anon fellowship.

Over the years, I've participated in Al-Anon in many ways. I don't think one role is more important than any other. The member who makes sure the meeting room is unlocked and set up is just as important as the area delegate. We are a fellowship of equals.

But we do have to continue to participate in order to continue to grow. I currently serve as district repre-

OUR LEG
WORK IS
PARTICIPA-
TION

sentative and area literature coordinator. I never meant to serve two positions at once, but when assembly asked me to serve at the area level, I knew my Higher Power must have something in store for me. In the years since I agreed, my mother has had a breast removed due to cancer, my daughter left home to marry, my son branched out in what I consider scary directions and my husband relapsed after more than 12 years of sobriety. It's been an eventful year. Service work has always helped me keep the focus on myself, so I'm grateful God gave me the opportunity to participate in service at the area level. The district and area have brought new Al-Anon friends into my life. They've shared their personal recovery as well as their service recovery with me.

There have been conflicts along the way at group, district, and area levels, but because we all practice the Traditions and Concepts, we always seem to come to an understanding. I always seem to gain new insight as we participate in these discussions. Often an Al-Anon conflict, discussion and resolution will help me better understand a personal conflict going on at home. To find the courage to speak up when needed, the maturity to keep silent when I feel like attacking and the ability truly to listen to the other person's point of view all bring about the harmony and spiritual growth offered in Concept Four.

I've been a part of a group conscience at my home group, in my district and in my area and have always felt the presence of my Higher Power. One of my area Al-Anon friends reminds me, "God is in charge of Al-Anon." And He is! Our leg work is participation at all service levels. I think between our participation and His guidance, we'll always find harmony.

IN GIVING, I RECEIVE

THIS CONCEPT has certainly been true for me. I was not one who participated in very many things and it was scary to start putting myself in this role. But through the program I felt that it was not fair to allow one or two persons in our group to share all the responsibility, so I stepped in and I've met new people and rebuilt confidence in myself that I knew I had. This is allowing me to give some of my program to others – what truly helps me the most.

I WAS listening to a barbershop quartet recently and marveled at how good it sounded, how the music carried such a good message and was so upbeat. When the quartet finished playing, I felt so happy and satisfied. I noticed that no two persons in the quartet sang the same notes. Sometimes they weren't even singing the same words at the same time. But I recognized the harmony the group had because they were all participating in the same goal – to entertain the audience.

LEARNING TO PARTICIPATE

As I thought of how I was encouraged to participate in Al-Anon service, I noticed that I wasn't asked to carry the whole load either. Someone was a secretary; someone else was group representative, or chairperson, treasurer or literature person. When the meeting began, each person did his or her part to start the meeting, make announcements, suggest literature to the newcomer, select a topic or share. Each one of these jobs alone didn't make the meeting wonderful, but the combination of them did.

As a newcomer to Al-Anon, I was afraid to take part. What if I said the wrong thing? Would I look dumb or foolish if I didn't do it right? Then I noticed that those who were in charge had some booklets or papers to use when they shared or made an announcement. I also remembered my experiences in other organizations. I was recognized as someone who could organize and was asked over and over to organize. No one else volunteered, and no one else was asked. In my Al-Anon meeting, terms were announced for the offices: sometimes three months, sometimes three years. When the person finished the term, the group thanked him or her and looked for someone else to share those duties. "Aha," I said to myself, "it is safe to volunteer," and I did.

Participating in Al-Anon, which is called service, opened a new dimension of personal recovery. I wasn't the solution to the group's misery, but I was a welcome addition to our family. Every time I was asked or I volunteered to do something, the position I held had a solution to a personal dilemma. When I spoke to a group of teens, I got a new measure of understanding of the problems that my own children had in growing up with sick parents. When I accepted the post of group treasurer, I realized that I could take care of my own finances if I could take the responsibility of the group's funds. When I was the group representative, I found out that it was important to speak to my group about Al-Anon's efforts beyond the group level. It was also important to listen to the group's position on these same matters.

As time went on, I found that groups that have a lively discussion about a topic are more healthy. These groups took the time to make sure that everyone had a chance to voice their opinions, and that no one took offense to the lonely dissenter. Just as the barbershop quartet creates its best harmony when each person has a different voice, so does Al-Anon. The result is harmonious.

Members of Al-Anon showed me through their own sharings that I could try the Al-Anon principles in my home, with my family, friends and coworkers. I found it very interesting that by sharing my thoughts with them without commanding their acceptance, I could listen to their ideas. Together we were able to listen to each other's desires or concerns and come to an agreement on what we wanted to do together. When I didn't get my way, at least I knew I was heard.

Participation also means that I am willing to commit to a task in Al-Anon. The commitment becomes an opportunity to learn and experience events in which I was previously unable or unwilling to participate. Thanks to each of my new friends in Al-Anon, I have experienced more new pleasures, been able to share my pains and to learn that participation leads to harmony. And thanks to listening to a group of singers, I am able to understand that I don't have to do everything in order to participate in Al-Anon's recovery.

Working Concept Four

Participation is the key to harmony.

* Am I an active participant in Al-Anon? Why, or why not?

* What can I do to participate more fully?

* What can I do to encourage others to share their opinions freely?

* Is there a situation in my life today where those concerned do not participate equally in all decisions?

* What can I do to make such situations more harmonious?

* Am I willing to hear all that others may share?

* How am I willing to learn more about myself as I share with others?

* Am I willing to risk discovering that I have more to offer others than I thought?

* Can I trust that there is more than one good or right way to do something? Give examples.

* In what areas of my life can I apply Concept Four?

* What might the results be?

Concept Five

The Rights of Appeal and Petition protect minorities and assure that they be heard.

Al-Anon is a fellowship in which anyone who believes his or her personal life has been affected by a problem drinker can be a member. Individual freedom and belonging are both of enormous importance to us. We never take these rights away from each other. Concept Five protects both our freedom and our belonging at all service levels by assuring each of us that we can expect respectful consideration whether we fit into the majority or the minority at any point in time. The Right of Appeal assures that dissenting opinions will be heard; the Right of Petition assures that any trusted servant can always petition for resolution of a grievance.

The Right of Appeal found in Concept Five reminds us that we need to listen with consideration to everyone and encourage those with differing opinions (minorities) to state their views. Inviting those in the minority to speak out and listening to them with full hearts and consideration helps us maintain unity. When we hear, understand, value and incorporate minority opinions into our decision-making process, we may avoid mistakes that can occur when we are angry, hasty, misinformed or rigid. Practicing consideration compels a thorough debate, keeps us all focused on the issue at hand and validates the worth and dignity of each member.

We recognize by applying Concept Five that even substantial majorities sometimes can be wrong, and that we are all served best by encouraging a full and fair discussion of issues. A minority in Al-Anon that feels strongly that the majority is in error has not only the right, but also the duty to speak out or to file a report stating their views (a minority report). It takes courage to speak up when we are in the minority. Having permission and even the obligation to do so without prejudice or fear of reprisal often strengthens our courage.

Sometimes in the heat of debate, we can only see things in terms of winning or losing. Sometimes we become so attached to our own solutions that we lose our creativity. Listening to a minority voice may bring to mind a solution we have never even thought about that serves all parties better than a compromise. Practicing consideration and courage helps us seek resolution where everyone wins.

An example of such a win/win solution is the story of the two people who wanted a single orange. Recognizing that if one got the whole orange, the other would be unhappy, they agreed to compromise. Each took half of the orange. One promptly peeled her half, threw the peel away and ate the pulp. The other peeled the half he got, grated the peel for a recipe, and threw away the pulp. Had they listened more closely to each other, they could have discovered a solution in which each won the whole part of the orange they wanted, and none of it would have been wasted.

When we are open to hearing minority voices and listen with full consideration, we all benefit because everyone is respected and included. Mistakes are frequently avoided, and solutions that please everyone are often found. In cases where substantial unanimity still overrules the minority members, respectfully hearing and carefully considering their suggestions assures each of us that we will always be a valuable participant.

In addition to the Right of Appeal, we want to be sure that those who serve us, whether paid employees or volunteers, can feel safe from any unjust use of power. Our Right of Petition permits anyone to petition to be heard in a personal grievance and to carry the complaint all the way to the Board of Trustees without prejudice or fear of reprisal. The Right of Petition may include writing a report or letter and submitting it to an area assembly, to the Policy Committee (Concept Eleven) or to the World Service Conference. The existence of the Right of Petition, even if it is not often used, restrains the abuse of authority. While we recognize the need for directions and discipline in doing our various jobs, abuse of power and control is unacceptable and no one ever need silently endure it.

Trusting minority opinions has other advantages. Tradition Two establishes that the group conscience is the main guide for our fellowship. Situations can arise involving details of operation in which the general membership is not nearly as well informed as a service committee, whether it be a local information service board or the World Service Office (WSO) Board of Trustees. It can be difficult for an uninformed group conscience to make decisions effectively, particularly when emotions on an issue run high. Faith in our trusted servants means sometimes deferring to their greater knowledge and ability in certain areas, even when they are in the minority.

In Al-Anon, we carry respect for the minority even further. We extend minority rights in our elections. For example, in the selection of delegates to the World Service Conference (WSC), if no candidate receives a two-thirds vote after a number of ballots, the names of the candidates may be placed into a hat and the delegate drawn by lot. We are all equal in Al-Anon, and we trust that such candidates are equally capable of serving the fellowship. While majority vote usually prevails and often we even achieve unanimity, in cases where we continue to disagree, we trust our Higher Power to help us sort it out. Going to the hat in this way assures minorities they have an equal chance to be represented.

Even when we agree and establish a majority, we may still choose to discuss an issue. It is necessary to see that everyone feels included, that no one feels railroaded by a quickly made decision and that no one holds back an important idea that could benefit the group. The inclusion and consideration of every member's opinion in our fellowship of democracy fosters our unity.

Members Share Experience, Strength and Hope

FOR YEARS after coming into Al-Anon, the Concepts made no sense to me. I had become involved in service outside my group, gotten myself a service sponsor and was told I needed to use the Concepts, so I read them. I thought it was a bunch of gibberish and I didn't understand a thing I read. Our group never read them. Many felt that the only help was found in the Steps and Traditions. Fortunately, a couple of die-hards kept saying, "Read the Concepts" at every business meeting. So back I went to the *Al-Anon/Alateen Service Manual* on the Concepts. A light in my brain went on. Concept Five said quite plainly that we needed to listen to these people. Maybe if this Concept fit, the rest did, too.

The first Concept meeting was chaired by a new-comer. She read the history and introduction. She then started asking questions about each one. There were a lot of blank faces on some of the members who had not wanted to hear these ideas, but gradually everyone got involved. If the group could use these, maybe I could use them at home, too. Novel idea! I read Concept Five again and thought, maybe if I listened to the alcoholic, I would indeed learn something. Until now, I had ignored most of his comments and felt it was just the booze talking. A very surprising thing happened when I began to listen. I began hearing all sorts of things that I had been rejecting. I realized that the only time the alcoholic in my life can talk about feelings is when he is drinking. It has taken me a long time to get to this point, almost 17 years in this wonderful program, but the more I practice this Concept at home, the better I understand not only my husband of 41 years but also myself. You all know me, that wonderful helpful member who has been around so long that you all consider me cured. Well, I'm not cured, but I am

I LISTENED
AND
LEARNED

working at it one day at a time by using all our legacies, including the Concepts.

A MINORITY
REPORT WAS
FILED

A SMALL group felt that an action taken by our Area World Service Committee (AWSC) on a motion to be presented to the assembly was not in the best interests of our area or Al-Anon as a whole. With Concept Five in mind, a minority report was filed. At a special meeting of the AWSC, the matter was discussed and both sides were heard. After a thorough review, a vote was taken and the committee voted with the minority opinion. The motion for AWSC was changed before being presented to the assembly. This was truly Concept Five at work.

WE ACCOM-
MODATED
EVERYONE

NOT TOO long ago, a young girl who was studying at the local university came to our closed Al-Anon meeting. She said she had an assignment to observe an Al-Anon meeting and asked to sit in on ours. Whether she actually had any problems with drinkers in her family or among her friends, I do not know, but she said she didn't and that she simply wanted to observe to fulfill her assignment.

We told her about our group conscience and that we would have to discuss it. Everyone in the group agreed it would be acceptable except one member, who was quite upset. Even after we voted, she was visibly uncomfortable. Remembering our commitment to practice the Concepts, I suggested we invite her to share her opinion one more time. She had come with a lot to share and just didn't feel comfortable sharing her thoughts in front of anyone who was just an observer and not a participant.

Most of us still wanted the young woman to stay. Some of us thought that, given the nature of denial, she might even discover she had been affected by alcoholism. We were becoming quite uncomfortable about the time it was taking us to decide when a solution was offered that made everyone happy. We invited the young woman to stay for the first 50 minutes of the meeting and closed the last 10 minutes so that our member could share safely.

I am so glad we took the time to listen to our minority member's voice. She may even have represented another of us who didn't have the courage to speak at that time. This way, everyone was accommodated and no one had to go away unserved.

Working Concept Five

The Rights of Appeal and Petition protect minorities and assure that they be heard.

* When I am in the minority, how willing am I to speak up?

* What would make me more willing?

* How do I encourage others to voice their opinions?

* Do I truly listen to those with whom I disagree?

* How can I extend consideration to those with whom I disagree?

* How can I keep an open mind to different ideas?

* What are the benefits of encouraging minority reports and discussing issues even when the majority agrees? What disadvantages keep us from doing it?

* How willing am I to listen in Al-Anon?

* How willing am I to listen in my family?

* How willing am I to listen at work?

Concept Six

The Conference acknowledges the primary administrative responsibility of the trustees.

THE PRINCIPLES of delegation, authority and responsibility within Al-Anon are paramount to the understanding of Concept Six. The members of the World Service Conference (WSC), while providing Al-Anon with guiding principles, cannot in a one-week annual meeting begin to become involved in the administrative duties of the World Service Office (WSO) or services worldwide. Without a method of delegation and assignment of responsibility, the members and groups of Al-Anon would not be able to fulfill their primary purpose, to help families and friends of alcoholics.

We learn in Concept Two that the groups delegate their administrative and operational authority to the Conference, and in Concept Six we learn that the Conference delegates specific authority to the trustees. The Conference depends on the trustees to guide and oversee the business of our fellowship throughout the year.

Who are our trustees? "The Board of Trustees of Al-Anon Family Group Headquarters, Inc., is composed of qualified members of Al-Anon groups. The Board elects its own successors, with nominees subject to the approval of the Conference or a committee thereof. The Board is the chief service arm of the Conference, which is the guardian of Al-Anon's Twelve Traditions" (*Al-Anon/Alateen Service Manual*). Our trustees take care of much of Al-Anon business at their quarterly meetings and they implement policy decided at the Conference. Therefore, they must have considerable freedom to decide and act so that our other service arms do not get bogged down and become ineffective between meetings of the Conference.

The Board of Trustees receives quarterly reports from the WSO staff detailing activities and events of importance. The Board in turn reports to the delegates, who report to the members of their area world service committee (AWSC) and each Al-Anon group.

Most AISs are managed by members of the

districts they serve. These members elect trusted servants (service boards) who meet on a regular basis to assure the groups that the business of paying rent and other bills is carried out in a timely manner. Financial reports as well as activity reports from the office manager are usually reviewed. This information is conveyed to the groups via the information service representative (alternate group representative) or other trusted servant.

Although Concept Six is specifically about the relationship between our delegates, our trustees and WSO staff, it also reminds us to acknowledge where the primary responsibility lies, to grant others enough freedom to do a job and to provide workable guidelines that keep visions and goals clearly in mind.

As the groups delegate their authority to the Conference and the Conference to the trustees, it is helpful to distinguish the differences between overseeing, supervising and overmanaging. Overseeing an operation requires clear general policies, while supervising a task or method of operation is left to those doing the actual work. At each level of our service structure, we try to treat our employees and volunteers as we would like to be treated by providing clear guidelines and not nit-picking or overmanaging each minute detail.

One of the important principles of good management, whether of a large corporation such as Al-Anon Family Group Headquarters, Inc., a small business or our families, is linking the responsibility of the job with the authority needed to do it. Responsibility without power is both ineffective and unhealthy. Power without accountability is an invitation to dominance. In Al-Anon, we combine the responsibilities we assign with enough authority to carry them out within established guidelines and policy. Accountability means jobs are overseen so that the work fits within the guidelines.

Al-Anon's primary purpose is to help families and friends of alcoholics. Efficient and effective business operations help us achieve our primary purpose. We want our resources used to achieve maximum spiritual aims, and we need people with many talents as well as deep dedication to Al-Anon, to make this happen. Our trustees, the active guardians of our Traditions, function as business leaders. We ask a lot from our trustees, and we want to attract qualified members to serve. The power of Concept Six assures each member that our Traditions are guarded with the same love for the fellowship found in Al-Anon meetings worldwide.

Members Share Experience, Strength and Hope

ACTION IS
THE MAGIC
WORD

EACH APRIL, delegates representing 67 areas in the United States, Canada and Puerto Rico meet with committee chairpersons, trustees, Executive Committee members and the WSO staff at the World Service Conference (WSC). It is a stimulating time of mutual sharing and careful scrutiny of Al-Anon's role – from its close personal contact with each individual and group to its worldwide function. Many issues of our fellowship are discussed so that the group conscience can be fully expressed and clearly delineated.

Now what? The worldwide service work of Al-Anon Family Group Headquarters, Inc., continues. Who has the authority to make day-to-day decisions in a fellowship of equals? Concept Six makes it clear: just as the groups entrust their responsibility for Al-Anon as a whole to the WSC, the Conference gives the Board of Trustees the responsibility for policy, service activities, worldwide public relations, guardianship of our Twelve Traditions and prudent management of finances. With the trustees actively overseeing things until the WSC meets again, we can be sure that service will be available when any group or individual anywhere in the world asks for help.

When I first heard this Concept, I felt it made

Al-Anon sound like some sort of a corporation, not a spiritual program. As I became more involved in service, I realized that although our objectives are spiritual, our aims are best achieved through efficient business organization. Action is the magic word, and our trustees must function like directors of any large business.

Then I thought, if all the trustees are Al-Anon members, can we really trust the confused families and friends of alcoholics to run something of this size and importance? My service sponsors pointed out to me that we Al-Anons run the Al-Anon Family Group Headquarters, Inc. (AFG). We all participate from making coffee to making policy and administrative decisions. The reality is that, while our objectives are spiritual, we must trust someone to make things happen in order for our business to function. Trustees are members elected by members, and their qualifications are carefully considered.

In my group life, I realize there are realistic matters to be taken care of: rent, literature, refreshments, group representative expenses, contributions to our information service, district, area and WSO. In my personal life, I have to face reality. I need to recognize my limitations – financial and physical. I need to come to grips with family finances. Should I take a job? Are we adequately insured? Do I have a will? Am I making necessary things happen? If not, I can be so spiritual that I'm no earthly good.

Now I can understand how Al-Anon can be both a corporate entity and a spiritual program.

Working Concept Six

The Conference acknowledges the primary administrative responsibility of the trustees.

- Do I know what region my area is located in?

- Do I know who my regional trustee is?

- What administrative responsibilities are required of my group in order to continue operating?

- Does my group delegate these administrative responsibilities? To whom?

- Does my group hold business meetings on a regular basis?

- Does my group expect the treasurer to give regular reports on our income and expenses?

- How is this Concept a spiritual principle?

- How can I apply this Concept to my work life?

- How can I apply this Concept to my family life?

- How does this Concept relate to Concept Three and Al-Anon's "links of service"?

CONCEPT SEVEN further clarifies the relationship between the World Service Conference (WSC) and the Board of Trustees. The Board is entrusted with administrative responsibility for Al-Anon's world services, including guardianship of our legal status, rights and finances. The Conference is guided by the group conscience of thousands of Al-Anon groups. This spiritual guidance through the large group conscience of the Conference works well with the trustees' duty to keep Al-Anon on track with its legal obligations and fiscal responsibilities as a nonprofit organization. As guardians of our Traditions, the trustees consult the Conference for guidance whenever important matters are considered.

Ideally, the principles contained in our legacies bring sufficient consideration to any issue so that equitable agreement can be found. Usually this is the case in both personal and group life. However, we still have the rare occasion in which agreement cannot be reached and conflict follows. What then?

When considering traditional authority, we turn to our Steps, Traditions and Concepts. In our personal lives, we turn our will and our lives over to the God of our understanding (Step Three). In our Al-Anon groups, there is only one authority, a loving God who guides our group conscience (Tradition Two). At the world service level, the group conscience of our many groups is delegated to the group conscience of the WSC.

In Concept Seven we address the practical authority given to our trustees to ensure that decisions of the Conference are consistent with the laws that govern us and the well-being of our fellowship as a whole. The trustees can say no to a Conference vote or ask the Conference to reconsider if the action goes against our Charter or bylaws or appears reckless. Likewise, if an action would seriously impair our financial health or has become unworkable because of an unforeseen change in circumstances, the trustees can override or

Concept Seven

The trustees have legal rights while the rights of the Conference are traditional.

amend a Conference motion. Our trustees, having "complete legal power over Al-Anon's funds and services" (*Al-Anon/Alateen Service Manual*), do have veto power to keep us within the law. However, the trustees seldom use this power and usually turn instead to qualified sources, including the Conference, for advice and direction rather than resorting to a veto.

Interpreting the laws as they apply to Al-Anon is part of the trustees' job. These legal rights help our trustees keep the business of Al-Anon running smoothly and legally, while not requiring that each delegate become versed in all of the intricacies of the law. Our trustees are selected, at least in part, for their expertise and experience in these areas.

Our spiritual democracy is maintained because the respect for the Conference's traditional authority is backed up by the power of the groups and all the experience we have acquired to date. When the Conference acknowledges the rights, duties and legal responsibilities of the trustees, and the trustees remember the traditional rights of the Conference representing the group conscience of our fellowship, a harmonious and respectful working relationship can be maintained. Each is important and neither becomes a rubber stamp for the other.

Members Share Experience, Strength and Hope

MY UNDER-
STANDING
WIDENED

ANY UNDERSTANDING of Concept Seven that was not a contradiction in my mind was a long time in coming. I really thought that the Seventh Concept wiped out the first one, the second one and seriously confused Concept Six. Once again my very narrow understanding of certain words, my untrusting nature and my limited experience in matters of faith were my hang-ups.

I had been in service long enough not to put our delegates on pedestals. When I had interacted with them and other area trusted servants, heard them share and saw and felt the faith of these individuals, I knew their combined faith was the group conscience – our collective ultimate authority. I had grown enough through working the Steps to trust. How I missed elementary information about our structure and the trustees, I don't know. I suppose that it was my trying to study and learn rather than trying to learn by doing and listening and being a part of.

For me there simply came a time when this Concept made perfect sense. My doubts and questions were no longer with me. I reminded myself that Al-Anon is a set of principles with a spiritual base. I cannot grasp the written words through study, using my head and my limited comprehension. It is imperative that I use the spiritual principles and acknowledge that they highlight and weave through all the words.

I practiced this Concept without knowing it as I did my very best to follow the winners in the program. I am also aware of my growth, only by looking backwards. Each time I study a Concept and assess it, I learn its worth.

My better grasp of this Concept became clear to me as the matter of WSO's relocation was widely discussed among my fellowship friends. Questions and opinions came up. There were some pretty firm opinions and some strong debates among some of our members. I remember thinking to myself that some of the attitudes I observed could well have been mine, if I had not grown enough to totally trust the structure and the collective ultimate authority. I was glad to know that the wishes of the membership would be checked by the trustees for all legal aspects, by the Conference for all traditional aspects and by the guidance of a Higher Power that would see to us all. This Concept provides for cross-checks. It balances our program on a healthy spiritual basis.

My introduction to the Twelve Concepts came
when my service sponsor put me on a panel for a
Concepts workshop. My fourteen-year-old daughter,
who was in Alateen, had participated with me in
many service opportunities prior to this workshop, so
it was natural for me to include her in the adventure
of exploring Concepts Seven and Eight. Her reaction?
"Aw, Mom! Nobody in Alateen does Concepts! It is
soooo uncool! I don't want to look stupid!"

After some fast backstepping and quick amends, I
reassured her that many members were unfamiliar
with the Concepts, so we couldn't go wrong.

We spent the next few weeks preparing. My
daughter focused her attention on the Seventh Concept as I focused on the Eighth. We discussed our in-
terpretations and researched every possible avenue. I
cannot remember what we said in our presentation,
but we not only prepared for the workshop, we prepared for an incident in our family life that would
bring us face to face with the powerful insight and
wisdom of Concept Seven.

Several years later, my daughter very calmly announced to me that she was moving out of our home.
Her rationalization was thoughtful. She presented me
with the pros and cons and then added the zinger
that, though I may not be comfortable with her
choice, it was hers to make and I could not control
the outcome. As I listened I could not discount any
of her seventeen-year-old-using-the-principles-of-the-
program reasoning. This was one of those instances in
which I was not a grateful member of Al-Anon. I felt
that ignorance of the Al-Anon principles would have
been more comfortable. As my daughter was busy
packing her belongings, I was searching frantically
through my heart and mind for how to respond. I
cannot recall the trigger, but all of a sudden I thought,
"Hey, wait a minute! I'm the Board of Trustees in this
family!" Not knowing what to say, just knowing the
truth of that thought, I invited my Higher Power to

go with me to my daughter's room. After being granted entrance and hugging her, I asked her if she could remember back to that Concepts workshop and all the work we had put into the preparation so we wouldn't look stupid. I reminded her of the difference between the legal rights of the trustees and the traditional rights of the Conference. I reminded my thoughtful daughter that the trustees are still very much a part of Al-Anon and not separate from, nor more authoritative than, the Conference. As my daughter looked at me with that "yeah, so what?" look, I went in for the scoring point.

"In this family, I am the Board of Trustees. I remain a member of the family (the Conference), but a Higher Power, who is also a part of this recovering family, made me the Board of Trustees. I have been granted legal rights to guard and protect our family and, if necessary, override any decision made by the Conference (you, Daughter) that would endanger the legal and financial well-being of the entire family. Moving out before you are of age, no matter how sound the rationalization may seem to you, is out of the question. I will continue to be held legally liable until you are of age." I ended by saying to her, "This means that I am the Board of Trustees, you are the Conference, and I say 'No, not at this time.' Any questions?" She shook her head and said, very calmly, "Okay."

I couldn't believe how easy it was! There was no screaming, no tears, just calm reasoning and drawing on the experience of shared family recovery. My daughter did not for one minute debate my decision because she had been gifted with the wisdom of the Seventh Concept when she was fourteen.

There had been a time when I thought the Traditions were rules for the Al-Anon and Alateen groups and didn't apply to the family. I found out otherwise. I had already seen the Traditions as an avenue for reinforcement of my personal recovery gained through the Steps. Now I had a clear picture of the personal and family recovery found in the Concepts.

Working Concept Seven

The trustees have legal rights while the rights of the Conference are traditional.

* What does "legal rights" mean to me?

* What are "traditional rights"?

* Who holds "traditional rights" in my group? Who holds "legal rights"?

* What are the legal responsibilities of the members of our group? The members of our district? The members of our assembly? As an intergroup or literature distribution center? In other service positions?

* In what situations in our group might it be advisable for our leaders to say "no" to the will of the group?

* How can I apply this Concept to my home life?

* How can I apply this Concept to my work life?

* Is anything out of balance in my life? If so, what?

* What can I do to balance my spiritual aims with my practical living situation?

"THE AL-ANON Concepts record the 'why' of our service structure in such a way that the valuable experience of the past and the lessons drawn from that experience can never be forgotten or lost" (*Al-Anon/Alateen Service Manual*). Concept Eight, more than any of our Concepts, reflects the growth of Al-Anon and the need for the delegation of authority.

In the early 1950s, Al-Anon's headquarters was in its formative years. Volunteers were used for a variety of duties. With incorporation in 1954, a Board of Trustees was created to administer the World Service Office (WSO). In 1957, the Board appointed an Advisory Committee to provide guidance in matters of policy and finance, while the trustees fulfilled their duties, later defined in Concepts One through Seven. Over time the committee structure changed, and the Advisory Committee was replaced in 1964 by the World Service Conference (WSC) who became the permanent guardian of Al-Anon's Traditions and services. From its beginnings, our structure has always been guided by the Twelve Steps and Twelve Traditions.

The Board, recognizing its role as the overseers of policy, leadership, finance, group and public relations, then assigned administrative functions to a seven-member Executive Committee. This committee is comprised of three volunteer Al-Anon members, the World Service Office Executive Director, another WSO staff member and the volunteer Chairpersons of the Budget and Policy Committees.

It simply is not practical for a volunteer group, no matter how dedicated, to manage all the work necessary to serve a fellowship as large as Al-Anon. Al-Anon's trusted servants decided to keep our trustees as volunteers and have paid staff work in the office. Our paid employees provide a year-round office where the phones are answered regularly, information is available, literature is produced and disseminated and other needed services are provided.

Concept Eight

The Board of Trustees delegates full authority for routine management of the Al-Anon Headquarters to its executive committees.

Our trustees possess long-range vision for our future and delegate the routine management and details to our paid employees. We strive to keep a balance between our volunteer fellowship and our need to provide dependable service on a day-to-day basis.

As the principal long-range planners, the trustees are responsible for all final decisions within the guidelines of our Conference. Our World Service Conference (introduced in Concept Two) meets annually. Our Board of Trustees (discussed in Concept Six) meets quarterly. In Concept Eight we learn that oversight of the operations of Al-Anon's headquarters is delegated to the Executive Committee, which meets monthly.

To delegate with confidence, the groups, the Conference members and the Board of Trustees learn to choose competent leaders, assist in setting the direction and tone desired and then allow those designated to do their jobs.

At each level of service, we need both leaders and managers. We need leaders to hear us and provide the big vision, and we need managers to lay out the steps that make accomplishing that vision possible. With faith in our policies, we extend that faith to each other and find that we do not have to attend to every detail personally. Whether at home, at work or in our Al-Anon business meetings, we learn to trust others – none of us have to do it all. Each of our skills complement those of others. This makes it possible to keep Al-Anon consistently available.

Members Share Experience, Strength and Hope

THIS CONCEPT, to me, denotes consistency. The World Service Conference (WSC), which meets once a year, makes many decisions on what needs to be done in Al-Anon. The WSC can decide that new public information fliers need to be developed, that new literature for younger Alateens is necessary or that a new video is needed. (This list could be endless). The Conference lasts less than a week, and then everyone goes home. The trustees meet periodically throughout the year, but they are not full-time – they are not on call daily. Then who gets the work done? The Conference realizes it must rely on someone else to do the daily management (see Concept Two). For example, what if during the year a TV movie is being made in which the main problem is alcoholism and its affect on the family? The producers cannot call on delegates or trustees; they must be able to go to the World Service Office (WSO) and ask the committee managing Public Information matters for assistance. Thus, these committee members take care of the nitty-gritty, getting things done that need to be done daily. These are the people who insure consistency. Al-Anon's work is done day by day, not just at the once-a-year Conference or at the quarterly meetings of the trustees.

WE MUST HAVE VISIONS

How does this apply to my personal life? Before Al-Anon, I remember how many big plans I was always making. If you had heard me talk, you may have thought I was going to be the first woman president! I was going to write a book. I was going to redecorate my entire house. I was going to re-landscape my yard. I was going to lose weight. I was going to begin a consulting agency. These were all very good decisions to make – I believe that we must have visions of what we can do and what we can be. But after making all these plans, did I consider the day-to-day activities that were necessary to make any of these big plans happen? It is wonderful to plan the forest, but I must also be very sure that I make some provision for taking care of the trees. Have I thought about who is going to plant, water, prune, and fertilize? Big plans are great, but they won't ever happen unless I am able to take care of all the little things, daily.

Is this another reminder that I must live "One Day at a Time?" If I do, my life then can become consistent.

I DELEGATE RESPONSIBILITY

By taking Concept Eight into my home, I learn that life can be enjoyed by everyone.

My husband and I have three boys. I'm the homemaker and my job is to keep the household running smoothly – meals made, rooms clean, beds made, laundry, dusting and vacuuming. The list is endless. I can do it all myself and go crazy, or I can delegate some jobs to their owners – like bed making, filling the hamper, keeping a clean bedroom – and retain some sanity. I then have time to prepare interesting meals, be the taxi driver and spend quality time with my husband.

When things are put in perspective and I delegate responsibility, I can meet the end of each day with relative calm, knowing that everything got done in its own time without my frazzled attention.

I HAVE THE SATISFACTION OF BEING OF SERVICE

Concept Eight lets Al-Anon's trusted servants lead by example. On the surface the Concept tells us something about how the Board of Trustees functions. But underlying this explicit meaning is a valuable principle: that of delegating authority and responsibility. This principle can be applied by any of us to any part of our lives.

I was recently asked to become a member of the Recreation Committee at my workplace. The Recreation Committee runs the company picnic, holiday party and other social events. At first, I was uneasy about getting involved because I was afraid it would take too much time and effort and I would get overwhelmed. But I decided to give it a try.

Shortly after I joined the committee, the chairperson resigned, and we had a meeting to select a new chair. Some members expressed anxiety that no one would be willing to take the job. The previous chairperson did more work than anyone else on the committee and found the responsibilities a burden. Everyone assumed that it had to be that way.

My recovery in Al-Anon has taught me that I have choices. Nowadays, when I hear that something has "always been this way" or "can't change," I question it and wonder if a changed attitude would make a difference. As I sat in this meeting, I decided that there is nothing in the definition of chairperson that says you have to do all the work. So I said that I would be willing to serve and that my approach would be to act as a facilitator, delegating almost all of the footwork to others. My fellow committee members gladly accepted me on that basis.

We have already put on one event, and all I did was speak to other committee members and ask them to take responsibility for individual tasks. I am convinced that I do a better job this way. Not having to worry about details, I can easily make sure each event has a set-up crew, a clean-up crew, someone to purchase refreshments, someone to put up notices and so on. As a result of my growth in Al-Anon, I have the satisfaction of being of service to my co-workers without running myself ragged.

This experience has taught me that Concept Eight is about letting go and trusting others. If I couldn't trust that my fellow committee members could handle the responsibilities I delegate to them, I would be paralyzed. I would obsess on whether they were doing things right, perhaps interfere with their tasks or give up and do everything myself. I am sure that this is what would have happened to me before

Al-Anon. I was brought up to believe "if you want something done right, you have to do it yourself." Now I know that other people can do a good job – maybe not exactly the way I would have done it, but as well or maybe even better.

Working Concept Eight

The Board of Trustees delegates full authority for routine management of the Al-Anon Headquarters to its executive committees.

* What are some of the many routine functions performed by our WSO employees to fulfill our primary purpose?

* What are the management tasks in my group? My district? My area?

* How are these tasks delegated?

* What are the management tasks in my home life? How are these tasks delegated?

* What are the management tasks in my work life? How are these tasks delegated?

* What responsibilities or jobs am I willing to delegate to others?

* Once I delegate a task, am I willing to trust the results?

* In what areas of my life have I had difficulty trusting?

* What are the spiritual principles embodied in this Concept?

In our study of the Traditions and Concepts, the importance of leadership is repeated and emphasized. Leadership is introduced in Tradition Two, "Our leaders are but trusted servants; they do not govern," and Tradition Nine introduces service activities found in "service boards or committees directly responsible to those they serve." In Concept Three our leaders are provided with the Right of Decision, and in Concepts Four through Nine, we learn the different duties of leaders.

Because we practice the Twelve Steps and carry the message of recovery to families of alcoholics, it is necessary for Al-Anon's growth that we develop good personal leadership. Each and every member of Al-Anon has the potential to become a leader. Because of our service structure and the way Al-Anon rotates service positions, members have many opportunities to develop their leadership qualities. In world service, leadership is provided by the Board of Trustees in recognizing, understanding and defining the message of recovery and in making the vision of recovery available locally and throughout the world.

Each Al-Anon member is also the member of a family unit. Within that unit, leadership is needed, plans are made, action is taken. Parents, for instance, take a leadership role in providing health care and assuring education is given to their children. In Al-Anon, our fellowship grows when we choose, teach and encourage leaders on a continuous basis. We choose our leaders carefully and recognize their talent and values. In every way we encourage our leaders, knowing that with each new role, they are growing – "One Day at a Time."

Some mistake the idea of "principles above personalities" to mean that we shouldn't have leaders, or that they should have no opinions and simply do what the fellowship says. This is unrealistic and undesirable. We realize that some jobs require no special talents while other jobs require experience and expertise.

Concept Nine

Good personal leadership at all service levels is a necessity. In the field of world service the Board of Trustees assumes the primary leadership.

Each person brings their own talents to the job, and no two people will do a job the same way. We practice the slogan "Let Go and Let God."

Natural leaders are people with such vision and enthusiasm that we want to follow them. In addition to vision, to be truly excellent, they also need to be responsible, tolerant, stable, flexible and of good judgment. Every Al-Anon member possesses some of these qualities. Practicing the Al-Anon program while we lead enhances them. Developing our leadership qualities helps us lead satisfying lives and helps our fellowship thrive as well. Thus we all benefit when we participate in service.

Within the Concepts, the role of leadership in every level of service – from group representatives, district representatives, delegates and trustees – is discussed. With the study of these Concepts, each level of service has also been discussed: the groups, districts, areas, regions and now world services. Concept Nine guides us in understanding the importance of the trustees in the leadership needed for our world service.

The development of the Al-Anon service structure provides excellent examples of the primary leadership of the Board of Trustees. The Board led the way in the establishment of our World Service Conference (WSC) in 1960, successfully combining members from the United States and Canada into one body. As Al-Anon General Service Offices (GSOs) develop around the world, they seek the experience, strength and hope of our World Service Office (WSO) staff and the Conference, including our Board members. As the number of GSOs grew, in 1980 the Board initiated a biennial International Al-Anon General Services Meeting (IAGSM). Delegates from all over the world attend, united in our primary purpose: to help families and friends of alcoholics.

Just as their term of service is concluding, many a leader in Al-Anon has been quoted as saying, "I just figured out what I was supposed to be doing, and now it's time to turn it over to someone else." Our leaders, our election process, the rotation of service, our democratic thought and action are all the necessary ingredients that make Al-Anon so very unique and special. Rotating service – from changing group treasurers on a scheduled basis to imposing the maximum term a trustee can serve – assures us that no one person gains control over Al-Anon and that the joys found in service can be shared by many.

In *Lois Remembers*, Lois W., Al-Anon's co-founder, wrote, "We believed that Al-Anon leadership should initiate ideas, offer choices, and perhaps emphasize aspects but leave it up to the fellowship to make the decisions." A detached, clear-headed ability to respond with courage and creativity is a quiet strength we seek in our leaders and in ourselves.

How do we select our leaders? In the *Al-Anon/ Alateen Service Manual*, World Service Handbook section, the suggested election procedures for our trusted servants are outlined. Experience and careful thought have produced these procedures which are seen by many to be spiritual in direction. Guided by the principles found in all of our three legacies – the Steps, Traditions and Concepts – leaders are selected on the basis of Al-Anon membership, eligibility, special skills and willingness to serve. Selecting a delegate by a two-thirds vote or by lot reduces the possibility of personalities interfering with principles and assures the newly elected delegate of member support.

In our *Al-Anon/Alateen Service Manual*, Al-Anon members will find a powerful essay by Bill W., the co-founder of AA. This essay on leadership defines the qualities that we seek for Al-Anon as well. Key points from the essay include:

"A leader is a person who can put principles, plans, and policies into such dedicated and effective action that the rest of us want to back him up and help him with his job."

"A good leader originates plans and policies for the improvement of the fellowship."

"Good leadership knows that a fine plan or idea can come from anyone, anywhere."

"Leadership should always have good reasons and give them."

"Leadership is often called upon to face heavy and sometimes long-continued criticism – an acid test."

Leadership qualities may seem overwhelming to some. Having service sponsors is helpful to all members at all levels of service in overcoming any feeling of self-doubt. Leadership begins with attending Al-Anon meetings on a regular basis and taking on group service positions. Good personal leadership at all service levels also means welcoming the newest member into our fellowship and listening. One of the most valued service positions is that of answering the phone and listening to a member in need. If we remember that we seek progress rather than perfection, we can accept our human limitations while striving for the very best we can do for ourselves and for our fellowship. We are all leaders at one time or another, and we can practice those qualities that will make us excellent leaders in all the service jobs in Al-Anon.

WATCH CHILDREN at play. Even with very young ones, you can pick out the natural leaders. They are the ones who are having such a good time that every other child wants to do what they are doing. You can contrast this with the child who is controlling, bossy, domineering and so concerned with making rules and making everyone else follow the rules that the other children lose interest, rebel or start their own game.

When I was in high school, I wanted to be elected to whatever, not because I had a plan or program to implement, but because I needed the assurance that I was liked and accepted. I would win the popularity contest, but then be frightened of the responsibility.

As I got older, I still didn't want the responsibility, but I wanted to be part of the in crowd. I took a position in whatever organization I was involved in. As the disease of alcoholism progressed in my family, I didn't have time for any positions because I had to worry about and take care of the alcoholic. I thought I was providing leadership in my family, but actually all I was doing was controlling.

When I came into Al-Anon I heard Tradition Two, "Our leaders are but trusted servants, they do not govern." My first interpretation was that Al-Anon had no leaders. But without leadership, everything ends in chaos. The Tradition is saying that we have no authoritarian figures or dictators. We do have leaders, and they are to use the abilities God has given them to serve the fellowship rather than for individual power, prestige or property.

I believe that in our Fourth Step we learn what our strengths and weaknesses are and how God can take our weaknesses and turn them into strengths. Because of financial insecurities in my childhood, I developed an interest and ability in financial matters. I have been able to use this in serving the fellowship. When I

WE ALL
SHARE
LEADERSHIP

became district representative, we had ten dollars in the treasury. Today our district treasury has enough funds to support the telephone service, do Public Information work, have an anniversary picnic, a monthly calendar, pay for some of our district representative expenses and do other special projects we conceive.

I also know my weaknesses. Every so often I decide to do something creative. I try a craft project, but I rarely finish it. One of our big fund-raisers is a craft fair in October, and I am very thankful that other creative people come forward and are willing to be leaders. We need to know each other well enough to know each other's strengths and weaknesses.

I like Concept Nine, as it is one that I can understand and apply to my Al-Anon service, my personal life and my work life. It explains leadership better than any of the text books I have read, and I recognize myself and others in it.

I MUST
EARN
TRUST

I LOOKED up the word trust in a dictionary. The definition read, "a confident reliance on the integrity, veracity, or justice of another; confidence; faith; also the person or thing so trusted."

Before Al-Anon I confused trust with gullibility. I would believe what I was told regardless of how many times it was proven untrue. This Concept points out mutual trust. The Al-Anon groups trust the Conference and the trustees to carry out duties and to be accountable to the groups. They can hardly be accountable unless the groups maintain an interest in hearing that accountability through reports from delegates, the Conference Summary and "Inside Al-Anon." Recently I received my copy of the Conference Summary. I turned to the back and read both the motions that were passed and those that were not passed. I noticed in those motions some things that will alter the descriptive text on the Concepts and some that will alter other portions of the Service Manual.

Therefore it is important that I understand the Concepts and Manual and examine these changes and, when I have a question, seek answers.

Before Al-Anon I would have thought that I must simply accept without question or without further investigation. Concept Nine tells us to seek answers. A part of my trust must be trusting that the person or thing will be accountable and thus willing to explain their answers. We place our faith in our Higher Power. Then we trust our leaders to act in our best interest – to fill their responsibilities. Leaders earn our trust. Within the fellowship we have the means, through group conscience, to remove a leader who breaks the Traditions or misuses group funds. In my everyday life, this Concept means a lot to me. I can have faith in my Higher Power that He will show me what I need to know. My job is to keep conscious contact with my Higher Power and to learn to be aware of His messages. God gave me some intelligence to use the knowledge available to me.

Before Al-Anon I had unfounded, irrational fears. One aspect of my disease is fear that made me think I had to take care of everything or it wouldn't get done. On the other hand, I was gullible, not seeking knowledge of His will.

Today I don't walk constantly in fear, but I have an awareness of it. Fear is a normal human emotion, and to me, a lack of trust stems from fear. Like any other emotion, fear can cripple me. I can swim and I'm not afraid of water – that would prevent me from swimming – yet I have an awareness that swimming could be dangerous unless I think and use necessary precautions.

Before Al-Anon the failure of others to meet my expectations was like having a rug jerked from under my feet. On the other hand, I jerked a lot of rugs, too. As a leader it is my responsibility to be accountable and earn others' trust.

Good personal leadership at all service levels is a necessity. In the field of world service the Board of Trustees assumes the primary leadership.

* What is "good personal leadership"?

* What are the leadership positions available in my group? In my district? In our local Al-Anon information service (AIS) or intergroup? Our local literature distribution center (LDC)? In our area? At the World Service Conference (WSC)? At the World Service Office (WSO)?

* Who assumes the primary leadership in my group? My district? My area? Our AIS? Our LDC?

* How can I use Concept Nine as a practical, spiritual yardstick for choosing leaders? Roommates? Employees?

* What are the differences between leadership and management tasks in my life?

* In what situations have I served as a leader?

* What qualities of leadership do I have?

* Which ones would I like to develop?

* Am I hesitant to be a leader? Why or why not?

* What does it mean to have vision? How can I share my vision?

* Do I have a service sponsor?

When we look at the Concepts in order, each one builds upon the principles established in the last. We know that the groups have ultimate responsibility and authority for Al-Anon world services. The groups entrust the Conference with administrative and operational authority. The Conference knows that the trustees will handle administrative responsibility. The trustees delegate management of the World Service Office (WSO) to the Executive Committee. The importance of participation and good leadership is established. The Rights of Decision (Concept Three), Appeal and Petition (Concept Five) provide guidelines for handling disagreement. Each level of world service has clearly defined responsibilities and recourse back through the chain of leadership if there are problems.

Our "carefully defined service authority" ensures that no two people or groups will be equally responsible for the outcome of any project. But sometimes a goal requires the participation of two or more important groups. For example, a project that may affect policy and requires considerable expenditure of funds needs direction from both the Policy Committee and the Budget Committee. Their responsibilities are equal in importance to the project. If the Board of Trustees was not given the service authority to make the final decision, and if the committees disagree, they could issue conflicting directives, creating "double-headed management." As things are, they can refer their concerns to the Board of Trustees, where the final decision rests in the area of our world services. The committees present their findings and recommendations, along with their minority reports if any, and the Board will settle the matter or take the issue to the Conference for further input.

In all areas of our lives, we need to be clear about what our responsibilities are. Limits to one's power should be clearly spelled out in the description of a job. With an organization composed of many people,

Concept
Ten

Service responsibility is balanced by carefully defined service authority and double-headed management is avoided.

there must also be a clear understanding of who has the final "service authority." Double-headed management can happen when no one is in charge or when two people or two groups are charged with overlapping responsibility and authority.

A worker is empowered when given the responsibility to do a job, as well as the carefully defined authority to do it. With the freedom and the right to decide the best way to get a job done, the person doing it is both trusted and held accountable for the outcome. If we are given large responsibilities and no clear authority, we can't lead. Without the necessary authority to complete a task, it is natural to assume less and less responsibility or to pass the buck.

In a family it must be clear who sets the rules. If children can get a different answer from each parent to a request to stay out late, this is "double-headed management." If Dad prefers to defer to Mom on such matters, the entire family must know this. Then the children will know that they can't manipulate Dad to stay out late. Likewise, Dad must have respect for Mom's ultimate authority in this matter, trust that she will fulfill her responsibility in the best interest of the family and not interfere.

Throughout all levels of Al-Anon, clear lines are drawn between ultimate authority and delegated authority. We are accountable for our accomplishments and report to those we serve. If the job is poorly done or conflicts arise, there need to be clear lines of authority that can be used to correct the mistakes or even to replace the people who do not fulfill their responsibilities. This is the proper use of ultimate authority. Ultimate authority should be clearly defined in all situations, but seldom used.

One of the most important principles of using ultimate authority is the recognition that when delegated authority is working well, it is best to leave it alone. Trusted servants need to be given the respect and trust to accomplish their jobs efficiently.

Excessively detailed management or checks at every step of the way is not only inefficient, it can also cause demoralization and resentment. Thus in Al-Anon ultimate authority is never used unless our trusted servants are in serious error, are clearly ineffective or interfere with others' work.

In practicing Concept Ten, we set clear goals and trust each other to accomplish them. We recognize that there are many ways to do a job. When we accept responsibility and are willing to be held accountable for the tasks we have agreed to undertake, we are empowered. We know that ultimate authority will not be exercised unfairly.

Delegating both responsibility and carefully defined service authority is evident at every level of Al-Anon service. Each time responsibility is delegated, whether to an executive or to a clerical worker, what goes with it is the power to carry out that responsibility. By clearly defining the job and who has the final say at each level of operation, our trusted servants are free to create the best solutions and still be accountable to the organization for the outcome.

Members Share Experience, Strength and Hope

THIS CONCEPT, to me, means clarity. In our Al-Anon World Service Conference Charter (see *Al-Anon/Alateen Service Manual*), there is nothing legally binding, but there is an implied contract between all the Al-Anon groups and the Conference. Our group conscience is our ultimate authority, but our trusted servants have delegated authority. Usually the ultimate authority functions more in terms of influence than in terms of power. Thus the ultimate authority is never used except when our trusted servants are (1) in error, (2) are ineffective, (3) exceed their purpose. When delegated authority is working well, *leave it alone*. In our program we must avoid

I AM
ACCOUNT-
ABLE

personal clashes, confusion and ineffectiveness. There is confusion if two people are trying to do the same thing. However, nothing gets done if no one decides to do anything. Thus, in the group, in the district, in the area, and at the Conference level, each person has his own job to do. Each person counts.

I must also remember that, when authority is delegated to me, I am not only given responsibility but I am also accountable for the results. I am supposed to be able to report, "This job was mine to do. I did the job. This is the result." If I am a group treasurer, I am responsible for collecting the money, paying the bills, etc. This authority has been given to me by the group, but I am also accountable to the group and give reports on what has been collected and what has been spent.

In my personal life I must remember that I need to do my job and no one else's, yield if I need to, stand up when I need to. Each of us in Al-Anon and in our personal lives must neither dominate (all jobs are mine) nor cave in (no job is mine, you do it). Clarity appears in my life. I know what I am supposed to do. If it is my job and I do not do it, it will not get done. When I have completed my job, I am accountable to others and report the results.

How wonderful it is to know that I have a place in life, I have a job to do – a job that counts – I am responsible, I am accountable. This clarity brings me closer to knowing, "This is who I really am." I continue on my path to recovery.

I WANTED
AUTHORITY,
NOT
RESPONSI-
BILITY

I WAS a newcomer. I consider that a good excuse for the time I wanted others to bear all the responsibility while I hung on to the authority to make decisions.

My Al-Anon life began when I found 30 recovering Al-Anon members clustered around long tables in a school cafeteria on Saturday evenings, sharing experience, strength and hope. I loved the warmth and energy. I stayed and made it my first home group.

Eventually I realized that most of us were pretty new to the Al-Anon way of life.

Each meeting had five minutes for Al-Anon announcements and five minutes for group matters. If group matters needed more than five minutes of discussion, a special meeting was called, usually scheduled to follow a regular meeting.

A few members tried to attract us to participate in the group conscience discussions, announcing the dates and topics for weeks in advance, so everyone could plan accordingly. But, as it turned out, most of us would go to any lengths to avoid participating in any discussion of a group matter. So those special meetings often consisted of three or four members.

One night during the five minutes for group matters, we were informed what the prior week's group conscience meeting had decided and why. I didn't like their decision at all. Butterflies flew loops in my stomach. I raised my hand. "I'm unhappy with that outcome," I said, "and here's why." I began explaining. "The five minutes are all used up!" someone interrupted.

"But wait," I persisted. "I don't think the group conscience meeting gets to dictate to this whole group. It should be like an advisory committee and then this whole group gets to vote on the final decision."

The meeting moved on, and I got to sit there with my feelings. I looked at my sponsor, whose eyes were closed, apparently in quiet reflection.

After the meeting, my sponsor explained that group members decide how to make group decisions. We could vote to spend more than five minutes on group matters during our regular meetings, providing us group time to discuss options researched and proposed by an advisory committee. That used to happen in this group, but discussion often took half an hour or more, so members preferred to assign decisions to the group conscience meeting where all members were invited, but not forced to participate. The group conscience meeting had been made responsible for researching, discussing and reaching an informed group conscience. It had been given the carefully defined authority to make the decision, carry it out and inform us all. My sponsor said we could reopen the subject of how to handle group matters if I'd like to bring it up.

Did I want to start spending half an hour or more of meeting time on a group conscience process? Really? Nah. The truth is I wanted it both ways. Without taking responsibility for doing any footwork at all, I wanted final veto power on their informed group conscience. I wanted authority without responsibility. Apparently, Al-Anon wasn't offering me that option. Now I participate in group conscience meetings and am grateful for Concept Ten.

Service responsibility is balanced by carefully defined service authority and double-headed management is avoided.

* Is service responsibility carefully defined in my group? In my district? In my area? At our Al-Anon information service (AIS), intergroup or literature distribution center (LDC)?

* What is double-headed management? Why do we want to avoid it?

* In what ways am I willing to delegate enough authority to carry out the job?

* Am I involved in any double-headed management?

* Am I involved in any situations where one person has the responsibility while a different person has the authority?

* What kind of guidelines and definitions of a project would I find helpful before accepting a responsibility?

* How do I define guidelines for others?

Concept Eleven

The World Service Office is composed of standing committees, executives and staff members.

SPIRITUAL PRINCIPLES guide us as we learn and work each Step, Tradition and Concept. Concept Eleven provides us with good business practices and a structure as we put our Twelfth Step work into action. Concept Eleven describes how the World Service Office (WSO) serves our groups by coordinating and carrying out many different aspects of Al-Anon service. It shows how the various parts of Al-Anon's structure fit together, the organizational principles that make service accessible to all and how we can use the WSO as a model for organization and unity in our groups, districts and areas. Many a member has also found this Concept to be a guiding principle, applicable in all of their affairs outside of Al-Anon.

Our WSO is organized into standing committees composed of volunteer members and paid staff, who are charged with overseeing and administering the operations. The work is organized so that services can be provided on a continuous basis to our members. With the participation of talented, capable volunteers and staff, the work is divided into manageable segments.

There are currently 12 committees that make recommendations to guide Al-Anon. The *Alateen Committee* provides guidance for the activities of Alateen. The *Archives Committee* collects and organizes our historical material, giving us a sense of our past which then provides us with information helpful in planning our future. The *Budget Committee* sees that we remain solvent and keep money in its proper perspective. The *Conference Committee* plans and arranges for Al-Anon's yearly business meeting, the World Service Conference (WSC). The *Cooperating with the Professional Community* Committee reaches out to professionals and agencies that help alcoholics and their families find recovery. The *Institutions Committee* helps us reach families and friends of alcoholics in hospitals, treatment centers, correctional and residential facilities. The *International Coordination*

Committee helps keep the WSO connected to individuals, groups and services outside the United States and Canada. It considers requests for permission to translate Al-Anon literature. The *Literature Committee* oversees the creation and revision of all our Conference Approved Literature (CAL). The *Nominating Committee* helps the Board of Trustees fill the volunteer positions that open up each year. The *Policy Committee* has jurisdiction over all projects and problems that involve Al-Anon policy. It defines and clarifies how we represent ourselves to the world. The *Public Information Committee* keeps Al-Anon available to the public through radio, press, film and television, so that we can attract those still in need of our services. Finally, the *Regional Service Seminars Committee* helps coordinate service seminars throughout the United States and Canada, which are open to all members who wish to learn how to keep the hand of Al-Anon available to families and friends of alcoholics. Together these committees oversee all of our services worldwide.*

The Executive Committee supervises the administration of the WSO and has legal and financial power delegated by the Board of Trustees. *The Forum*, our monthly magazine, has its own committee which works with staff in determining the editorial content and policy of the magazine.

Whatever Al-Anon seeks to accomplish, we need good leaders to manage it. We want employees who possess the rare qualities of being able to inspire by example, act firmly but fairly and stay abreast of the large tasks without losing track of the small ones. We want our staff to take the initiative in planning without controlling others to achieve their objectives. To attract and keep good executives, Al-Anon needs to reward competence with praise, appreciation and

---

* A revised committee structure was put into place for a three-year trial period beginning in 1996.

reasonable financial compensation. The same principles apply to all our service jobs.

We want to attract competent staff members who will be happy in their jobs. We compensate our workers at wages similar to those paid for similar positions outside Al-Anon. To expect them to work for less is not in line with our principle of being fully self-supporting. In this way our workers are treated fairly. They receive our respect and they achieve their own self-respect.

No organizational structure can ensure absolute harmony and protection from the conflicts that are inevitable whenever a large number of people work together. No amount of organization can substitute for competence and cooperation among the people involved. Only sustained practice of all our spiritual principles can accomplish this and create harmonious cooperation in Al-Anon. Honesty, fairness, respect and willingness to keep spiritual principles uppermost in our minds is our best guarantee of continued friendly, efficient service in Al-Anon and in our lives.

Members Share Experience, Strength and Hope

I'M BECOMING
MORE HUMAN

I'LL NEVER forget the look on my sponsor's face the first time I showed her my schedule in black and white. I had written it out calendar-style and asked if she had any insights about how to make it work better. "Sweetie, no human being could fit this much stuff into one life," she said quietly.

"Really?" I asked. Part of me was relieved that my problem hadn't been just my imagination, but I was also dismayed that now I needed to fit one more project into my life: a realistic look at my concept of scheduling. "What'll I do?" I asked.

She smiled and told me what she had done. She had asked herself what was the primary purpose of her life. I thought about my life and said, "I think my primary purpose is to keep growing into the best possible member of the family of humanity I can be. How? Love, learn and grow; earn an honorable living, and help my family love, learn and grow."

Then my sponsor wrote down her purpose and dated it. I did that too. Next she asked me, "What do I need to be doing in order to accomplish this life purpose?" "Laundry!" I said. She laughed; "Okay, what else?" she asked. I listed play time, personal alone time, family quality time, Al-Anon and other spiritual meetings, job commute, job, on and on I went until I stopped for breath. That was when she suggested I read our Service Manual's Concept Eleven, which groups together certain activities needed to carry out Al-Anon's primary purpose and divides the work into manageable committee jobs. Wow, what a simple idea!

She suggested I go home and ask my family members the same questions she had asked me. She thought they might find it as inspiring as I had (she said this could improve conscious contact with fellow humans as we understand them).

Well, I did share the idea with my family and we had a lot of fun with it. Our equivalent of Concept Eleven is "Our family structure is composed of family teams, supervisors and do-ers, no prima donnas, and everyone gets treated fairly." Our team members rotate often, and most teams consist of one person with a helper or two. We have six rotating family teams – family policy council; family time council (plans birthdays, daily quality time, spiritual time); home maintenance (laundry, housecleaning, furnace); daily life maintenance (food, mail, supplies, phone messages); transportation; finance.

This has brought a new level of humor, dignity and mutual trust to our family life and completely changed how I think about my own scheduling. Al-Anon's Concept Eleven gave me simple tools to improve how I cooperate with the people in my daily life. The most exciting bonus of all is that it's helping me love, learn and grow. It's helping me help my family love, learn and grow. It's helping me to earn an honorable living and become a more human being.

THE SECOND longest Concept in our handbook did not come alive for me until I was sitting at the WSC during my second year as delegate. Another delegate shared a simple statement and I experienced the aha that many of us experience when we finally get it. I realized that as a delegate I am a member of one of the twelve standing committees, which include Policy, Alateen, Budget, Conference, Institutions, Nominating, Public Information, Archives, Literature, International Coordination, Cooperating with the Professional Community and Regional Service Seminars.

For the past year, I had been receiving mail from the WSO staff member of my committee asking for input and had given my approval for a new piece of Al-Anon material. On the Conference floor, I had listened to my fellow delegates work through such issues as revising the *Al-Anon/Alateen Service Manual* or approving new brochures. I sat through committee discussions during the Conference and realized that as a trusted servant I had worked with all the people described in Concept Eleven and was indeed one of them. I was a member of the Conference which approved the budget prepared by the WSO and the Treasurer of the Board.

I had to smile to myself. Even though they are called *standing* committees there is a lot of sitting, reading, writing and hard work. In fact, I realized that the standing committees are replicated at the area level through our coordinators and area officers, at a district level through our district representatives and district committees and at a group level through our group representatives and group-selected service workers.

In my area the officers meet at the area world service committee (AWSC) meetings to set the agenda for our assemblies. Similarly the WSO Executive Committee meets with the Executive Director to consider budgets, policies and new projects.

Concept Eleven discusses the principles that operate within the WSO and Al-Anon worldwide. The first principle defines the qualities of a good Al-Anon executive as "responsibility of authority without favor or partiality," fairness and being an Al-Anon member. Most Al-Anon areas seek these same principles in choosing their delegates and area officers. The second principle talks about paying fair compensation for efficient quality service much like we are paid in our employment. The third principle talks about the full participation of paid workers on our committees. The experience and knowledge of our paid workers is much like the sharing of our longtime Al-Anon members at our home group meeting. The wisdom they have as they share their experience, strength and hope is invaluable.

The closing discussion of Concept Eleven in our *Al-Anon/Alateen Service Manual* states, "No organizational structure can fully guarantee our WSO against the possible damage done by clashing personalities. Only sustained willingness to practice spiritual principles in all our affairs can accomplish this." Not only has Concept Eleven come alive for me, now I also understand its spiritual nature for Al-Anon worldwide, in my area, district and, most importantly in my home group. Without our committees and the many trusted servants that serve on those committees, I doubt that Al-Anon would have survived.

Working Concept Eleven

The World Service Office is composed of standing committees, executives and staff members.

* What does our World Service Office (WSO) mean to me?

* What does our WSO mean to my group? Does my group consider the WSO to be a part of our Al-Anon family?

* How many area coordinators does my area have with positions similar to those at the WSO?

* What committees serve my district? Our Al-Anon information service or intergroup? My group?

* Do I respect the amount of time my group, district and area trusted servants commit to Al-Anon service work?

* Have I shown my appreciation to our trusted servants for all that they do for Al-Anon?

* If my area has Al-Anon information service staff members, do we pay them fair wages? Are these employees treated with respect? Do we thank them for their efforts?

* Have I studied this Concept with my service sponsor to gain a better understanding of its meaning to my group? Our district? Our area?

* Am I a student of the *Al-Anon/Alateen Service Manual?* If not, am I willing to study it now? Have I ever introduced a new Al-Anon member to the Manual for its guidance?

* Do we value our past trusted servants for their wisdom and seek their continued participation?

* As a trusted servant, do I share openly by passing on my experience to others?

* What does this Concept teach me about delegation? About turning things over?

* How is Concept Eleven applicable to my personal life?

* How is Concept Eleven applicable to my work life?

Concept Twelve

The spiritual foundation for Al-Anon's world services is contained in the General Warranties of the Conference, Article 12 of the Charter.

THE GENERAL WARRANTIES:

In all its proceedings the World Service Conference of Al-Anon shall observe the spirit of the Traditions:

1. that only sufficient operating funds, including an ample reserve, be its prudent financial principle;

2. that no Conference member shall be placed in unqualified authority over other members;

3. that all decisions be reached by discussion, vote and, whenever possible, by unanimity;

4. that no Conference action ever be personally punitive or an incitement to public controversy;

5. that though the Conference serves Al-Anon, it shall never perform any act of government; and that, like the fellowship of Al-Anon Family Groups which it serves, it shall always remain democratic in thought and action.

We may have thought the Steps, Traditions and Concepts were overwhelming and/or confusing at first glance. Now we have Warranties to consider in Concept Twelve. Their close examination, one by one, reveals the wisdom to be found here. The Warranties reinforce the principles set forth in our Traditions and Concepts, offering final guidance for the application of our legacies. They remind us of the importance of each Al-Anon Family Group (AFG) for their support of our fellowship as a whole, both financially and in service leadership.

Examining the Warranties one at a time, Warranty One states, "that only sufficient operating funds, including an ample reserve, be its prudent financial principle." It is difficult to discuss finances in a spiritual light: "There is no romance in paying the landlord" (*Al-Anon/Alateen Service Manual*). Money is necessary for Al-Anon to survive and grow. Our groups pay rent, purchase literature, support a group representative; our service meetings incur travel, meeting and printing expenses; our World Service Office (WSO) and some information services have occupancy costs, salaries, printing, telephone and other expenses. Being prudent with our finances means we are conservative and thoughtful in our planning. We maintain an ample reserve to cover our future needs, yet we don't accumulate a significant excess. Our available funds serve Al-Anon. We will continue to thrive with the continued support of our many members. Warranty One reminds us to take care of ourselves financially without excessive spending or stockpiling.

Warranty Two states, "that no Conference member shall be placed in unqualified authority over other members." Our Concepts detail the ultimate and delegated responsibilities of our service arms.

In Al-Anon, absolute authority is never in the hands of one individual, but is in our group conscience as guided by the God of our understanding. Those among us who have positions of "authority" in Al-Anon find that leading by example is preferable to leading by force. Service practiced with humility and enthusiasm is easy to follow. Warranty Two guides us away from seeking prestige and power over others and instead reminds us that the spiritual power of our fellowship is found in our group conscience process, not in any one individual.

Warranty Three states, "that all decisions be reached by discussion, vote and, whenever possible, by unanimity." Concept Four provides us with the principle of participation, and Concept Five protects minorities and assures that they will be heard in any discussion. Warranty Three reinforces these principles. Whenever possible, issues are discussed until there is certainty that all minorities have been heard and most people can support the decision. While unanimity implies agreement by all, experience shows that such full agreement is often not realistic. Hence our pioneers embraced the term "substantial unanimity." There will be less room for criticism of a decision when all have fully participated and most are in favor of it. "Substantial unanimity" is decided by the group or groups involved; two-thirds is a common figure. When the World Service Conference convenes each April, a vote is taken to establish the ratio needed for substantial unanimity for that year.

Al-Anon has always recognized the value of seeking consensus rather than settling for a bare majority. There are times, however, when a decision must be made, despite the lack of substantial unanimity. In these cases, the group conscience can decide whether a simple majority will decide the question or if further discussion is warranted. As long as the principles laid down in our Traditions and Concepts have been followed, Warranty Three is satisfied. Warranty Three guides us to consider all viewpoints carefully in the group conscience process, and to strive for substantial unanimity.

Warranty Four states, "that no Conference action ever be personally punitive or an incitement to public controversy." In Al-Anon we uphold the individual liberties of our members. As individuals and groups, we willingly follow unenforceable principles and guidelines. We don't make rules and punish those who break them. We know that when we do not follow our Traditions, it is we who suffer. Growth halts or declines; our groups sometimes fold. Should Al-Anon ever be unjustly attacked, we most likely would not respond, because defending ourselves could incite further attack and lead to controversy. We avoid public quarreling, which might give Al-Anon an unfavorable public image. When we keep our focus on our spiritual principles, even in the face of strong controversy, we discover our protection is in God's hands.

Warranty Four guides us to maintain "principles above personalities" in our service work. We have no doctrine to maintain, no prestige to defend, no power, pride or property worth fighting over. We protect our fellowship and its principles, but not through revenge or punishment of individuals. If their criticisms are well-founded, we are best served if we thank them and take our own inventory. Peace is our goal, and we believe the best defense is to set a good example.

Warranty five states, "that though the Conference serves Al-Anon, it shall never perform any act of government; and that, like the fellowship of Al-Anon Family Groups which it serves, it shall always remain democratic in thought and action." Warranty five encourages democracy among us, reminding us to strive for mutual respect, consensus and equality of rights, opportunity and treatment for all.

Being democratic in thought means keeping an open mind, granting the same dignity to others' ideas as we do to our own. Democracy in action requires us always to remember the greatest good – what will be best for Al-Anon as a whole. Democratic actions incorporate prudent financial management, keeping principles before personalities and welcoming and creating a place for all who wish to belong to our fellowship. We act with firmness and kindness, without anger, haste, recklessness or control. We ask our trusted servants in the Conference to model these highest democratic ideals rather than to rule through use of their authority, and then we willingly give them our trust because they have earned it.

The full text of the Al-Anon World Service Conference Charter can be found in the *Al-Anon/Alateen Service Manual*. The first eleven articles detail the purpose and composition of the Conference, its relationship to Al-Anon and to the WSO, the purpose and composition of area assemblies, recommendations on elections and terms of offices, meeting schedules, scope of the Board of Trustees and Conference procedures. These sections are a working document which the Conference can amend as needed.

Article Twelve, the General Warranties of the Conference, is protected just as our Steps and Traditions are. Written consent of three quarters of all registered Al-Anon groups would be required to make a change to these Warranties. Some people say the Warranties are Al-Anon's bill of rights, which assures a prudent and responsible balance of power in our organization. As guardian of our Traditions, the Conference is expected to observe the spirit of our Traditions and to lead all of us by their principles.

Al-Anon's five Warranties give our Conference guidelines to prevent problems of money, property, power or prestige from diverting us from our primary spiritual aim. These Warranties insure that our Conference limits its own power in the spirit of the Traditions. Our Conference operates with humility, maintaining a healthy balance in matters of finance, personal authority and decision-making. It refrains from personal punishment or public controversy and remains ever democratic in thought and action. We find that we can follow similar paths in our personal, family and work lives by holding before us these five ideals that form the spiritual foundation of Al-Anon's world services.

Al-Anon has guiding principles, not musts. These principles represent a healthy balance each of us can practice daily in all our affairs. We do not strive for perfection; but to the best of our ability, we will walk the path of these principles because we receive the greatest benefits when we do.

I NEVER really thought of using the Concepts in my personal life until I joined a Concepts Study Group. Concept Twelve and the General Warranties proved to be great principles for guiding family life. For a point of reference, the four members in our family include a father, step-mother, teenage son who lives with us and daughter who lives with her mother. Here's how I am trying to incorporate the Concepts.

IT IS ALSO OUR RESPONSI-BILITY

1. *Sufficient operating funds and reserve.* Applying myself to my profession will provide about half the operating funds for our family. My husband supplies the rest. It is my responsibility to save money for emergency repairs, vacations and retirement. The more I am able to save and properly invest now, the more comfortable I will be later. It is also mine and my husband's responsibility to teach our children by being a good role model, explaining our financial decisions and guiding them with their own financial decisions.

2. *Unqualified authority.* This Warranty reminds me that all members of my family are human beings with feelings, that hierarchy leads to rebellion, and that communication within the family is vital. This is not always easy with stepchildren. I am forever grateful that we each have programs to work and sponsors to work with us, and that my husband has an excellent rapport with his children. I have had to face many of my childhood issues with my own parents which has not been easy and has impacted how I interact with our teens. This Warranty reminds me that there is one unqualified authority, our Higher Power, and He works with and for each of us.

3. *Decisions:* Our teenagers are reaching the age of wanting to do their own thing. This Warranty helps us remember to take their plans into consideration. A major decision – moving across the country – was

discussed among us all before we decided it was not right for us. Individual needs are discussed, prioritized and accomplished as soon as funds are available.

4. *Personally punitive/public controversy.* This speaks to me of respect and trust. The building blocks for respect and trust are courtesy, consideration and following through on commitments. I have found that the disease of alcoholism destroys respect and trust for both the parents and children, and that it takes a long time to rebuild, or in my case, build respect and trust. I have to work on not taking comments and actions, or lack of actions, personally. It is not a reflection on me. It is a reflection on that person and their sickness and self-esteem. This lesson helps me not to hold a grudge and not to punish the child. The saying "don't sweat the small stuff" is finally making sense! It leaves me much more room to relax and enjoy our life together rather than to be upset because some chore was not done.

5. *Democratic in thought and action.* This is the result of working the four Warranties above. It's the natural flow. With the help of the program, we as parents can be more stable. We can be grateful that our son and daughter do not drink or use drugs and that our son is happy in Alateen and school even though studying is hard. Instead of unrealistic consequences for missed commitments, we can have reasonable consequences that are known in advance and allow the children to make informed decisions.

Although I may not be able to practice this with every situation, this Al-Anon guidance has been invaluable to me. The majority of time, I do not react with verbal or silent anger and I can grow through each new experience.

ALL OF the Steps, Traditions and Concepts have helped me to have a yardstick as a guide for better living, but it is the five Warranties of Concept Twelve which have had the greatest impact on my life. They are the entire program wrapped up in just a few words.

"Only sufficient operating funds" helps me to understand that wealth is not a necessary goal in my life. Although it may be what I think I want, it is not what I need. What I need is enough to survive, to keep a roof over my head (not a palace), to have food for nourishment and to have heat, water and light. Swimming pools, stables, and tennis courts are wonderful dreams, but in and of themselves, they will not improve my life.

"An ample reserve" means saving enough to cover an emergency if it should arise. A reserve is a way of helping me not to overextend while still relying on a Power greater than myself to resolve any problems. I do the footwork, make the plans and then leave it in His hands without planning the results.

This Warranty has helped me to eliminate waste and to conserve energy. The word prudent, for me, is wisdom with balance. I do not have to go overboard with either saving or spending. This is true with finances and also with my physical, emotional and spiritual well-being. Taking things one at a time with some order of importance is being prudent. Conserving my energy when I am hungry, angry, lonely or tired is prudent. Good physical exercise in accordance with my age and ability is prudent. Time for rest and leisure is prudent. An excess of any of these things is not only unwise but is also wasteful.

No "unqualified authority" by any one individual means that I can be free when I also allow others to be free. I let others live their lives as they are comfortable so that I may live my life as I am comfortable. I am less judgmental. What freedom this gives to me and others. No one except my Higher Power has the right, authority or need to take control of me, and I turn others over to their Higher Power. Mother may know best – but usually only for Mother. However, I must also realize that sharing my experience, strength and hope may help another, and listening to them may help me. I also need to remember that authority does not always mean a title or a job description, although both may be necessary to avoid confusion. Today the true authority in all my affairs is a power greater than myself as He speaks to me through others. This Warranty brings balance into my life.

"Decisions reached by discussion, vote and unanimity" is a rough one for me. I am grateful that this Warranty comes after Warranty Two, which gives me some practice in freedom, authority and fairness. A spirit of unanimity does not mean that we have no differences, but that we discuss our differences and hopefully arrive at a solution that leads to what is best for the majority. This helps me to hear what others have said, gives me permission to disagree and allows me to abide by a vote that is contrary to my personal wishes. Unanimity does not mean that I may not share a dissenting opinion or contrary point of view. I may share my personal feelings, ideas, experiences, strengths and hope, but once I have shared, I am not free to insist that others agree, adhere or even listen. Today my family most often discusses decisions to be made, rather than each of us running off in our own direction and thereby creating confusion and chaos.

By giving myself permission to disagree, I am learning to accept the disagreements of others without feeling that I am being put down, insulted or called a fool.

"Unqualified authority" and unanimity are opposite ends of my pendulum. As prudence provides balance in Warranty One, so does a balance of authority and unanimity in Warranties Two and Three provide prudence.

Warranty Four is my think-principle. In order for

my actions not to be "personally punitive" to myself or others, either in public or in private, I must think before I speak or act. I need to put my brain in gear before I step on the gas or run the engine. Again, balance is the word which seems to come alive in this Warranty. The risk of "an incitement to public controversy" at any level has helped to make me less demanding, more accepting, and no longer disagreeable just to be different or to get attention. Today I need knowledge, experience, and facts before I take an action, make a decision or even a statement. I am also finding that I listen to others much more closely when what they are sharing is more informational and less emotional. I know that, when I am emotional, I frequently cannot say what it is that I really need to express, and so now I try to give others (as well as myself) time to calm down before having a discussion or making a decision.

The democracy of Warranty Five is, for me, the Al-Anon program in action in my life. Through democracy, I become a better trusted servant without being a rubber stamp. I am able to let others do a job with their ability and not mine and I am less critical of results that are different than what I anticipated. Being "democratic in thought" is keeping an open mind, especially with ideas that are new or different to me. Being "democratic in ... action" means not being forced to do the bidding of others or forcing them to do mine. Today I can accept that I am not your Higher Power and that no one else is mine. With true democracy comes freedom, acceptance and unity.

As I keep each of these Warranties in mind, I become aware that they are a balance of principles, not musts. This has given me a goal to aim for rather than a prison in which I must live. When I hear that there are no musts in Al-Anon, but a lot of "you betters," I realize that what is really being said is to use the Warranties in all my affairs. These truly are the spiritual principles on which not just the Traditions but my whole life is based. I practice each Al-Anon principle (whether Steps, Traditions, or Concepts) until I am able to work it. I work it until I am able to use it. Now with the Warranties, I am able to apply each of them to my life.

WE WANTED
TO DEMAND

WHILE ALL the Steps and Traditions have helped me in different ways and at different times, Concept Twelve has definitely changed my perspective and understanding. Warranty five of Concept Twelve was a real eye-opener.

We were having countless complaints about a group in our district. Several of us Al-Anon "experts" decided to march right into that meeting and show them the error of their ways. We wanted to demand that they follow Traditions (control), and if they refused (we were projecting), we would (unknown to them, of course) stop inviting them to district meetings and sending them district information (why waste time and postage on a rebellious group?), take them off our meeting directory, tell the local information service they disbanded (who would want newcomers to go to such a bad meeting) and maybe even tell our area and WSO they disbanded. That would show them!

Warranty five taught me that no penalties are to be inflicted for nonconformity to Al-Anon principles. It also taught me to abstain from any act of authoritative government that would curtail others' freedoms to act with mutual love and respect: to take no action in anger, haste or recklessness; to take no punitive action, and to guard against tyrannies (after all, that was how we were acting).

We now continue gently and lovingly to service every group in our district – even those who fail to follow the Traditions and policies. We never know when a member may decide to take an interest and become group representative (GR). We need to keep the door open. This also is helpful in personal areas of our lives. We are not the authority on the right way of doing things and need to be loving and supportive of others even when our feelings and methods differ.

Working Concept Twelve

The spiritual foundation for Al-Anon's world services is contained in the General Warranties of the Conference, Article 12 of the Charter.

The General Warranties:

In all its proceedings the World Service Conference of Al-Anon shall observe the spirit of the Traditions:

1. that only sufficient operating funds, including an ample reserve, be its prudent financial principle;

2. that no Conference member shall be placed in unqualified authority over other members;

3. that all decisions be reached by discussion, vote and, whenever possible, by unanimity;

4. that no Conference action ever be personally punitive or an incitement to public controversy;

5. that though the Conference serves Al-Anon, it shall never perform any act of government; and that, like the fellowship of Al-Anon Family Groups which it serves, it shall always remain democratic in thought and action.

* How does my group practice financial prudence? My district? My area?

* How do I practice prudence in my financial affairs?

* In what other areas of my life could I practice prudence?

* What docs authority mean to me?

* Do I ever assume unqualified authority? Does my group allow this?

* Can I listen to all sides of a discussion before making a decision?

* What is substantial unanimity in my group? My district? My area? In my family? My job?

* Can I keep principles above personalities at all times? Why or why not?

* Do I like to stir things up? If so, why?

* Does my group practice democratic thought? My district? My area?

* How is my family democratic in thought? In action?

* Is my workplace democratic in thought and action? How?

* How has study of the Concepts improved my understanding of my role in my group?

* How has study of the Concepts improved my understanding of my group's role in our district? In our area? In worldwide Al-Anon?

* How can I apply the Concepts to my personal life? To my work life?

Epilogue

Epilogue

OFTEN WE hear someone say, "You can't keep it if you don't give it away." We find that, when we serve each other and the fellowship, we can only give away those aspects of recovery we learn to practice in our own lives. As we serve, we contribute to the unity of our group, our own recovery expands and we have more and more to give away.

When we serve we are not alone. We have all three of Al-Anon's legacies, the Steps, Traditions and Concepts, to guide us and each of them connects us to our own recovery and spirituality. When we go to a business meeting and are tempted to say, "Let's hurry up with this business so we can get to the real program," someone reminds us that our "real program" is to help families and friends of alcoholics. We share what we have received in order to keep it for ourselves – that is a basic spiritual principle. As we walk our paths to recovery, by understanding and using our legacies we find that Al-Anon is really about all of life. Recovery, unity and service are found in all the principles we share.

WHEN I was a newcomer, my sponsor led me to try an approach to the Steps, Traditions and Concepts that made all of them relevant in my life. He had me learn them horizontally rather than vertically.

With Step One I also studied Tradition One and Concept One. With Step Two I studied Tradition Two and Concept Two, and so on. My sponsor said if I did a Step, Tradition, or Concept without being able to relate it to the other parts of the program, I would miss understanding a great deal of my recovery in Al-Anon. He also wanted me to relate each Tradition and Concept to my own life, not just the Step. He didn't want me to think of them as just abstract ideas

A MEMBER PUTS OUR THREE LEGACIES TO WORK

that related only to Al-Anon groups or to the World Service Office (WSO).

As I work the program horizontally, I look at Step One, Tradition One and Concept One as three discussions of power. Step One says I do not have power, that my life is unmanageable. Tradition One discusses the power inherent in our group, that our unity gives us the strength that we do not have as individuals. Concept One discusses the power that all of the groups have over the world services organization. All three legacies discuss the power of unity instead of the powerlessness of each individual acting alone.

I experience the power of unity when I gather with one or more Al-Anons, when I talk with my sponsor, or when I talk with one of the people that I sponsor. The strength of emotion, character and ideas that we generate surpasses the strength that any of us produces by working alone. Inherent in this process is the guidance that comes from a power greater than ourselves. This guidance is what I call my Higher Power.

A combination of the first Step, first Tradition and first Concept reveals to me the overriding spirituality of the Al-Anon program. The reason I need to rely on it is that it takes my life from unmanageable to higher-powered. I experience the Higher Power interaction of the Step, Tradition and Concept when I express my unity with other Al-Anons. When I act alone, I deprive myself of the inspiration that comes from others. As a result my life remains unmanageable. With unity, however, I can find manageability and even serenity in all my affairs.

My sponsor used to say there was another thread in Al-Anon that held all of the Steps, Traditions and Concepts together. This special thread was a Higher Power that expressed itself as love. Without love the whole fabric of recovery would unravel.

My sponsor's guidance in understanding the Steps, Traditions and Concepts has helped me look at many relationships in my life. I now find that as often as a

Step may solve some question for me, a Tradition or a Concept may also be the answer. Now, if I have a question about a personal relationship, I usually look first to the Traditions to clarify my position in the picture. If I have a business question, a Concept is probably where I will begin to find my answer.

This way of looking at the Steps, Traditions and Concepts has made it easier for me when I sponsor, too. I can often help a sponsee find understanding more quickly and with less hassle than by just looking at an individual part of the program. It has also given me a clearer understanding of why I can be of use only when I share experience, strength, hope and unconditional love – but not advice or direction. Understanding these relationships has allowed me to observe my own uneven performance as a sponsor. Sometimes I can even see my own growth coming as a result of working the Al-Anon program with those I sponsor.

I always try to remember my sponsor's wise saying: "The Steps show me how to love myself; the Traditions show me how to love others, and the Concepts show me how to love the world that I live in."

Index

A

AA, Alcoholics Anonymous, xi, 4, 8,
11, 77, 94, 131, 132, 139, 163, 164,
166, 167, 169, 172–174, 175, 180,
182, 184,186–188, 190–192, 227,
229, 230, 232, 233, 247, 249, 303
Abuse, 25, 26, 95, 159, 224, 279
Acceptance, xi, 9, 18, 34, 42, 53, 56,
57, 64, 65, 72, 73, 90, 99, 121,
125, 141, 154, 162, 177, 200, 236,
276, 333
Accountability, 285, 306
Accusations, 86, 222
Admitting (our wrongs), 54, 58, 62,
63, 103, 110
Advertising, 232, 258
Advice, 57, 120, 127, 151, 172, 178, 209,
213, 215, 225, 290, 348
Al-Anon principles, 40, 121, 135, 154,
156, 158, 188, 212, 221, 227, 238,
268, 276, 292, 334
Al-Anon World Services, 245, 249,
250, 253, 309
Al-Anon/Alateen Service Manual, vi,
148, 187, 189, 212, 232, 247, 257,
264, 266, 267, 269, 281, 284,
290, 295, 303, 320, 321, 322, 324,
327
Alateen, ix, 40, 138, 149, 156, 158, 168,
174, 187, 225, 248, 292, 293, 316,
320
Alateen Fourth Step Inventory, 40, 103
Alienation, 25, 161, 179, 221, 272
Amends, 3, 4, 81– 85, 87–95, 97–106,
108, 121, 292
Anger, 14, 25, 33, 46, 52, 56, 57, 68, 78,
85, 139, 149, 175, 226, 235, 238,
293, 307, 327, 330, 334
Anne B., 184, 207, 249
Anonymity, 131–133, 227– 240
Anxiety, 54, 299

Area assemblies, 163, 194, 202, 213,
250, 261, 263, 327
Area delegates, 146, 250, 193,
Area meetings, 163,194, 202, 250, 284,
321
Assets, 35, 41, 42, 48, 53, 63, 69, 70,
72, 74, 97, 126
Attitudes, v, 5, 19, 41, 44, 78, 99, 123,
131, 170, 171, 181, 198, 266, 291
Autonomy, 163, 164, 165, 166, 168,
169, 170, 173, 213, 26568, 85, 96

B

Baggage, 68, 85, 96, 102
Belonging, 106, 125, 156, 158, 180, 187,
190, 221, 270, 273, 278, 327
Bill W., 303
Blame, 54, 68, 84, 86, 87, 100, 151,
153, 17 7, 8, 42, 51, 53, 175, 203
Blueprint for Progress, 40, 43, 44, 103,
123, 260
Board of Trustees, xiii, 206, 245, 271,
279, 280, 284, 286, 289, 292, 293,
295, 296, 298, 300, 301, 302, 308,
309, 317, 327
Business meetings, 212, 215, 254, 255,
257, 261, 262, 268, 138, 191, 201,
288, 296

C

Carrying the message, 78, 94, 107
Change, 5, 9, 11, 12, 16, 20, 22, 52, 69,
73–75, 79, 80, 87, 90, 91, 98, 99,
102, 113, 115, 124, 140, 141, 148,
176, 181, 223, 234, 264, 299,
303,319, 334
Chaos, 9, 57, 145, 218, 305, 332
Choices, 15, 19, 23, 28, 35, 169, 184,
299, 303
Clarity, 311, 312

D

U

W

Notes

Notes

Notes

Notes

Notes

Notes

Notes

Notes

Notes

Notes

Notes

Notes

Notes

Notes

Notes

Notes